Tourism, Leisure and Recreation Series

Series Editors
Gareth Shaw and Allan Williams

D0808975

Urban Tourism

Urban Tourism

Attracting Visitors to Large Cities

Christopher M. Law

MANSELL

First published by
Mansell Publishing Limited. *A Cassell Imprint*

Villiers House	387 Park Avenue South
41/47 Strand	New York
London WC2N 5JE	NY 10016–881
England	USA

Reprinted in paperback, 1994 © Christopher M. Law 1993

British Library Cataloguing-in-Publication Data
Law, Christopher M.
Urban Tourism: Attracting Visitors to Large Cities. –
(Tourism, Leisure & Recreation Series)
I. Title II. Series
338.4791

ISBN 0-7201-2129-9 (Hardback)   ISBN 0-7201-2253-8 (Paperback)
Library of Congress Cataloging-in-Publication Data
Law, Christopher M.
Urban Tourism: Attracting visitors to large cities/by
Christopher M. Law.
p.   cm. – (Tourism, Leisure and Recreation series)
Includes bibliographical references and index.
ISBN 0-7201-2129-9 (Hardback)
ISBN 0-7201-2253-8 (Paperback)
1. Tourist Trade. 2. Cities and towns. I. Title. II. Series.
G155.A1L377 1993   93-17220
338.4'791-dc20   CIP

Printed and bound in Great Britain by Biddles Ltd, Guildford and King's Lynn

Contents

List of Figures

List of Tables

Preface

There is a very extensive literature on cities by academics and planners. Because of their size, complexity and problems, cities have attracted much attention. Almost every aspect of the life and organization of cities has been described and evaluated, with the apparent exception of tourism. There is a literature on tourism in particular cities, but this usually consists of consultants' and official reports and has neither been synthesized at a general level nor made more publicly available. Most textbooks on tourism either ignore cities or give only a brief passing mention. Until the 1980s this was understandable, since tourism was not important in most cities. However, since the early 1980s cities across the Western world have been attempting to expand their tourist industry. In most cities this endeavour is still in its early stages and it is premature to suggest that a full evaluation can be made at the present time.

The author hopes that this book will fill a lacuna that exists in the literature, and thus be useful both to the academic world, lecturers and students, and also to practitioners. While tourism is increasingly taught by subject specialists, it is also studied and taught by economists, geographers, planners and sociologists. Because of the general absence of material on the subject, this book will seek first to describe the situation before making an evaluation and assessing the role of tourism in urban change. It will also seek to determine why some cities have been successful in developing the industry, and why others have not, and what practical lessons can be learned.

The author wishes to thank the many people who have made this book possible, but who, of course, are not responsible for any of the opinions expressed. In late 1984 Councillor Peter Scott, then Chairman of the Planning Committee of the late Greater Manchester Council, asked me to write a report suggesting how the development of tourism could benefit Manchester. It was this project which first stimulated my interest in the subject. Since then very many tourist organizations, too numerous to mention, have helped my studies by supplying material and granting an interview when one has been requested. The Geography Department at Salford University made this book possible by granting a sabbatical term in autumn 1991, and also by making the usual facilities available. Gustav Dobrynski drew the maps and Marie Partington and Moira Armit helped with the typing. Lastly I must thank my wife Elizabeth and children Katherine and Nicholas for their support, as over the years they have been dragged around many cities. For a natural urban tourist like myself there can be no greater job satisfaction than writing a book on the topic.

1

Introduction

Large cities are arguably the most important type of tourist destination across the world. They have always attracted visitors but until recently, with the exception of capital cities like London and Paris, the tourist industry has not been perceived as a significant one, nor have these cities been classified as tourist centres (Blank and Petkovich, 1987). With a large population, facilities such as museums, shops, theatres and sports have been developed to a high standard for local people, and these would have drawn visitors from at least the wider region. City councils have certainly advertised these amenities to non-locals for many decades, but little time or finance were put into this effort or into developing the resource base for tourism.

The 1980s witnessed a significant shift in attitude by cities towards the tourist industry. For reasons which will be discussed in greater detail in the next chapter, more and more cities saw the tourist industry as one which should be encouraged. Among the prime reasons were the decline of long-established economic activities and the need to introduce new ones or face either contraction or high unemployment, the perception of tourism as a growth industry, and the hope that the development of the industry would result in physical regeneration and the revitalization of the city centre. The perception of tourism as a growth industry was based on the idea that with leisure increasing, the population becoming more affluent and transport easier there would be a follow through to greater travel for pleasure and work. This shift in attitude by cities was very widespread, affecting not just those with an obvious resource base. Old industrial cities with a poor image and scarred landscapes also sought to develop the industry. Where there was already a nucleus of the industry, this was to be greatly expanded. The aim of tourism promotion was, then, partly to boost the city, partly to revitalize the city, and partly to physically regenerate areas. From old industrial cities like Baltimore, Cleveland, Detroit and Pittsburgh in the USA and Bradford, Birmingham, Liverpool and Manchester in the UK, to cities like Duisburg and Lyon in continental Europe, the movement for urban tourism was very widespread.

This change in policy quickly became visible on the ground. In the cities of the USA, convention centres, aquariums, domed stadiums, festival market-places and atrium hotels were built and waterfronts were redeveloped. In the UK, many new museums have been opened and concert halls built, and waterfronts redeveloped. Similar trends can be seen in continental Europe.

The aim of this book is to describe, interpret and evaluate the tourism industry in large cities. The focus of this book will be on large cities in North America and western Europe, but much of what is written is relevant to large cities elsewhere in the world. By large cities is meant metropolitan areas that have a population of over 1 million. However, much of what is written in this book is applicable to smaller cities, ones that have half a million population, and perhaps some of even a quarter of a million. Large cities are a diverse group. Because of their size they usually have a varied economic structure, although this does not prevent them from being strong in certain sectors and playing a dominating role in some. As has been mentioned above, the tourism industry already exists in these cities. In some capital and/or historic cities, tourism is well developed. In other large cities, such as the industrial city, tourism has only recently been recognized, and has been selected for expansion. A special theme of this book is to examine the task which these older industrial cities face in attempting to develop the industry. Is the growth of tourism in these cities feasible? Another special theme, often connected with the above one, is to examine the role of tourism in the regeneration of the city centre and inner city. While reference will be made to historic cities and resorts, whether large or small, it is not the aim of this book to discuss the tourism industry in these types of urban area. For the former, attracting visitors is relatively easy, while for the latter, tourism is the *raison d'être* of their existence. It is much more difficult to transform the image of a city from the negative to the positive and to win large numbers of visitors.

The study of tourism in large cities, or urban tourism as it will be referred to, has not attracted much attention in the academic literature (Ashworth, 1989; Pearce, 1989, p. 84). There are a few case studies of tourism in large cities, some of which were brought together in a book by Vetter (1985). One obvious reason for this lack of interest is that the topic appeared to become relevant only in the 1980s. This was the time when older industrial cities were losing jobs on a large scale, and the potential of tourism to create new employment was recognized (English Tourist Board, 1980). Articles began to appear about tourism and the inner city, and a little research was undertaken (Jansen-Verbeke, 1986, 1988, 1989). At this time the potential of tourism to regenerate areas was considered not just for large cities, but for smaller industrial areas as well (Buckley and Witt, 1985, 1989).

Academics studying cities have given very little attention to the role of tourism. This is true even for large cities like London and New York, where the industry is responsible for hundreds of thousands of jobs (Fainstein *et al.*, 1992). This lack of attention almost certainly arises from the contemporary fashionable methodological approaches. In the past, economic/export base theory suggested that the prime sector of the urban economy was manufacturing, which drew in income from the rest of the world. More recently it has been recognized that parts of the long-neglected service sector are capable of generating export income, but interest has focused on producer services such as finance and insurance. One reason for the lack of attention given to tourism is its invisibility. Employment generated by tourism does not appear within one Standard Industrial Classification order or heading, and without detailed research it is difficult to estimate its importance.

Researchers have also frequently written tourism off, wrongly perceiving the jobs as being seasonal and part-time. In fact, tourism is a very important export industry for cities and most of the jobs are permanent.

Academics studying tourism have also neglected the large city as a type of destination, while seeing it mainly as the origin of tourist flows. This neglect may be because most attention has been given to holiday tourism. Trips for business and conferences and to friends and relatives are often hardly recognized, as are short breaks and day trips, all areas where the city is important. While it has been recognized that urban landscapes and museums attract tourists, it has been difficult for the tourism researcher to distinguish the locals from the visitors and therefore evaluate precisely the importance of the industry. Pearce suggests that tourism researchers are naturally more interested in the delights of resorts and mountains and therefore neglect the subject (Pearce, 1987, p. 180). However, this must surely be a personal view; it is not borne out by the widespread interest academics have shown in cities, and ignores the fact that most universities are located in cities.

While the academic world may have ignored tourism in cities, many reports have been produced by or for the industry. Unfortunately, many of these reports are not easily available to the outsider, sometimes because only a few copies are produced, or because their contents are considered confidential. This is a problem for anyone studying the industry. The industry is also better at producing action plans than it is at commissioning research. Accordingly, many of these reports should be read with a critical eye, distinguishing hard facts from hard sell, and reality from wishful thinking. Often, surveys undertaken for these reports are based on very small samples, making them of doubtful validity. Nevertheless, such reports may be useful in following the aspirations of a city, some of which may be realized.

Table 1.1 Travel by US residents over 100 miles from home

	Person trips (millions)		Share of total (%)	
	1981	*1988*	*1981*	*1988*
Total	1152.0	1232.5	100	100
Purpose				
VFR*	421.0	425.8	36.5	34.5
Other pleasure	412.3	502.1	35.8	40.7
Business and				
conventions	157.3	211.7	13.7	17.1
Other	161.4	92.9	14.0	7.5
Other characteristics				
Vacation	737.9	830.9	64.1	67.4
Weekend	545.7	560.0	47.4	45.4

*VFR, visiting friends and relatives.
Source: US Travel Data Center (Washington, DC), National Travel Survey (Annual), quoted in the *Statistical Abstract of the United States*, 1990, 238.

Definitions

So far the word 'tourism' has been used as if it were unproblematic (Gilbert, 1990). As in other fields, even this simple term has different meanings in the USA and Britain. In Britain the word 'tourism' covers all travel for whatever purpose, whereas in the USA it refers to leisure travel only. In this book the British use of the term will be adopted. The tourism industry covers what in the USA is variously referred to as the visitor industry, the hospitality industry, the travel industry or the convention and tourism industry. The importance of the different types of tourism as classified by purpose of trip in the USA can be seen in Table 1.1. Just over one-third of all travel is to visit friends and relatives. During the 1980s the share of pleasure travel grew to reach over 40 per cent, while business travel also increased in importance to 17 per cent. About two-thirds of all travel takes place as a vacation and nearly half at the weekend. In Britain, which is a smaller country and therefore might have fewer overnight stays, 18.6 per cent of trips in 1991 were to friends and relatives, 6.7 per cent for business and work and 65 per cent for all types of holiday.

The World Tourism Organization definition of a tourist is someone who moves away from home on a temporary or short-term basis for at least 24 hours, whether travelling in his or her own country (domestic tourism) or going to another country (international tourism). The growth of the latter is illustrated in Figure 1.1, where the vast increase in foreign travel in the postwar period is shown. Since the size, shape and proximity of countries one to another varies enormously, these figures do not give a very precise indication of the distances over which tourists are travelling. To be useful, surveys of travel need to measure the distance moved, the length of stay

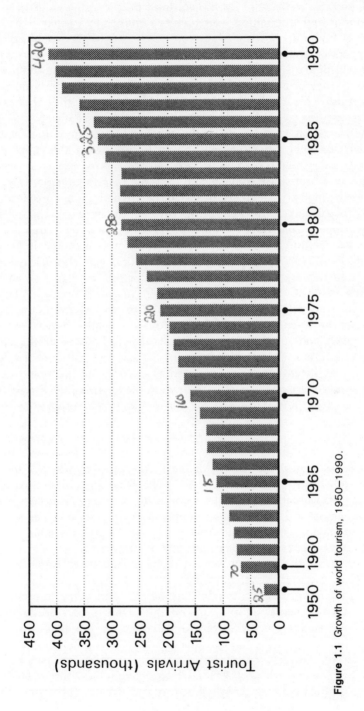

Figure 1.1 Growth of world tourism, 1950–1990.

and the purpose of the trip. Even then, most people in the industry or those who study it find a definition which limits a 'tourist' to a person who spends at least 24 hours away from home too restrictive. Many would argue that day trippers or excursionists should be included. In Britain these have been defined as people spending at least three hours away from home and involving a round journey of at least 20 miles which they do not regularly make, thus moving outside the area of their normal daily journeys (Office of Population Censuses and Surveys, 1991). However, any distance used is open to discussion. As travel has become easier, the boundaries of commuting areas have increased. For some cities this may be up to 100 miles, although for most people 10 miles might be a more appropriate figure. Excluded from this definition of a tourist are students and workers migrating temporarily. Some people in the industry, in an effort to avoid these definitional problems, have resorted to using the word 'visitor' to cover both the overnight stayer and the day tripper. Unfortunately the word visitor has a very common usage and cannot so easily be redefined. The definition of a tourist is illustrated in Chadwick's (1987) diagram (Figure 1.2). At first sight this discussion may appear academic and irrelevant, but definitions are important when assessments are made of the impact of tourism. Then it is necessary to define tourists in order to count their number, and to use surveys of expenditure to estimate the revenue generated by the tourist industry. Several definitions can be given and there may be no right answer because of the different purposes of various studies. In particular, the size and nature of the destination area may determine who is counted as a tourist. In this book the focus of attention is cities, and generally this means the metropolitan area, covering the central city, the suburbs and the surrounding commuting zone.

The Tourism System

There has been much discussion in the literature as to whether there is a tourism industry as such (Gilbert, 1990). This is because, compared to, say, the motor vehicle industry, the boundaries are not very clear-cut. Many of the firms associated with tourism supply both tourists and residents, and there is no way of recording the division of trade. Again, an industry is often defined on the basis of a product, but how is this defined for tourism? Some writers have avoided the term 'tourist industry' and taken cover in what is described as the tourist system (Gunn, 1988). Such a terminology uses the notion of components which would include the tourist, the transporter, the attractions, the ancillary facilities, and the planners and promoters of a place. However, there is some merit in retaining the simple ideas of supply and demand, and product and consumer (Ashworth and Goodall, 1990). The product is what attracts the tourist to a place. For cities, products have been defined by Jansen-Verbeke (1988) as historic buildings, urban landscapes, museums and art galleries, theatres, sports and events. She defines these as

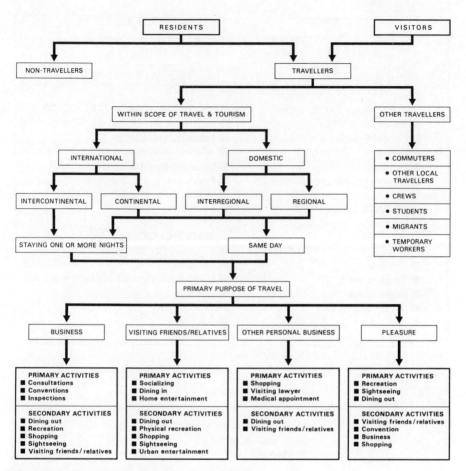

Figure 1.2 Classification of travellers (after Chadwick, 1987).

the primary elements (Figure 1.3). There are also other facilities which are important for the experience of the tourist, but are unlikely to be the cause of the visitor coming to the city. These include hotels, shops and other services and are described as the secondary elements. Cities offer what can be described as either a product or a bundle of products. Some visitors travel to the city to purchase one product only, while others are attracted by the possibility of consuming several products during their stay. Many of them are unique to a city, and these include historic buildings, museums and special events. They can only be consumed by travelling to the city where they are found.

Just because these attractions are unique does not mean that tourists will come. While individuals have specialist interests for which they will travel a long distance, most people will only travel for something that they perceive as really impressive. Within the popular mind there is a hierarchy of attractions

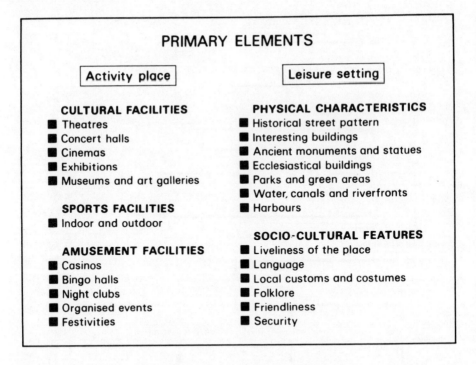

PRIMARY ELEMENTS

Activity place

CULTURAL FACILITIES
- Theatres
- Concert halls
- Cinemas
- Exhibitions
- Museums and art galleries

SPORTS FACILITIES
- Indoor and outdoor

AMUSEMENT FACILITIES
- Casinos
- Bingo halls
- Night clubs
- Organised events
- Festivities

Leisure setting

PHYSICAL CHARACTERISTICS
- Historical street pattern
- Interesting buildings
- Ancient monuments and statues
- Ecclesiastical buildings
- Parks and green areas
- Water, canals and riverfronts
- Harbours

SOCIO-CULTURAL FEATURES
- Liveliness of the place
- Language
- Local customs and costumes
- Folklore
- Friendliness
- Security

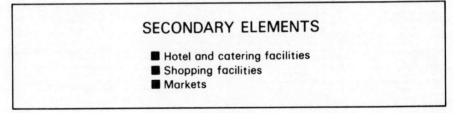

SECONDARY ELEMENTS

- Hotel and catering facilities
- Shopping facilities
- Markets

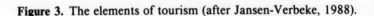

ADDITIONAL ELEMENTS

- Accessibility and parking facilities
- Tourist facilities : information offices,
  signposts, guides, maps and leaflets, etc.

Figure 3. The elements of tourism (after Jansen-Verbeke, 1988).

which is illustrated by the Michelin Guides' starring system, where three stars are for worth a journey/highly recommended, two stars are for worth a detour/recommended, and one star is for interesting. Butler (1991) has suggested that there is a hierarchy of attractions as follows:

1 International recognition. Many elements of appeal and attracting people from all over the world, e.g. London and Paris.
2 International recognition. Limited or special appeal, such as the Pyramids.
3 National recognition with wide appeal.
4 National recognition with specialized appeal.
5 Regional appeal.
6 Local appeal.

The higher up the hierarchy a product is classified, the more it is able to attract visitors from a distance. The appeal of a city is not fixed for all time. New products can be developed which add to the existing ones and raise the appeal of the city in the outside world. Alternatively, the existing products can be promoted so that they become more widely known. Of course, it is also possible that some products will become less attractive for various reasons, including fashion, and it will be necessary for a city to find replacements. There may be a life cycle for some products. Cities have many products which are not unique, or at least do not appear unique to the outsider. This does not mean that they are valueless for tourism. They may be useful for people who have come to the city primarily for another reason, such as business, or visiting friends and relatives. The enjoyment of their trip can be enhanced by visiting one of these lesser-ranked attractions. In the past, the city product was the outcome of the decisions made by a number of actors, perhaps over many centuries. Little thought had gone into designing a product which would have appeal. Today this situation is changing as cities aspire to be tourist centres and plan their resource base and marketing programmes.

The second main component of the tourism system is the consumer who supplies the demand, in this case the tourist. The development of a tourism industry in a city will depend on being able to appeal to the potential tourist, and this in turn requires an understanding of their wants and requirements.

Types of Tourism

Definitions of tourism are based on the concept of travel for whatever purpose. Some have argued that this is a chaotic concept (Hughes, 1991), and needs to be refined. But as we shall see, this is not always easy to do. It is possible to divide tourists into two main types on the basis of purpose of trip, i.e. business and leisure. The business tourist is one who travels as part of his or her work. This may be to sell or buy goods and services, to undertake management functions, to receive or give training, and to attend conferences and exhibitions. The conference and exhibition business is also described as conventions, congresses and meetings, and is a key part of urban tourism.

Table 1.2 US business trip characteristics

Characteristics	1980	1985	1988
Total (millions)	97.1	133.3	155.6
Average household members on trip	1.5	1.4	1.4
Average nights per trip	n/a	3.6	3.1
Average miles per trip	n/a	1180	1100
Mainly car travel (%)	56	51	54
Air travel (%)	42	44	44
Stay in hotel (%)	66	62	67
Also vacation (%)	10	13	8
Income more than $40 000 (%)	n/a	42	52

Source: As for Table 1.1.

However, whilst many delegates are attending as part of their work, there are also meetings held by voluntary organizations, which could not be described as business. Again, conferences may be held in places noted for their leisure opportunities, for which delegates may stay on afterwards and also bring a partner. Overall, about 20 per cent of all tourism is accounted for by business and conference travel (Clevedon and O'Brien, 1988).

The main characteristics of business tourism in the USA are shown in Table 1.2. During the 1980s the number of trips grew by more than 50 per cent. Surprisingly, another member of the household often went on the business trip, which is partly explained by the fact that in about 10 per cent of the cases the trip was also a vacation. Two-thirds of the business travellers were men and the average income was high. About two-thirds of the trips also involved a stay in a hotel.

The term 'leisure travel' clearly applies to what people do in their spare, free or non-working hours, but once again this can cover several purposes. Most obviously it applies to what people do on holiday, even if it is only a day's holiday. This holiday travel is also referred to as pleasure tourism. But the term leisure travel may also be used for visits to friends and relatives, and conducting personal business. The pleasure tourist is attracted to cities because of their historic buildings, interesting urban landscapes, museums and art galleries, theatres, sports events and other entertainments, the primary elements of Figure 1.3.

The main characteristics of the pleasure tourist in the USA are shown in Table 1.3. Compared to the business trip there are more household members in the party, more nights are spent away from home, there are more car trips, but there are fewer stays in hotels, fewer males and lower incomes.

The urban tourist can be classified in various ways. Chadwick's diagram (Figure 1.2) suggests four main types, namely business, visiting friends and relatives, personal and pleasure. His diagram also hints that many trips combine a number of reasons. Thus the primary purpose of a trip to a city might be to attend a conference, but the delegate might also have secondary

Table 1.3 US pleasure trip characteristics

Characteristics	1980	1985	1988
Trips (millions)	342.8	384.4	455.3
Average household members per trip	2.2	2.1	2.0
Average nights per trip	n/a	5.6	4.6
Average miles per trip	n/a	1010	940
Mainly car travel (%)	80	73	77
Air travel (%)	16	21	18
Stay in hotel (%)	34	39	39
Also vacation (%)	75	80	80
Male (%)	n/a	48	50
Income more than $40 000 (%)	n/a	27	30

Source: As for Table 1.1.

purposes in sightseeing or visiting friends and relatives. Given the range of opportunities in a city, this is not surprising. Accordingly, it can be suggested that while some urban tourists have a single purpose, others have a prime motive with secondary aims and yet others come with several purposes and no overriding one. The latter visit the city because it has a number of attractions which add up to make it worth visiting.

Leisure Tourism

The growth of leisure travel has been greatly facilitated by easier travel, increased wealth and more leisure time. This latter aspect is a product of a shorter working week and longer paid holidays. In Britain the length of the normal basic working week has been reduced from about 44.4 hours in 1951 to about 38 hours in 1990, although the actual hours worked has fallen only from 47.8 hours in 1951 to 43 hours in 1990 (*Social Trends*, Volume 22, 1992). At the same time the number of days worked each week has gone down from about 5.5–6 to 5 and some people on special shifts may only work 3 or 4 days a week. For most people there is a definite weekend which can be used, if they wish, either for day trips or a short holiday. Holiday entitlement has also steadily lengthened during the twentieth century. In Britain a 'Holidays with Pay' Act was passed in 1938, and by 1939 11 million workers were covered by this legislation. After the war most employed people had about two weeks' a year holiday entitlement, and this has steadily increased since then. In 1961, 97 per cent of manual workers had two weeks' holiday. By 1990, 90 per cent had at least four weeks (*Social Trends*, Volume 22, 1992). In the USA the average length of holiday increased from 1.8 weeks in 1960 to 2.6 weeks by the end of the 1970s. Today, holidays are often expressed in terms of days of leave, with many people having between 20 and 25 and some up to 30 days a year. The latter may occur either because of the length of time worked with a firm or because of seniority in the organization. These figures do not include what in Britain are referred to as Bank Holidays, where there are eight days, and elsewhere as public holidays or holy days. With so many days of leave there is a mix of possibilities as to how they can be taken. Most people will keep some days for various personal uses, such as shopping (particularly before Christmas), decorating the house or working in the garden, attending weddings and other such events, or dealing with other personal business. Some of these uses may involve travel. The remainder of the time can be used for some form of holiday, whether it be day trips, short breaks, long holidays or just lazing around at home.

Another cause of the increase in leisure travel is earlier retirement coupled with better pensions and longer life. Retired or semi-retired people form an important section of the travel market. They have greater flexibility in the times when they can travel and so are important in the off-peak seasons.

Motivations

For business travel the reason for travelling is usually obvious and unproblematic. This is not so for leisure travel, where there may be both explicit and implicit reasons. As with all migration, there may be both push and pull factors. Many people perceive leisure and holiday periods as a time to escape from the normal routines of life; to do, to see, to experience something different. Leisure tourism is often crudely divided between sunlust and wanderlust (Gray, 1970). Sunlust covers the traditional seaside holiday, which has lengthened its reach in the last 30 years as a result of cheap flights and the desire for sunnier, warmer and more reliable weather. We may link with this category outdoor holidays involving walking, skiing and mountaineering, although these are not strictly sunlust. Beach and outdoor holidays appeal particularly to young people and families with young children. All of these types of travel have little relevance for urban tourism.

Wanderlust is more relevant to urban tourism, and raises the question why people want to travel to see different places. Psychologists, sociologists and others have sought to understand this phenomenom. It is apparent that some people are keener to travel than others. Plog (1987) classified people on a psychographic continuum, ranging from allocentric to psychocentric. The term psychocentric is derived from psyche or self-centred, meaning the centring of one's life on one's thought or concerns over the small problem areas of one's life. Allocentric, on the other hand, derives from the root word 'allo', meaning varied in form. An allocentric person's interest patterns are focused on varied activities. Such a person is outgoing and self-confident in behaviour and is characterized by a considerable degree of adventure and willingness to reach out and experiment with life. Travel becomes a way for the allocentric person to express inquisitiveness and satisfy curiosity (Gupta, 1984). These characteristics and the resulting behaviour may be affected by income and education. Low income will constrain the desire to explore, while education will have widened the knowledge of what there is to do. Psychocentrics do not necessarily make shorter journeys. They may be carried along by their families and friends, and perhaps find the security they want in coach trips.

Another method of classifying people on a psychographic continuum is by lifestyle segmentation using the values and lifestyles system (VALS). This divides the population into three main groups. Those described as 'sustenance driven' are security minded and family centred and form 28 per cent of the population, and are least likely to want to travel (Jones Lang Wootton, 1989). A second group termed 'outer directed', forming 34 per cent of the population, search for esteem and status, and may travel if this achieves these objectives. The third group are 'inner directed' and form 38 per cent of the population, and are most likely to travel to learn and discover.

The fact that people want to explore does not tell us anything about the kind of places they will choose to visit. At a simple push level, many people just want a change. They do not want to stay in the same place all the year round and are looking to go and see another place. Boorstein (1964) suggested that people seek to escape from the real world and the security of the familiar to something extravagantly strange. They are drawn to pseudo-events and landscapes of illusion. MacCannell (1976) has suggested that people travel to authenticate their lives. So often the familiar, ordinary everyday life is downgraded, and judged to be of no value; in order to experience the 'high life', people must travel. They want to feel that they have visited the famous places. After they have visited these places their life has become valid and put in contact with world history. In fact, as MacCannell emphasizes, tourists rarely see a 'natural attraction'. Their minds will have been prepared beforehand by what they have read about the site, and the site itself will have been 'marked' out in some way. This is 'staged authenticity' according to MacCannell. This still leaves the question of what places people will want to visit. Places obviously vary in their interest and attractiveness, but what constitutes these factors is culturally determined (Urry, 1990). Potential tourists learn about the world from the media and from literature. Most importantly, they learn from television and films, which provide potent images of places. In news reports and in films, particular places will appear many times. These places will almost certainly include capital cities like London and Paris. Famous buildings like London's Houses of Parliament and Buckingham Palace, and Paris's Eiffel Tower, will become well known to people around the world. These places become a powerful draw for the travelling tourist. Historic cities attract people a great deal, from Florence and Venice in Italy, to small cities like Bath, Chester and York in England. Some places, because of their good preservation, become representatives of history or urban landscapes. Of course, culture is broader than this. It covers urban landscapes made famous by literary and historic figures, as with Stratford-upon-Avon. The most famous and largest art galleries are also able to attract patrons from around the world.

Some writers have compared the tourist with the religious pilgrim who feels compelled to leave home and travel to a distant shrine and there worship. With the large numbers involved there may be the same sense of bonding between the travellers as there was with the pilgrims in the past. With the secular decline of religion, pilgrimages are less popular today, but the modern educated person may be driven by a sense of duty that he must learn, even when on holiday, and thus wander from one cultural experience to another. This will include visiting the world-famous cities and seeing the 'sights' which they contain.

Conclusion

The power of cities to attract visitors will obviously vary. Some cities are at the top of a hierarchy in terms of their ability to attract tourists because they are well endowed with the tourist resources mentioned above. Other cities are lower in the hierarchy because they have fewer resources, but they may wish to develop the tourist industry. This is possible to a certain extent. Some resources, such as historic buildings or art collections, either are impossible to create or could be created only at enormous expense. There is also the question of attracting media attention so that people know of the city and want to visit it. It is almost inevitable that only a limited number of places can have world stature. Other cities will have to struggle to obtain publicity, and then they may not have the right image to attract tourists. A hierarchy of cities as tourist attractors exists and will almost certainly continue to exist.

Urban tourism, then, is a complex of activities which are interlinked in a particular milieu and enable cities to attract visitors. There is not necessarily one key factor, as with a beach in a resort. The study of urban tourism involves understanding the principal elements (Figure 1.3), always remembering that they do not stand in isolation from each other. None of these components is necessarily unique to cities (Figure 1.4). These activities take place in cities and elsewhere, and so in this respect cities are in competition with other types of places. To understand tourism in cities, it is necessary to study the geographical pattern of these elements across space, and the processes which are affecting change.

Understanding tourism can involve several disciplines, but the perspective of this author is primarily that of a geographer. In many respects tourism is the geography of consumption outside the home area; it is about how and why people travel to consume, whether it be historic buildings, landscapes, art and museum collections, or sports and entertainment. It is concerned with what makes tourists travel, what determines how far and in what direction they move. On the production side it is concerned to understand where tourism activities develop and on what scale. It is concerned with the process or processes whereby some cities are able to create tourism resources and a tourism industry. How far is this primarily a political process and to what

	TYPE OF AREA							
	CAPITAL CITY	LARGE CITY	HISTORIC CITY	SMALL TOWN	SEASIDE RESORT	SPA	SKI RESORT	RURAL AREA
HISTORIC URBANSCAPE	●	?	●	?	?	●	~	~
ATTRACTIONS	●	●	~	?	●	?	~	?
URBAN FACILITIES	●	●	?	~	?	?	~	~
CONFERENCES & EXHIBITIONS	●	●	●	~	●	●	~	?
SUN/SEA	~	~	~	~	●	~	~	~
EXERCISE	~	~	~	~	●	~	●	●
OPEN SPACE	~	~	~	~	~	~	●	●

Figure 1.4 The tourism matrix.

extent do existing resources and potential ones influence the outcome? These and many other questions will be considered in the rest of this book. Before these wider questions can be considered, it is necessary to begin by placing tourism in cities in the context of urban change and the challenge facing cities.

2

The urban context

The aim of this book is to examine the role which tourism does play and might play in the economy of large cities. Within North America and western Europe, there are over 60 metropolitan areas with a population over 1 million. It is important, therefore, to understand how cities are changing in order to be able to place tourism in this wider context. In this chapter the changes that are taking place to cities, both in their relationships to each other and with respect to the patterns within cities, will be reviewed. The response which cities are making to this changing environment and how successful their policies have been will also be examined. Very little mention will be made of tourism, and many of the implications of these urban changes for tourism will become apparent only in later chapters. However, this urban context is essential if the growth of tourism and policies for tourism are to be understood.

Changing Patterns of Urban Growth

Geographers have long sought to understand the pattern of cities, why some places are important and others less so. While there have clearly been some chance factors, it is also possible to see some general forces at work. Two influences in particular can be mentioned. Firstly, there is the importance of what is called the urban economic base. Cities grow because they are able to export goods, and the income derived from this enables them to import more materials and goods and develop a higher standard of living. For many centuries, cities lived primarily on the basis of trade, either short distance, to be discussed below, or over a longer distance. However, from the eighteenth century onwards industries evolved and developed to become of great importance in the economies of cities. It was the growth of industries in the nineteenth century and the first half of the twentieth century that caused most cities to grow, and the terms industrial city and industrial age to be used. The exact character of industry varied from place to place, depending on local resources, communications and the character of the population, including the skills and innovative abilities available. Thus there were steel towns, shipbuilding towns, cotton towns, motor car towns, and so on. Because the resources, both natural and human, used by industry were unevenly distributed, there was no simple geographical pattern of cities. While there was some concentration of urban growth on coalfields and other natural resources, industry was also found elsewhere at ports, existing cities, and new centres where innovators lived.

A second influence on the pattern of cities focuses on what is technically called 'central place' theory. As mentioned above, towns developed to trade with their surrounding areas. They provided services, such as retailing, which could not be justified in every village because of the small population. A regular pattern of towns developed every few kilometres to serve rural areas. However, these small market towns could not supply all services, and so larger towns emerged less frequently to meet the need for these 'higher order' goods and services. Most countries do (or did) exhibit an urban hierarchy, moving down from the largest city supplying a very wide range of goods and services over a very extensive area, to the lowest level of town offering a limited range of goods and services to a small rural area round about. As the population grew in the nineteenth and twentieth centuries, this urban hierarchy both changed and was reinforced. In some regions industrial cities increased rapidly in size and moved up the urban hierarchy; an example is Manchester overtaking Chester. However, many existing cities maintained their status. In some cases the new forms of communication focused on them, giving them added advantages to attract industry. Similarly, new utilities, such as gas supply or telephones, were often first based there, again giving them advantages to attract industry. Also, for the larger cities their size often encouraged industrial innovation, from which emerged new industries (Pred, 1966). For these reasons, the urban hierarchy appeared relatively stable in the first half of the twentieth century. Once a city had achieved a certain size and status in the urban hierarchy, it appeared able to maintain this role without threat from neighbouring rivals and safe from the competition of cities further away because of the friction (cost) of distance.

Since the mid-twentieth century these verities have been changing owing to a number of forces. Firstly, the industrial structure has been evolving. Overall, manufacturing employment is far less important than it used to be. Increased mechanization and automation mean that goods can be produced with much less labour than in the past. This increased productivity has affected the primary and secondary sectors far more than the tertiary (or services) sector, with the consequence that an increasing share of employment is found within services. One response to this shift is to talk of a post-industrial society and the post-industrial city. The loss of jobs in industry is obviously a problem for those cities which are not able to increase employment in the tertiary sector. While many industries have been shedding labour, some industries have been expanding. The history of the period since the industrial revolution is one of a series of innovative waves throwing up new industries. As these appear, the industrial structure changes and the old industries go into relative decline. Today's new industries include certain types of chemicals and electronics, the so-called high-technology industries, which require much research and development. Once again, the location of the growth industries does not often coincide with the areas where industrial employment is declining most rapidly, so causing problems.

Another change within industry has been the occupational shift. The structure of employment within manufacturing firms has shifted away from blue collar shopfloor manual workers towards white collar non-manual and professional workers. The different units of the manufacturing firm which once coexisted on the same site may now be located in different places, with the factory in one place, the head office somewhere else and the research and development laboratory in yet another location. The linkages between activities may mean that these different types of work may concentrate together in particular types of location, producing a spatial division of labour (Massey, 1984). All of this has significant implications for the economies of cities.

The tertiarization of the economy, or the growth of services, has also not been without spatial implications. Not all services have experienced employment growth. Jobs in railways and ports have disappeared rapidly, while the location of some activities, such as wholesaling, has changed. For many years after World War II, the main growth activities involved public services, especially education and health. In recent years the most notable growth has been in finance and business services. While education and health services are widely distributed according to the population, finance and business services are more localized. Consequently, cities with advantages for business have gained jobs while those without this benefit have performed poorly. Leisure and tourism jobs have also grown and these will be the subject of discussion in the rest of this book.

Another factor which has affected city growth in recent years has been improvements in communications, both physical and telecommunications. This has undermined the local base of cities, enabling cities to compete against each other through the widening of spheres of influence. Previously, cities would have been protected from competition because of the cost of movement. Now companies may be able to serve distant areas using the telephone, or dispatch goods from a central warehouse rather than having numerous small ones to serve each local area. With computers and telephone lines, work that was previously done locally can now be done centrally. As a consequence of these improved communications, the relationships between

Table 2.1 Population and civilian employment changes in the USA

Region	Population (millions)			Civilian employment (millions)		
	1970	1989	Change (%)	1970	1988	Change (%)
North-east	49	51	+4	20	25	+26
Midwest	57	60	+5	24	30	+25
South	63	86	+37	25	41	+64
West	35	52	+49	14	25	+79
USA	203	248	+22	83	122	+46

Source: *Statistical Abstract of the United States*, 1990.

Table 2.2 Population and employment changes in the UK

Region	Population (000)			Employment (000)		
	1971	1991	Change (%)	1971	1991	Change (%)
South	22 681	24 372	+7.5	9 278	9 835	+6.0
Midlands*	11 474	12 167	+6.0	4 582	4 537	−1.0
North	21 360	21 109	−1.1	8 258	7 864	−4.8
UK	55 515	57 649	+3.8	22 122	22 235	+0.5

Source: OPCS and Department of Employment. *Midlands = East and West Midlands and Wales.

cities are changing, and there is now greater competition. The location of economic activities can now take place over wider areas with business people having more choice of location.

Studies of the changing pattern of employment and population have drawn attention to two broad trends (Champion and Townsend, 1990). Firstly there is a drift from north to south. In the USA this is seen in the difference between the sunbelt and the frostbelt (or rustbelt) (Table 2.1). There is a shift of population and employment from the north and east to the south and west, from states like New York and Pennsylvania to states such as California and Texas. In Britain there has been a shift from the north and west to the south and east (Table 2.2). A similar shift has occurred in Germany, where Bavaria and Baden-Württemberg have gained, while in France the southern areas have again had high rates of growth. The second broad trend is the shift away from large cities towards rural areas, sometimes called 'counterurbanization' (Berry, 1976; Champion, 1989). In North America and western Europe, aggregate statistics show that the very largest cities (or conurbations) are either losing population or growing less rapidly than other types of settlement. Surprisingly in view of demographic history from 1850 to 1950, many remote rural areas, after decades of decline, are showing growth again, often at the highest rates. Because of this reversal of roles, Berry also used the term 'the inversion of geography'. The outcome of these trends is that older industrial cities in the 'north' are often experiencing decline and stagnation, while those in the 'south' are more likely to be buoyant and growing.

Any explanation of these spatial trends must involve many factors, some of which have listed location constraints and some of which have pulled development in particular directions. In the past, cities had many advantages for economic activities, because of good communications, public utilities, a large labour force with varied skills, and a complex of industries which could provide services to each other. In contrast, rural areas offered few of the requirements of industry. Today, however, rural areas have all the basic utilities, are often near motorways, and have plenty of land for development. Living in a rural area today does not mean cutting oneself off from the benefits of civilization as it once did. Television at least gives access to the rest of the world. Meanwhile, conditions in cities have changed. Land and labour are expensive and congestion may add costs. At least for a period up to the 1970s, land was often in short supply in Britain's greenbelt-encircled cities. These conditions have encouraged people to move away from cities and to the rural areas. This shift has been accentuated by the decline that has taken place in many cities through deindustrialization and increases in productivity, mainly since the late 1960s.

A feature of both trends is the apparent shift towards environmentally attractive areas, either in the 'south' with its warmer climate, or rural areas with their open landscapes. With more activities spatially footloose and with retired people free to live where they want, one interpretation is that many people are choosing to move away from cities, which they think are dirty, unsafe, expensive and congested, towards what they regard as more pleasant and less stressful surroundings. Many of the social changes that are taking place in society and that produce problems impinge most severely on cities. The rise in unemployment and the creation of an underclass is one phenomenon that appears to produce rising crime rates and other social problems. These are further incentives for people and firms to leave cities.

Social scientists studying cities see them as being in a much more fluid situation than in the past. There are some general trends but these will not rigidly determine which cities grow and which decline. Economic activities are growing and declining and also relocating. Cities must perpetually strive to attract economic growth or else they will face the prospect of decline. In this they are in competition with a large number of other cities both near and far away. Not surprisingly, given this context, the actions of some cities are described as proactive and entrepreneurial (Harvey, 1989). To attract growth they must create an all-round environment which is likely to appeal to those who make decisions about where to locate business. This must cover not just the basic economic requirements, such as good communications and sites for industries and offices, but also the general environment and amenities which will make the city a good place to live in, involving both housing and lifestyle opportunities. They must also 'sell' the city to a wide audience so that its advantages are known. In a large and competitive market-place, cities must 'shout' loudly, using innovative ways to obtain a high profile.

Given the fluidity of economic change, it is likely that most cities will seek a diversified economic base, although this will not preclude their playing to any particular strength which they have. At the present time the growth industries appear to be high technology, finance and business and tourism. Inevitably a large number of cities will be attempting to create an environment in which these activities can grow and flourish, picking on components of these sectors in which they feel they have a comparative advantage. In recent years it has become commonplace for cities to prepare economic development strategies in which they set out their goals and objectives, and their pro-grammes of action. Some cities have been able to articulate a strategic vision much better than others, reflecting various internal political factors, including the quality of the leadership. Often, slogans and images are used to indicate the vision which the city has, such as 'international city', 'business city', 'high-tech city', and so on. Such phrases are often regarded as mere hype, but can assist in the realization of goals.

Intraurban Patterns

The postwar period has also witnessed significant changes in the internal geography of cities. From being relatively compact and monocentric (i.e. focused on the city centre), cities have decentralized and become polycentric, with consequences for the core areas. Cities have always been focused on the city centre, and the coming of the railways reinforced this tendency. They gave the city centre great nodality both for people and goods, and as a con-sequence cities were often structured around this core of accessibility. Shops and offices, which needed to draw in people from a wider area and which could outbid other land uses in paying high rents, came to dominate the city centre. Around them were found warehouses and manufacturing industry, which needed to be near the railway goods yards from where goods were dispatched by horse and cart. Further out were the residential areas, with the poor living near the centre at high densities to be near their work, whilst the rich lived on the periphery with larger houses and gardens and were able to afford to travel back to the centre. Of course, cities did not show an exact concentric pattern or a complete segregation of land uses. Without planning, some mixing up of land uses was inevitable, and the physical geography of cities meant that transport and industry were often pulled towards particular areas such as river valleys.

During the twentieth century there has been an increasing trend of decen-tralization, made possible by easier transport, and in particular the use of motor vehicles. This has caused cities to sprawl outwards. Initially the predominant form of decentralization was of people, thus introducing a pattern of commuting back to the core. Later, as jobs decentralized, some people moved to be near their work, but at the same time journey to work patterns became more complex, with movements from suburb to core, core to suburb, and suburb to suburb. Many expanding industries found that their central city sites were too constricted, with no room for expansion, and thus came to look for sites on the periphery. Similar trends affected warehouses, where the change to horizontal rather than vertical buildings and congested inner city streets encouraged firms to look for sites on the periphery, near motorways. For a long time offices appeared to prefer to remain in the centre, where there was good accessibility, the possibility of face-to-face contact with firms in ancillary businesses, and external economies, but the high rents, the difficulty of recruiting staff and sometimes the wish to be able to use the car easily has now persuaded many firms of the benefits of the suburbs. Finally, there has also been the decentralization of retailing. As the population grew in the suburbs, so shops appeared, and as more people moved there, a wider range of shops could be found. As a few suburban centres began to offer a wider range of higher-order goods, so consumers began to switch their purchases away from the city centre.

The social patterning of cities is also important in understanding the inner city problem. The more modern and spacious housing of the suburbs has inevitably drawn the higher-income groups to the suburbs, leaving the poorer housing stock of the inner city to the less affluent. Here a cycle of deterioration often occurred as low returns on investment discouraged landlords from making repairs, so that the standards of housing declined even further. In Britain, slum clearance led to these houses being replaced by public housing, which has increasingly become the housing for the poor. Falling household size and lower-density housing has meant that the population of inner city areas has fallen considerably. In general, inner city areas are occupied by the poor, but one counter-trend has been 'gentrification', with a few middle-class people moving back into these areas. These are childless households, either young (yuppies) or older (empty nesters), who generally work in the city centre. Sometimes old houses have been upgraded while at other times new houses have been built.

Most large cities have some problems in their core areas, although the scale, nature and intensity vary considerably. In the city centre, retailing faces competition from suburban and out-of-town shopping centres, which in some cases has led to decline. This is particularly so in American cities, where some downtown traditional shopping districts have almost disappeared. In most city centres office activities remain important and may have grown significantly, although in all cases they face competition from suburban complexes. The wholesaling and manufacturing activities on the fringe of the city centre have generally declined significantly, together with transport and public utilities. This has often left behind vacant land and derelict buildings. What was once expensive land has now become much cheaper, although the owners are not always ready to accept this. In many city centres one of the main challenges for planning is to find new uses for these redundant fringe areas.

In the surrounding inner city there are similar problems. Industry and warehousing have declined. Many firms have gone out of business, others have relocated to the suburbs, while others which are part of larger organizations may have been closed as part of a rationalization process. There are now sites for industry available but these are not always perceived favourably, as skilled workers no longer live locally and there may be problems of crime and vandalism. As regards housing, there may be a mix of old housing in need of renovation and modern public housing deteriorating rapidly, and forming areas where there are often severe social problems. Given the poverty of these areas it is often difficult to get private investment except in a few favourable locations where gentrification may be possible.

There is no universal model of the decay of inner cities just as there is no one prescription. In general it could be argued that decline in the inner city is greatest in the USA, less so in Britain and least in continental Europe, but within each of these regions there is considerable variation. Detroit does offer the prospect of the (ringed) doughnut city, but there are many US cities such as Boston where the downtown area is still vibrant. In continental Europe the city centre has remained vibrant for several reasons. It has historic buildings and associations which attract people. The wealthy have never moved away from their apartments in the city centre and in the adjacent inner city as they have done in the USA and Britain. It retains lively social and cultural activities as well as good shops. Not least, it is served by regular and efficient public transport.

The combination of problems in these core areas, dereliction, low investment, poverty and unemployment, plus the desire of cities to revitalize their city centres to present a good face to the outside world, has meant that these areas have become the focus of urban policy since the late 1960s. The occasional riot has kept these zones in the news and reinforced existing policies. In the USA, central cities were recipients of several types of federal grants in the 1970s and 1980s, including community block grants and urban development action grants. In Britain a strong inner city policy has existed since 1978 and has included enterprise zones, city grants, urban development corporations and task forces. Inner city areas are often potential recipients of grants from other tiers of government from the level of the region to the supranational, such as the European Community.

Policy Approaches

Urban policies are concerned with both winning economic growth for a city and regenerating the core areas, goals which may not always be coincident. A difficulty in many areas is that the urban agglomeration is divided into numerous jurisdictions, most noticeably between the central city (the old urban area) and the suburban districts. This can exacerbate urban sprawl as suburbs compete to attract growth, often accelerating the process of decentralization. Without a metropolitan-wide organization it may be difficult to get all local authorities to work for the overall good of the entire urban area. Frequently the central city is attempting both to counteract the processes of decentralization, act for the entire urban area in various ways, and regenerate its inner city. Because the inner city problem first became apparent on a large scale in the USA, many policies were first pioneered there and subsequently transposed to Britain. European continental cities have less severe inner city problems, but their policies are often similar. Obviously the mix of policies in any city will be unique but it is possible to suggest some key elements in current urban policy, as follows:

1   An emphasis on economic policies. Notwithstanding the great social problems that exist in cities, particularly in inner city areas, and the pressure that democratic politicians are under to respond to these, most urban policies are primarily economic. In times of economic difficulty it is generally agreed that the priority must be to obtain economic growth rather than redistribute the inadequate amount that exists. This is not to say that there are no social policies. American politicians usually respond by offering something to the neighbourhoods.
2   An emphasis on obtaining private investment. The private sector is obviously concerned with economic investments and activities, and so if economic policies are to be regarded as successful then one test is how much private sector investment has taken place. Grants and other incentives are offered to private firms in an effort to 'lever' investment. Evaluations of public policy usually calculate the private to public ratio of investment, and the higher it is the more successful the policy is adjudged to be.
3   An emphasis on property development. Most grants are given for property development, so that leverage ratios are in effect measuring the success of property development. Most buildings are for economic activities so that employment will result, but this is a byproduct of policy rather than its first objective. Property development usually takes place on derelict land, or alternatively on sites which were underused or contained redundant buildings. Since these types of sites are one of the problems of inner city areas, property development does clearly result in physical regeneration, although the economic objective of providing employment may not be achieved. One of the problems of property-led regeneration is that it is very susceptible to changes in the economic cycle. In periods of strong national growth, regeneration will take place quickly, only to grind to a halt when the recession comes.
4   Public sector investment in the infrastructure. Usually one of the reasons why there has been inadequate private investment in the inner city is that the infrastructure is both obsolete and insufficient. It is often necessary for public agencies to be involved in these old-established areas, to reclaim much of the land and to provide new utilities and communications. This public sector investment must proceed before any private sector investment can be expected to take place; it is a precondition for private investment.
5   Public sector 'anchors'. In addition to infrastructure it may be necessary for the public sector to invest in certain key activities. With respect to tourism, these might be museums and attractions, and convention centres. When these anchors are in place they will draw people in, and this will encourage private sector investment. Thus a convention centre might stimulate

investment in hotels. This approach has been considered important in the USA (e.g. Baltimore) and in the cities of continental Europe, but during the 1980s in Britain this type of public investment was often proscribed. Many grants were available only if they levered private investment, and they could not be used for public facilities. However, sometimes grants for museums and similar facilities were available from other national funds.

Taking 4 and 5 together, it can be seen that public investment plays a crucial role in encouraging private investment by reducing risk and creating confidence.

6 A focus on the city centre. While the city centre is only a small part of the inner city, and generally, being lightly populated, has few social problems, it has tended to receive most of the investment, both from the public and private sectors. This situation has arisen because this is the zone where private investment is likely to earn its highest return, and perhaps the only place where it will be profitable. The city centre usually still has good accessibility by public transport, although this needs improving. It will have offices and shops, plus many other facilities from museums to nightclubs. These provide a basis on which to build. In contrast, the inner city areas may have extensive tracts of poor-quality residential areas containing low-income groups, and the prospect of a low return on investment. Consequently, in spite of the needs of this zone and its political weight in a democracy, investment has been skewed to the city centre.

7 Public–private partnership. Another American idea which has become orthodoxy in inner city policy is public–private partnership. In the past, cities have prepared policies and zoned land for different uses and then hoped that the private sector would respond and invest as and where the plan suggested. This has not always worked because the plans were unrealistic in terms of market conditions. However, in the USA, where there are often strong locally based companies, they have joined together to form organizations which put their own ideas forward, and press the municipal body to accept and implement them. In favour of this it can be said that business leaders may have a better idea of market possibilities than politicians and planners. Also, insofar as they may own property and companies in the inner city, they have a strong vested interest in the success of the city, and their support may be crucial in gaining the investment required. Against this, it may be said that they could move the city in a direction which is in their interest and not that of most of the people of the city, and also seek public funds for their own investments. Partnerships can take many forms, from those which embrace a wide spectrum of the private sector, to those which involve only one industry, such as tourism. Some partnerships are concerned with the whole city and others only with a small part of it, as with those working for the revitalization of the downtown district.

8 Semi-autonomous public agencies. A frequent criticism of municipal authorities is that they are slow, bureaucratic, frightened of taking risks with the taxpayers' money, and not sufficiently market orientated. One way of overcoming this is to set up agencies at arm's length from government with a clear mandate and let them get on with it. In the USA many cities have set up such agencies. They have land provided to them via compulsory purchase and are provided with resources. After that, they tend to function like a private development company. In Britain the Conservative government in 1981 set up urban development corporations, responsible to the central government, to undertake a similar task.

9 Flagship projects. A characteristic feature of many development agencies is the concentration of effort into one or two large-scale schemes, often referred to as flagship projects. The argument here is that one large scheme can have more impact than many small schemes, and that a flagship project will come to symbolize the renewal efforts, be good publicity, create confidence, and have spillover impacts in the area round about. In other words, it will be a catalyst for renewal.

10 Image. In order to attract new activities, older industrial cities must change their image, from the perception of the smokestack to one that is more appealing. This will not only help attract new investment but will also be a form of confidence boosting for local business and residents.

The last twenty years have witnessed strenuous efforts to revive the inner city, with varying degrees of success. A few cities, like Baltimore and Boston, have dramatically changed their urban landscape and have been hailed as successes, although critics point out that appearances can sometimes be only skin deep and that there is still a long way to go with these policies before poverty and dereliction in the inner city are removed. Many of the features of the revitalized American inner city have been transferred to Europe. They include waterfront redevelopment, festival market-places, covered shopping malls, convention centres, spectacular high-rise office blocks, sports arenas, multi-use buildings, atrium buildings and rapid transit systems. Many of these features are integral or relevant to tourism in cities and will be examined later.

Conclusion

The purpose of this chapter has been to show that the attempt to develop tourism in cities cannot be understood without reference to the changing economic, social and physical structures. In the post-industrial world cities must compete to attract new activities to replace those they have lost. In this race cities do not all start from the same position nor do they have an equal chance of being successful. Some inherit better resources, some are better located, and some have sites of greater potential. Perhaps of greater importance is that some cities have a social structure which is more likely to produce alliances, coalitions and partnerships which will take the city forward and from which leaders will emerge. Some cities appear to be able to develop a strategy and maintain it over many years, while other cities have barely recognized that they are in this competitive situation and have been unable to put forward a strategy. One thing that appears almost certain is that when a policy is developed it will focus attention on the city centre, where the greatest potential is perceived to be.

3
The strategy of urban tourism

During the 1980s policies aimed at developing tourism in cities became widely adopted both in North America and western Europe. At the beginning of the decade, Bradford in England, a city hitherto only noted for its woollen industry, surprised the country by advertising itself as a tourist centre. Could they be serious? When other industrial towns attempted to follow suit, the media had so little understanding of tourism that cartoons were produced of people sitting on beaches against a background of factories. However, what was considered a surprising development to many at the beginning of the decade has now become accepted orthodoxy. The aim of this chapter is to discuss the urban tourism strategy and the ideas behind it, and to examine its feasibility in terms of tourism markets.

The Strategy

The context for the proposal to develop tourism in cities has already been outlined in the previous chapter. Since the 1970s (at least) cities have been losing economic activities, and they need new ones which will generate income for the area and create jobs. This decline has left behind many derelict areas, and new activities are required which will also stimulate physical regeneration. Concurrent with this economic decline in cities, tourism appeared to be growing, and therefore invited examination to assess whether it could play a role in the economic and physical regeneration of cities. On the basis that there would be increasing affluence, easier travel and greater leisure time, it was quickly assumed that the tourism industry was bound to grow. It brought income into the area, so acting as an economic base, and was assumed to be able to give support to the local economy. Without much deep analysis most political leaders decided that tourism did have a role to play and began to introduce policies. Tourism was never perceived as a panacea for urban problems but as part of the solution.

However, it would be wrong to see tourism promotion simply as one component of local economic development policy, similar to either industrial or office development (Law, 1991a). The proponents of urban tourism have always suggested that it had much greater significance (Collinge, 1989), (Figure 3.1). Investment for tourism involves the development of facilities, activities, physical environments and infrastructure which will have benefits for the local community. It also involves marketing the city and selling an image which will assist in the attraction of industrial and commercial activities (Ashworth and Voogd, 1990). As was seen in Chapter 2, in order to attract mobile investment and activities, cities must first gain attention in an increasingly competitive situation (Ashworth and Voogd, 1990). Advertising the city and engaging in activities which will be described later in this book will raise the profile and visibility of a city, which will be of assistance to those engaged in economic promotion. Many of the activities being expanded, such as culture and sport, at least partly with an eye on the tourism market, will persuade potential residents, such as professionals and executives, that the city is a good place in which to live, that it has the right lifestyle opportunities. With the renewal of districts and the new image it will be easier to bring middle-class residents back to the inner city. The money which tourists spend at urban facilities, such as concerts and theatres, may make these activities more economically viable, which will be of benefit to the local community. Finally, the development of these facilities, the physical regeneration of areas and the arrival of visitors may increase civic pride, which is usually deemed a good thing. It is suggested that local residents who have civic pride will take much greater care of the environment.

Large cities are already tourist centres but if the industry is to play a larger role in the economy then it must be substantially increased in size. This will mean attracting hundreds of thousands of extra tourists to bring in the extra income that will create jobs. To bring in more tourists the tourism resources must be expanded. These, as was seen in Chapter 1, have been classified into two types (Jansen-Verbeke, 1988) (Figure 1.3). Primary elements are those which attract people, and consist of historic buildings and urban landscapes, museums and art galleries, concerts, spectator sports, conferences, exhibitions, entertainments and special events. It is not always easy to say what is the main reason why a person has visited a city. A person could be attracted by one element and use only that element. However, he or she could come to the city for one component and then use other elements as well. Alternatively, tourists come because of the mix of attractions. It is likely that for many urban tourists it is the range of opportunities which is important and that these linkages should not be forgotten. Secondary elements enhance these attractions or assist in the process of attracting tourists, and include

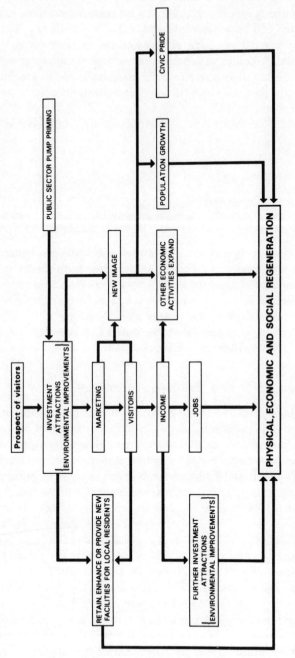

Figure 3.1 The strategy of urban tourism (after Law, 1992).

shopping, catering, accommodation, and transport and tourism agencies. Any expansion of tourism will involve the development of all these components. All these elements will be considered in later chapters in this book. In addition to these elements, cities may act as a 'gateway' to other areas. Today this applies particularly to cities which have major international airports. In Germany, Frankfurt acts as a base for tourists using its hotels and facilities to visit not only the city but also the Rhine gorge and historic towns such as Heidelberg and Rothenburg.

The prime visitor markets for urban tourism are considered to be:

business travellers
conference and exhibition delegates
short-break holiday makers
day trippers
visitors to friends and relatives
long holiday makers using the city as a gateway to the surrounding region
long holiday makers on a tour, stopping off for a short visit

With the exception of the last two categories and visits to capital cities, few long holiday makers stay in cities. The importance of the last two categories is clearly at least partly dependent on factors and conditions outside the city itself. A city such as Lyon in France which is on a main routeway has the opportunity to benefit from passing travellers (Renucci, 1992). If a city is to be successful as a tourist centre then it must make an impact in these markets. The feasibility of this strategy will be considered later.

The Adoption of Urban Tourism Strategies

While the strategy of urban tourism has been widely adopted, its path has not always been straightforward (Law, 1991b). Some critics, who sometimes include elected representatives, do not think that tourism is a 'proper' industry, and still look to manufacturing industry to restore the fortunes of cities. Given the near-universal shift in the employment structure away from manufacturing towards services, this approach appears increasingly irrelevant. Cities must seek to expand the service sector and thereby create jobs. Tourism is one part of the service sector which is growing rapidly. Another criticism of the strategy arises because tourism is often perceived as providing low-paid, low-skilled and seasonal jobs (Williams and Shaw, 1988). For urban tourism the latter is not true or is much less true than for the rest of the industry. Evidence to be presented later in this book will show that many of the activities of the industry, such as conferences, do not experience great seasonal variations, and that the hotel industry in cities has a very different seasonal profile from that in resorts. While many of the jobs are low skilled, this could be in tourism's favour when it is located in or near the inner city with its labour reserves of the unskilled. A strong argument against expanding the tourist industry is that it involves spending money on visitors when the priority should be to spend it on residents. For this reason many studies which will be reported later have attempted to prove that the community benefits from tourism and any public sector investment is worthwhile.

This ambiguous attitude towards tourism of some city councils has meant that funding has sometimes been either denied or limited, so that the promotion of tourism has varied from place to place. Of course, general attempts to cut public expenditure have impacted on the funding of tourism administrations and projects, and this has affected cities differentially.

Other critics perceive tourism as having adverse consequences for cities. Bringing more visitors to cities might add to existing congestion. More tourists will add to the wear and tear on facilities and increase the cost of urban management. Further, the influx of visitors may not be welcomed by local residents, and the facilities favoured by the tourist may not be those desired or needed by the community. Thus specialty shopping has been described as 'commercial gentrification'.

While the incorporation of tourism into city economic development strategies is fairly widespread, their articulation in published documents is often limited. Only a few cities in the UK have produced lengthy and comprehensive tourism plans, among them Belfast (PIEDA, 1987), Birmingham (Birmingham City Council, 1987), Bristol (Bristol City Council Planning Department, 1990), Cardiff (Tibbalds *et al.*, 1988), Glasgow (Pannell *et al.*, 1984) and Merseyside (Merseyside Tourist Board, 1987). Briefer documents have been produced by other cities, such as Manchester (English Tourist Board LDR, 1989), and in addition several British cities have produced 'tourism development action programmes', including Bradford, Bristol and Tyneside. Recently, Sheffield has produced a 'tourism initiative' (Heeley, 1990; Sheffield Joint Tourism Initiative, 1990). Tourism strategy documents usually combine a mixture of economic and physical planning, the latter containing a strong urban design element.

Elsewhere the role of tourism can be gauged from statements in economic development strategies and in structure plans. In Bradford, which early established a reputation in urban tourism, the tourism promotion unit has always been within the economic development department, and the principal statement of tourism policy is to be found in the city's economic strategy (Bradford Metropolitan District Council, 1991). However, sometimes there is a puzzling disjuncture between the tourism unit and the economic development unit, with the latter concentrating on traditional policies such as those of constructing industrial estates. In some cities tourism policies have not been formulated in official documents, but have nevertheless been articulated by city leaders in their speeches and are a sign of *de facto* policy. With or without tourism strategy documents, much tourism development is a product of pragmatic opportunism. It is impossible to foresee the opportunities that may arise, whether in the form of a mobile museum or special event, and it is the determination to develop the industry which is probably the critical element

Table 3.1 The structure of the US pleasure travel market

1. Visits to friends and relatives	44%
2. Touring	14%
3. Close to home leisure trip (mainly outdoors)	13%
4. Outdoor activities in a rural area	10%
5. A resort trip	8%
6. A city trip	7%
7. Theme park, exhibition or special event	3%
8. Cruise	1%

Source: Tourism Canada (1986).

in initiating a programme of tourism development. Tourism investment, like most property development, is cyclical. Several years of economic growth with resulting benefits to the tourist industry will encourage investment in tourism projects. Many of these schemes are linked with other types of investment, particularly in cities, and if these other activities are not viable then the whole project will not proceed. Thus urban tourism investment tends to be cyclical. In the downturn it may be very difficult for cities to get projects off the ground. In Manchester in 1990 two projects, a concert hall and a festival market-place, both depended on cross-subsidization from office development, and because of the recession it was difficult for the developers to obtain loan finance.

Tourism Markets: Leisure

The growth of tourism has been enabled by increasing affluence, easier travel and greater leisure. As was seen in Chapter 1, during the twentieth century leisure opportunities have increased enormously. The basic task of cities is to persuade tourists to come to them. Some assessment of this task can be made by examining the present patterns of leisure tourism both overall and through the different sub-markets. A study of the US pleasure travel market by Tourism Canada (1986) classified trips into eight types and found their importance to be as shown in Table 3.1.

At first sight the prospects for cities do not appear promising, as only 7 per cent of all visits are to cities, but visits to friends and relatives, touring and the theme park, etc. may all involve a city location. Thus while the purpose of the trip may not always be expressed as a city visit, it very often does include an urban component.

Long holidays

A long holiday is defined as 4+ nights away from home. British survey figures show that about 40 per cent of the population take no long holidays (Table 3.2). This proportion has not varied significantly over the past twenty

Table 3.2 Long holiday taking by the British

	Frequency of 4+ nights by British adults		
	1971 (%)	1981 (%)	1991 (%)
No holiday	41	39	40
All holidays	59	61	60
One holiday	44	40	36
Two holidays	12	15	16
Three or more	3	6	8
British Isles	49	46	43
Abroad	13	21	28

Source: British Tourist Authority (1991, 1992).

years, although, as could be expected, there is a small increase in years of recession, and a decrease in years of high growth. Again as could be guessed, those who do not take holidays are drawn more from the lower income groups, the elderly, the disabled and the poorer regions. Other people may not take holidays because of work commitments or because they do not wish to go on their own. About 60 per cent of the population do take a long holiday and this figure is composed of 35 per cent who have only one holiday, 16 per cent who have two holidays and 8 per cent who have three or more. Over the past twenty years the share in these last two categories has increased from 15 to 23 per cent, suggesting that with greater affluence there will be more holiday taking. Table 3.2 also shows that more British people are going on holiday abroad. Britain has a stable population and these figures suggest that the main growth in long holidays has been in those taking an additional one, many of which may have been taken abroad.

Most of these holidays took place in the five summer months, 77 per cent for those in Britain and 63 per cent for those abroad. Of holidays in Britain, about 50 per cent were self-catering, 30 per cent were in serviced accommodation and 20 per cent with friends and relatives. Of British holiday makers going abroad, just over half used serviced accommodation, about 30 per cent were self-catering, and the rest stayed with friends and relatives. Staying with friends and relatives may serve several purposes: seeing people, having a cheap holiday, and perhaps looking after a sick or elderly person. When families and friends are widely scattered it may be possible to see them only by using one's holidays. Long holidays are generally perceived as one stop, but they may take the form of a circuit with stops at several places, thus being the tour from which the word tourism is derived. This type of tourism commonly takes the form of visiting cities, as with the 'Grand Tour' in the past.

Cities have not generally targeted this type of holiday maker. With the exception of capital cities like London and Paris, cities have not generally appealed to the long holiday market. However, this may be changing. There are signs that the growth of the package tour to Mediterranean resorts has peaked. Tourists are beginning to look more widely, both in terms of destination and in terms of type of place. If the package tour was Fordism, then post-Fordism will involve greater variety and more self-designed holidays. With an ageing population, more people may be interested in cultural holidays (broadly conceived), and it is here that cities will have an advantage. As has been mentioned, some tourists visit capital cities such as London, but frequently only a part of the holiday is spent there. Trips are made to Windsor, Oxford, Bath and Stratford-upon-Avon. London is used as a base or gateway for a long holiday. Many other cities would like to perform such a gateway role. Whether they can will depend on how many attractions there are in the surrounding region, perhaps on having an international airport, and on having the kind of accommodation and other facilities which the tourist wants. In other cases the long holiday is broken down into sections, three or four days being spent in a different city. Many American cities are seeking the coach tour market, which often appeals to elderly citizens.

Short breaks

Cities are interested in the short-break market for a number of reasons. It is a type of business which operates throughout the year and is therefore attractive. It is also a type of business which operates throughout the week but which is particularly important at the weekends. Given that business travellers come mainly during the week, city hotels are looking for business to fill up their bedrooms at the weekend. Most city hotels offer special cut prices at the weekend, and may arrange tickets for entertainment at the same time. British cities have joined together to form the 'Great British City Break' to market these packages more widely. Except for the largest cities, many visitors would want to visit a city only for a short break, as they would be able to achieve all they wanted to do in that time. Many of the activities of the city are in fact likely to attract visitors only for two or three days, whether this be for a conference, festival or some form of entertainment. While cities prefer visitors who use serviced accommodation and thus make a greater impact, one of the principal types of tourist to the city is the visitor to friends and relatives, who often comes for the weekend.

A short-break holiday is defined as one of 1–3 nights away from home. These have not always been recorded by surveys, and often the small samples used mean that the results are not very reliable. In Britain there are between 30 million and 37 million short breaks a year taken by British residents. In the 1970s this appeared to be a growth area in tourism, as people used their additional wealth and holiday entitlements for this kind of holiday. However, in the 1980s the number taking this type of holiday stabilized. In 1990, of those staying in Britain, 44 per cent stayed with friends and relatives, 31 per cent were self-catering in some form, i.e. second homes, caravans and

Table 3.3 Short-break destination types in Britain

Seaside resorts	42%
Countryside	18%
Large towns	14%
Small towns	14%
London	7%
Other	5%

Source: MAS Research Marketing and Consulting (1989).

camping, and only 25 per cent used serviced accommodation. Nevertheless, the numbers using commercial serviced accommodation increased during the 1980s, perhaps another indication that with growing affluence people were using their wealth for this type of holiday (British Tourist Authority and English Tourist Board, 1988; Trinity Research, 1989). Not surprisingly, these short breakers tended to be drawn from the professional and managerial groups, childless households, and from either younger or older adult age groups. In continental Europe the short-break market appears to be growing (Lohmann, 1991). Short-break holidays take place throughout the year, with a higher incidence in spring and autumn. Similarly, they do occur throughout the week, but there is a higher incidence at the weekend. The short-break holiday is often described as supplementary or additional to the main holiday, although this is hardly true of visits to friends and relatives. As a supplementary holiday it is thought most likely to be axed in time of recession. However, while this may be true for most people, some prefer the short-break mode, such as, for instance, those whose work commitments do not allow them to take long holidays.

Some research has recently been undertaken on the location of these short breaks. In general, people do not want to travel too far for the short break as this will eat into the time available. A distance of up to 150 miles is common. This means that cities are likely to find that they have a predetermined hinterland for the packages that they offer. Of course, with air travel short breaks are being offered in foreign cities, including Paris, London and Vienna. When asked where they want to take a short break, most people say seaside resorts, historic towns or rural areas. Very few mention the large city. This may be because they associate a short holiday mostly with relaxation, although mention of historic cities suggests that there may be other motivations. A survey for the North West [England] Tourist Board found that respondents mentioned Blackpool first, Chester second and rural areas third, and that Liverpool and Manchester received only little mention. Another survey found the popularity of destinations to be as shown in Table 3.3. These surveys, which are not encouraging for city tourism, may understate the strength of cities, as perhaps respondents do not think of their visits to these places to see friends and relatives, or for football and concerts, as falling within the definition of short breaks.

Day trips

The usual definition of a tourist is a person who stays away overnight for 24 hours, which would exclude the day tripper. However, as has been shown, day trips are very important in terms of the numbers made, and it is clear that for many tourist centres a significant part of their business comes from day trips. Most studies of tourism therefore attempt to include them. While the expenditure of a day tripper will be less than that of someone who stays overnight, the large number involved means that the total income injected into a local economy can be large. One problem, however, is how to define them, even when they have come from the required distance. Should a shopper be included?

The leisure day trip market is an enormous one, although its size will depend on exactly how a trip is defined. OPCS (1991) used the liberal definition of a trip of more than three hours' duration and involving a round journey of over 20 miles. It suggested that there were over 630 million trips in Britain in that year, of which 23 per cent were to friends and relatives, 13 per cent were to to attractions, and 7 per cent for eating and/or drinking. Over half the trips took place at the weekend and not unexpectedly there were more in the summer months. The average round trip was of 68 miles, but just over one-fifth travelled over 100 miles. Not surprisingly, the likelihood of making a trip was correlated with income, class, education and car ownership.

Most day trips will take place from within a 100-mile (62-km) distance or two-hour drive. The widespread availability of the car and the construction of motorways has opened up many areas that were previously considered remote. It is much easier to get to cities now by car, although in the past and still today they are often well served by train. Given that the vast majority do only travel this distance, the effective day trip hinterland of a city is determined. However, some are prepared to travel further, as evidenced by the day trips made to London from up to 300 miles away. With air transport, much longer day trips are possible, and it is common today to see day trips advertised in Britain to places such as Vienna. Given the large populations of cities, it is likely that most day trips are made outwards from cities, but cities may attract from other cities.

A recent survey of day trips in Britain provides information about the location of these excursions (OPCS, 1991) (Table 3.4). Just over half of the trips were to an inland town or city, by far the largest type of destination. While the share of these trips in the total fell during the summer months, because there were more at this time of the year, the absolute numbers involved remained high throughout the year. This lack of seasonality contrasts with the other types of destination, such as the seaside resort. About a quarter of all trips were to friends and relatives. Other important purposes were shopping (16 per cent), the theatre (6.4 per cent), sightseeing (6.3 per cent), watching sport, eating in a restaurant, visiting a museum or cathedral, and

Table 3.4 British leisure day trips 1988–1989: destination

(a)

Destination	Share (%)				
		Quarter of year			
	All	*1*	*2*	*3*	*4*
Inland town/city	54	60	50	46	64
Inland village	13	13	14	13	12
Seaside	16	14	18	22	11
Countryside	15	11	16	17	11
Other	2	2	2	2	2

(b)

Destination	Number of trips (millions)				
		Quarter of year			
	All	*1*	*2*	*3*	*4*
All	630	129	177	178	147
Inland town/city	340	77	89	82	94
Seaside	101	18	32	39	16

Source: OPCS (1991).

going to a dance. Some of these are not regarded as being particularly tourism activities, but they show the role of the city as a place for enjoyment.

Visits to friends and relatives

Vast numbers of trips, whether long holiday, short break or day, are made to friends and relatives, but they have generally been discounted in studies of tourism. This is partly because they are largely invisible in the statistics and partly because it was thought that the expenditure was slight. While it is true that most visits to friends and relatives do not involve the use of serviced accommodation, those that last more than a few hours usually include either a visit to an attraction or eating and drinking out of the home, and therefore involve expenditure. A survey in Britain suggested that in 1986 visits to friends and relatives accounted for 42 per cent of all domestic trips and 17 per cent of all expenditure (British Tourist Authority and English Tourist Board, 1988). They were also the main reason for 21 per cent of visits to Britain by foreigners. In fact many visits to friends and relatives involve an important secondary motivation of having a holiday or leisure time away from home. Given the large numbers involved and the expenditure, this is clearly a market to be encouraged (Denman, 1988).

In theory the location of the visitors and friends market is the same as that of the population, but in fact the BTA/ETB survey quoted above did not find an exact correlation. It may be that people who live in attractive areas or near particular amenities will find that they have more visitors. With their large populations, cities will always have a large number of visits to friends and relatives, but this could be affected both positively and negatively by the perceptions of the public in terms of appeal. This presents a challenge to the promoters of city tourism to change the image of the city, to provide plenty of things to do and to create civic pride so that residents do want to invite their friends and are proud to show off their city when they come.

Tourism Markets: Business

With the possible exception of travel to conferences, business trips take place mainly to cities. Cities are where head offices, factories, business services and convention centres are usually found. The amount of business travel to a particular city cannot be neatly equated with its population size. Each city performs a different function in the world of business. World cities such as London and New York attract huge numbers of business people because of the functions they perform as the headquarters of national and international organizations, and as the largest financial and business service centres. Other cities with large populations may attract relatively few business travellers because they have few head offices and few business services which serve more than the local region, and can be described as predominantly branch plant economies. The particular form of business organization in a country may attract business travel. In the USA a system of marts is in operation in which retailers travel to a few major cities to examine permanent displays of consumer goods. With easier travel the number of major mart centres has been reduced to a few, which include New York, Chicago, Dallas, Atlanta and San Francisco. Travel to conferences and exhibitions is a special type of business travel which is dealt with in detail in Chapter 4.

Conclusion

The above comments present only a preliminary analysis of the markets identified in the urban tourism strategy. Some of the statistics quoted do not suggest that cities are well placed to attract tourists, but this may under-represent the situation as either respondents to surveys fail to remember their visits to cities or their answers are classified by purpose. It is likely that the real situation is more favourable. The success of cities in attracting tourists will be further examined as the various elements of the tourism strategy are discussed.

4
Conferences and exhibitions

Conferences and exhibitions are activities that are often regarded together as one of the staples of city tourism. In some cities up to 40 per cent of those staying overnight in serviced accommodation have come for this type of business tourism. Conferences and exhibitions are perceived to be growth industries in which the visitor spends an above-average amount, and which operate for most of the year. They are thus considered very desirable as the basis for tourism in cities. In the postwar period there has been a proliferation of new conference and exhibition facilities. Critics have suggested that they have been built as 'symbols of civic virility', and that there is a considerable overprovision of such facilities. Cities compete not only with other cities to attract the business but also with other types of urban area such as resorts. So, as Listokin (1985) has pointed out, 'the economic prize is great, but so is the competition'. This should make cities think deeply before investing in the construction of facilities.

Conferences and exhibitions can be considered as two separate kinds of event but there are increasing links between them. Many conferences include an exhibition so that the would-be conference centre now has to provide space for this purpose. Likewise, conferences are often held in association with exhibitions, and so once again exhibition centres are providing conference facilities within the site. In 1983 26 per cent of exhibitions held in Britain had an associated conference (Lawson, 1985a), while a survey of US conventions in 1981 found that 24 per cent had exhibitions (Petersen, 1989). The American convention centre illustrates these tendencies. It consists of a series of large halls which can be used either for exhibitions or with seating installed for conferences. The US model of a convention centre in a downtown area with hotels and other facilities adjacent is being adopted by many cities throughout the world. In the 1980s the Japanese government designated 25 cities as international convention venues, and between 1986 and 1991 16 centres were built. However, in the organization of exhibitions it is the German model of 'messes' which has proved most influential.

The aim of this chapter is to understand the development and location of conferences and exhibitions, and examine the role which they do and can play in urban tourism.

Conferences, Conventions, Congresses and Meetings

Conferences are convened for a number of different purposes, i.e. policy making, the exchange of information and ideas, training and selling. In addition, most conferences fulfil a social purpose, with delegates meeting old friends, making deals not connected directly with the purpose of the conference, and meeting people for the first time. There is also often a recreational purpose so that the delegates can have a short holiday either during or after the conference. Companies sometimes deliberately locate their conferences in exotic locations to facilitate this aspect, believing that such experiences will help motivate staff; this is referred to as incentive travel. Because of this recreational aspect many conference organizers make arrangements for partners to be able to come and lay on special programmes during the conference sessions.

Conferences are organized by or on behalf of a wide range of bodies which can generally be classified as either corporate or association. Corporate meetings are arranged by companies and other organizations to achieve their objectives. The association conference may involve educational, professional, political, religious and social organizations. Apart from achieving the objectives of the association, they are also a means of generating income which is often easier and less painful than raising subscriptions. Conferences vary from an intergovernmental summit, the convention of a political party, a company strategy meeting, a church synod, a symposium for scientists, to the annual conference of a trade union, or professional or social association.

Some conferences take place on a regular basis, such as the annual conferences mentioned above, while others are one-off and may involve a unique set of circumstances. Meetings may last from one day to a week or more. Conferences occur throughout the year, although there is a lull in the holiday periods of summer (July–August) and Christmas (including the New Year) (Astroff and Abbey, 1991, p. 57). This seasonal pattern makes the conference business attractive to seaside resorts.

Conferences vary in size from 10 people to over 20 000. The term convention is usually reserved for the larger meetings. Figures for Chicago (Table 4.1) show the breakdown between the different types of conferences and their various impacts. The vast majority are small and have fewer than 100 attenders. A significant proportion of all conferences are organized by

Table 4.1 Types of meetings in Chicago, 1990

Type	Number	Delegates	Share (%)	Average size	Spend per person ($)	Stay (days)
Convention	1 102	510 869	16	464	590	3.1
Trade show	145	1 769 160	55	12 200	892	3.1
Corporate	27 108	893 089	28	33	267	1.6

Source: Chicago Convention and Tourism Bureau.

companies, the corporate market, either for policy making, training or selling, and these are mainly small. It is in the association market, including political parties and trade unions, where the conference may be large, and could have up to several thousand delegates. As national and international organizations develop, so more large-membership associations are likely to come into being and there is the greater possibility of the mammoth-sized conference. These large bodies are also likely to have other meetings between their annual conferences as well as local and regional conferences. The larger the organization and the wider the area from which it draws its membership, and the longer the conference, the more likely it is that delegates will have to stop overnight, a factor of great importance when measuring the impact of conferences. In contrast to these large-association meetings, many corporate meetings are small in size, last only one day and often require no overnight accommodation. Of the 44 300 meetings held in Frankfurt in 1990, only 8100 required overnight stays. These day conferences are not necessarily for local and regional delegates. Nodal cities with good road, rail and air links can draw delegates from a wide area, and to facilitate this type of business, conference centres, often in hotels, are being built near airports.

While it is widely believed that the number of conferences is increasing, and similarly the number of people attending, it is often difficult to demonstrate this state of affairs with comprehensive and reliable statistics. Conferences do not have to be registered, so that the numerous small ones can go undetected by a tourist board which is attempting a count. Many hotels are unwilling to release details of the conferences they have hosted because of commercial confidentiality. Figures collected by the convention and visitor bureaus affiliated to the International Association of Convention and Visitor Bureaus (mainly North American) suggest a doubling in the size of the industry during the 1980s, but can in no way be regarded as an exact indicator of the whole scene (Figure 4.1). This buoyancy of the conference business argues against those forecasters who, years ago, predicted the demise of meetings because of the wider use of the telephone, teleconferencing and fax machines. There does seem a need for face-to-face contact for which machines cannot act as a substitute. The information explosion may be one reason why there is a greater need for conferences.

The basic accommodation requirement for a meeting is a large room or hall

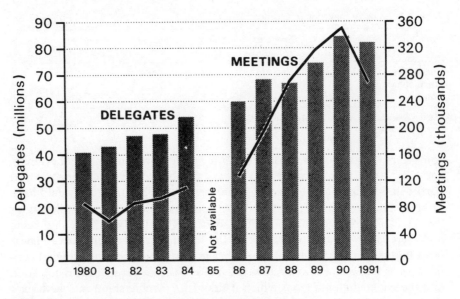

Figure 4.1 Growth of meetings and delegates.
Source: International Association of Convention and Visitor Bureaus.

of sufficient size to take the expected attendance, a feature which is widely found. However, increasingly, extra facilities are required in the form of special lighting, microphones and loudspeakers, projection equipment, the possibility of simultaneous translation, and catering, including banquets. Overnight accommodation does not usually need to be in the same building. As elsewhere, there are rising expectations and many conference organizers are looking for a high standard of venue.

Conference venues include:

1 Large halls, arenas, civic centres, concert halls and theatres, particularly found in major cities.
2 Purpose-built conference/convention/congress centres which have been provided by some cities in recent years. These not only have large halls for the main conference sessions, but also smaller 'break-out' rooms for other meetings.
3 Hotels. Most hotels have some large rooms, often built for banquets, which can be used for conferences. Of course, they can also provide catering and sleeping accommodation. In recent years new large hotels have been built with conferences in mind and have a high standard of facilities. In addition, starting in the USA and now spreading to Europe, special convention hotels have been built containing a large meeting room (perhaps seating 1600 people), smaller meeting rooms, and up to 2000 bedrooms, Such hotels can provide all the requirements for a conference with no need for delegates to leave the building. In the USA these hotels have been pioneered by firms like Hyatt and Westin, and in Europe by Maritim. Large hotel groups can build up links with companies and associations, and can be important influences on the location of conferences through this knowledge of the market.

4 University and other educational establishments where there are lecture rooms and possibly sleeping accommodation; these are usually only available outside the teaching year.

The importance of each of these types of venue will vary from city to city, depending on the characteristics of its conference business, including the breakdown between corporate and association, and between large and small. In Atlanta about one-third of all delegates coming to the city pass through the convention centre.

Conference organizers have a choice not only of type of venue but also of location. For some conferences, particularly if they are lasting only a day, a central location which is accessible to all participants is important. For longer conferences delegates will be prepared to travel further. Nevertheless, many associations move their conference around the country so that over a number of years travel is shared by those attending. In the USA conferences might rotate on a regular basis around the west coast, the centre and the east coast and possibly from north to south. In Britain the political conferences usually rotate between north and south, particularly between Blackpool and Brighton.

Surveys of how decisions are made as to where to locate a conference show that there are four main factors (Coopers & Lybrand Deloitte Tourism Leisure Consultancy Services, 1990; *Meetings and Conventions*, March 1992, 91–161; Table 4.2). Firstly, organizers must be convinced that there is a high standard of conference and accommodation facilities available. Secondly, there is the question of cost. Thirdly, there is accessibility, which becomes more important the wider the area from which the delegates are drawn. Cities with a major airport have a better chance of attracting international conferences, and within large countries such as the USA, cities with hub airports again have an advantage in winning trade. Fourthly, there is the attractiveness of the area. Attendance at the conference may be greater if the meeting is located in an area which is recognized as a tourist centre. Popular locations might be capital cities, historic cities, seaside resorts and rural areas. Unpopular locations might be industrial cities, and ones which have a reputation for being unsafe. Although the conference market is growing, there is great competition between venues to attract the business, and having the right ambience might be the key factor. Judd and Collins (1979) wrote, 'It would seem that tourist appeal is a prime consideration in convention site selection. Although many small and medium sized cities are competing for a share in the business, large cities with their multitude of entertainment, cultural and commercial attractions remain the primary cards for conventions.'

Some of the planning for conference facilities is in the control of the private or independent sectors. As has been seen, hotels have become very important providers of conference facilities and where there are conference centres, hotels provide the sleeping accommodation. Some conference centres have been built and operated by the private sector, such as the Wembley Conference

Table 4.2 US meeting planners' evaluation of destination choice factors 1991

Factor	Percentage agreeing very important	
	Corporate	Association
Availability of hotels and facilities	69	68
Ease of transport	66	57
Transport costs	56	47
Travel distance	46	50
Climate	31	19
Recreation	27	11
Glamour	10	8
Sights/culture	12	11

Source: *Meetings and Conventions*, March 1992, 91–161.

Centre in London. Universities and educational establishments also provide conference facilities, and they have in recent years been upgrading these and in some cases building all-year-round purpose-built centres. However, increasingly, it is the public sector which finances the main venues (Petersen, 1989). The public sector has traditionally provided large halls for meetings but in many cases they are no longer regarded as being of an acceptable standard. This has raised the question of whether public authorities should construct conference centres. The experience of many such facilities is that they lose money, as the building must be let at a low rent in order to attract business because of the competitive nature of the industry, and/or it is not used for sufficient days in the year for the overheads to be covered (Safavi, 1971). In spite of this situation, many conference centres have been justified on the grounds that they bring business to the community and that jobs are created elsewhere, as in hotels. As Petersen (1989) has noted, most convention centres have been built to make something else happen, to be a catalyst for urban regeneration. Notwithstanding this, the public in the USA have been wary of this proposition, as shown in bond issue referendums (Sanders, 1992). In recent years capital subsidies have become available to projects in inner city areas from local, regional, national or supranational institutions. Birmingham's International Convention Centre received a £41 million grant from the European Community.

The public sector may also have a role in planning the complex of facilities, namely the location of the conference centre, the hotels and other facilities. An example of this process is to be seen in Boston in the USA (Law, 1985b). The Boston Redevelopment Authority desired to improve the convention business. An existing building, the Hynes Auditorium, opened in 1965 with $14\,000\,m^2$ of space and a capacity of 5000 seats in the main hall, needed upgrading and extending, but there was also a need to provide hotel accommodation nearby. To achieve these ends a deck was constructed over an urban motorway and railway, and several hotels, including two convention hotels (Marriott and Westin), were built (Figure 4.2). These were linked by pedestrian walkways to the convention centre. In all, 5000 bedrooms were provided within half a kilometre of the Hynes Auditorium, as well as an upmarket shopping mall, Copley Place, for delegates. The whole complex is within walking distance of the historic core of Boston should delegates wish to explore the city. Boston illustrates how convention districts are being created in many American cities, and how these ideas have been exported to Europe, where cities like Birmingham are attempting to do the same. There is, of course, also a need for the public and private sectors to come together to market the facilities, a topic explored in Chapter 9.

Impact studies of the conference business are often crude. It has already been mentioned that there are few comprehensive figures for the conference business. The best estimates relate to conventions, where it is possible to obtain statistics on the number of delegates and, with surveys of their expenditure, derive an estimate of the income created, and possibly, through ratios, an estimate of the number of jobs created (for Orlando, see Brawn, 1992). Regular surveys of delegate expenditure are carried out for American conventions. Results for 1973 and 1988 show the breakdown of expenditure (Table 4.3).

In the case of the Birmingham (UK) International Convention Centre, an estimate of its likely impact was made at the planning stage (JURUE, 1983). Although only about 125 jobs would be created in the centre itself, it was estimated that 1959 jobs would be created in the area as a result of its establishment. As mentioned earlier, the impact of conferences is high because delegates are generally staying in hotels and have an above-average daily expenditure. But there are public costs, including subsidies to conference centres and security costs when political parties have meetings. A study of the Birmingham centre undertaken since it was opened argues that traditional impact analysis ignores the employment forgone through the cost of financing the debt on the capital expended (Loftman and Nevin, 1992). More jobs might have been created in Birmingham had the funds been used on education and housing, another responsibility of the city council. The study

Table 4.3 Convention delegate expenditure

Type of expediture	Percentage of total	
	1973	1988
Hotels (room service)	37.7	51.0
Hotel restaurants	16.0	11.0
Other restaurants	16.8	11.4
Shopping	10.3	8.2
Entertainment	9.5	5.0
Local transport		4.3
Other	—	4.0

Source: International Association of Convention and Visitor Bureaus, Delegate Expenditure Survey 1973 (quoted in Judd, 1979) and 1988.

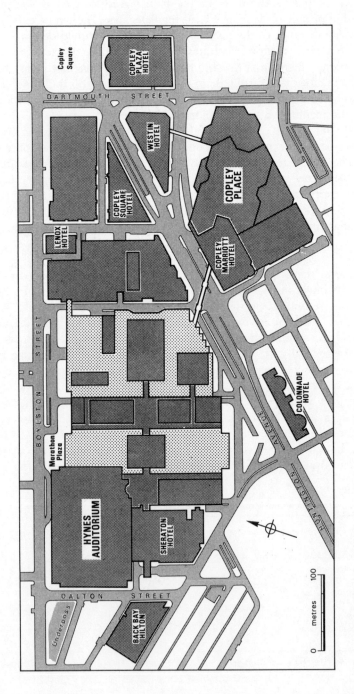

Figure 4.2 Boston's convention district (after Law, 1985b).

also found that although many jobs were low-skilled, and although there were training programmes for local people, in fact few inner city residents were recruited. However, this is a problem for all inner city projects and not just those in tourism.

One of the principal physical impacts of conference centres is the stimulus to the construction of hotels. A successful convention centre, as the example of Baltimore illustrates, quickly results in the construction of several hotels (see case study in Chapter 8).

International Conferences

Figures for international conferences are available from the Union of International Associations based in Brussels. This collects statistics from its members on the number of conferences held which have at least 300 participants, a minimum of 40 per cent foreigners, at least five nationalities, and a duration of at least three days. Its statistics show a steady growth in the number of international conferences: an average of 194 a year in the 1930s, 1272 in the 1950s, 1934 in the 1960s, and 3931 in the 1970s (Labasse, 1984). In 1979 there were 4345 conferences; by 1989 this had risen to 8207, and to 8559 in 1990.

Europe was by far the leading continent, with over 5225 meetings in 1990 or 61 per cent of the total, followed by North America (14.3 per cent) and Asia (12.9 per cent), with just over 1000 conferences each. However, in terms of countries, the USA was the most important, with over 894 meetings, followed by France (757) and Britain (722). Other important countries were Germany (505), the Netherlands (385), Italy (332), Switzerland (318), Belgium (303), Spain (294) and Japan (266).

In terms of the leading cities for international conferences, Paris has been the most important for many years, followed by London (Table 4.4). In the second tier are found Brussels, Geneva, Vienna and Berlin. Madrid and Singapore have been improving their ranking in recent years, while Rome

Table 4.4 International conference cities

City	Number of conferences							
	1983	1984	1985	1986	1987	1988	1989	1990
Paris	252	254	274	358	356	324	388	361
London	235	248	238	258	265	268	261	268
Brussels	145	201	219	157	160	159	165	195
Geneva	153	175	212	180	133	152	270	166
Vienna	142	146	127	106	88	91	129	177
Berlin (West)	62	76	94	100	134	141	160	166
Madrid	51	31	37	118	146	169	139	151
Singapore	77	68	74	100	91	109	111	136
Rome	73	85	91	69	97	122	108	91

Source: Union of International Associations, Brussels.

has fallen back. Other important cities include Amsterdam, The Hague, Strasbourg, Washington and New York. As other capital cities improve their conference facilities, it is likely that there will be a wider spread of international conferences within a growing total.

The explanation of the pattern shown by these figures is connected with the role of these cities in the world and national systems of organization. Many world organizations have their headquarters in cities like Paris, London, Geneva, Vienna and New York. Other cities, such as Brussels and Strasbourg, are headquarters for important supranational continental organizations, like the European Community. National capital cities may also be the head-quarters of large organizations which arrange international conferences. However, the quality of experience available in these cities may also affect the number of conferences which they attract. Thus Singapore in South East Asia attracts many conferences. In many countries other than federal states, the capital city completely dominated the pattern of international conferences (Go, 1991). For the UK in 1989 there were 700 meetings, of which 260 were in London, 43 in Brighton, 30 in Edinburgh, 27 in Cambridge, 27 in Birmingham and 19 in Manchester. In the future, as the number of inter-national conferences grows and other cities obtain good international air links, this dominance of capital cities may not be so great.

The USA

With a population of 250 million and a well-developed economic structure, there is a large conference market in the USA. In the early 1980s it was estimated that there were 25 000–28 000 national associations of which 80 per cent held an annual meeting. A more recent estimate for 1990 found nearly 22 000 associations, covering a very wide range of objectives (Astroff and Abbey, 1991, p. 55). In addition, subgroups within these associations, including regional bodies, might hold meetings. Many of the associations are very large and it has been estimated that 6000–7000 have an attendance over 500 and so require special facilities. This large group can be divided between: the very large, 10 000–15 000; the mid-sized, 5000–10 000; and the small, 500–5000. As mentioned above, national associations are likely to move around the country, but a few which are strongly based in particular regions may be less mobile. Thus organizations connected with the automobile industry may stay in the Midwest. In addition to associations, there is a large corporate market, with many of the world's major companies based in the USA.

Statistics on the convention market are collected by various organizations, such as the International Association of Convention and Visitor Bureaus (IACVB) and the magazine *Meetings and Conventions*, but unfortunately, because of the different sources and definitions used, the figures do not always agree. *Meetings and Conventions* relies on a survey of meeting planners, and because only about 70 per cent reply, the figures are generally considered an underestimate; however, unlike in the IACVB statistics, the corporate sector is identified (*Meetings and Conventions*, February 1986, April 1988, May 1990 and March 1992). Figure 4.3 shows the trends for the 12 years from 1979 to 1991. The total number of meetings increased from 752 000 to 1 031 400, and attendance increased from 64.0 million to 80.8 million. The main areas of growth were in the corporate and association meetings.

These figures provide further evidence of the growth of the industry, albeit at a slower rate than suggested by the IACVB statistics. They also show the effect of recession, evident in the decline between 1989 and 1991. The relative importance of the different sectors can also be observed. The corporate sector was responsible for 78 per cent of the meetings and 61 per cent of the attendance in 1991, but the average number of delegates was only 62. The major association meeting (conventions) had 1 per cent of the meetings and 11 per cent of the attendance, with a mean size of 843, while the other association meetings formed 21 per cent of the total, with 28 per cent of the attendance and an average size of 105. The attendance of delegates is supplemented by their partners. In 1983 the 63.4 million delegates brought 15.7 million partners, to give a total visitor impact of 79 million. The proportion of delegates taking partners with them was highest at conventions.

To supply this market, numerous convention centres and hotels have been built. At the end of World War II there were only a handful of convention centres in cities such as New York and Chicago (Graveline, 1984). According to Listokin (1985), between 1970 and 1985 over 100 convention centres were built. Var *et al.* (1985) also say, 'Before 1960 only about two dozen North American cities bid for the convention trade, but now the number is over one hundred.' Another indication of the scale of growth is that convention centre exhibit space increased from 6.7 million square feet in 1970 to nearly 18 million square feet in 1990 (Sanders, 1992). Nearly every major city which lacked such a facility sought to provide a purpose-built centre, nearly always at public expense (Safavi, 1971). Examples are Atlanta (1976), St Louis (1977), Baltimore (1979), Pittsburgh (1981) and Washington (1983). In those cities where a facility already existed, a new and more modern one was often added; examples are San Francisco (1981) and New York (1986). Many successful convention centres have been extended, often more than once. As mentioned above, the convention centre is a building which can be used both for conferences and exhibitions, having large halls where seating can be installed, and many ancillary 'break-out' rooms for smaller meetings. In the major cities most convention centres were built as part of downtown renewal schemes. Suburban communities are now beginning to construct convention centres, as at Valley Forge near Philadelphia and Gwinnett near Atlanta. A favourite suburban location for a convention centre is near an airport. One of the largest and most successful of these is found at Rosemont, near O'Hare Airport in Chicago. Many convention centres have been built

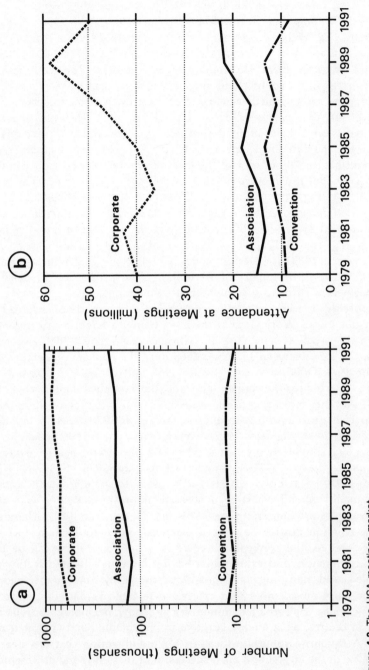

Figure 4.3 The USA meetings market.
Source: *Meetings and Conventions*, 1986, 1988, 1990, 1992.

Table 4.5 US convention cities

Rank	City	Delegates 1989	Metropolitan population (000s (rank))	Exhibit space (ft^2)	Hotel rooms
1	New York	2 934 000	18 087 (1)	755 000	40 000
2	Dallas	2 472 644	3 855 (9)	600 000	10 000
3	Chicago	2 273 763	8 066 (3)	1 625 000	22 352
4	Atlanta	1 800 792	2 834 (12)	940 000	10 300
5	Las Vegas	1 508 842	631 (60)	859 000	25 000
6	Washington	1 248 973	3 924 (8)	381 000	19 755
7	Orlando	1 215 457	971 (41)	300 000	19 300
8	San Francisco	1 204 000	4 821 (5)	442 000	22 000
9	Anaheim	1 062 000	2 257 (*)	685 000	16 000
10	St Louis	928 976	2 444 (17)	240 000	5 300
11	New Orleans	887 386	1 239 (31)	70 000	16 000
12	Phoenix	833 000	2 122 (20)	257 000	1 500
13	Atlantic City	788 271	309 (114)	436 000	10 000
14	Detroit	787 000	4 665 (6)	700 000	2 765
15	Los Angeles	726 000	14 532 (2)	750 000	7 629
16	Miami	600 000	3 193 (11)	350 000	2 500
17	Indianapolis	578 292	1 250 (30)	317 000	3 505
18	Columbus	558 139	1 377 (28)	180 000	2 000
19	Houston	542 042	3 711 (10)	935 000	2 570
20	Boston	525 000	4 172 (7)	200 000	6 766

*Part of larger metropolitan area.
Population = Census 1990.
Exhibit space = space in main convention centre.
Hotel rooms = number in downtown area or near convention centre.
Source: *Business Travel News*, 23 July 1990.

in resorts, which begin with the advantage of having a large hotel stock. Examples include Atlantic City, Las Vegas and the Disney theme parks at Anaheim in California and Orlando in Florida. There has also been a massive expansion of convention hotels, which may have up to 2000 bedrooms. The major chains include Hyatt, Sheraton, Marriott, Westin and Omni. Such hotels can host large conferences without the use of a convention centre. However, as mentioned above, often these hotels have been constructed nearby.

Statistics are also available for the distribution of convention and trade show delegates by city. Table 4.5 provides statistics for the 20 leading cities.

The main convention centres consist of the major cities and resorts. However, even for the major cities there is no simple correlation between population size and the number of delegates. Many large cities in the north-east, are missing from the list, such as Philadelphia. It is perhaps not too surprising that rustbelt cities like Cleveland, Buffalo and Pittsburgh do not figure prominently in the list, although Detroit's presence can be noted. In a similar way, there does not appear to be any simple correlation between importance and the amount of exhibit space or hotel rooms, although Petersen (1992) has suggested that the supply of hotel bedrooms is crucial and is determined by the strength of office activity. This underlines earlier statements that a number

Table 4.6 Types of location used by US meeting planners

Location	Percentage using						
	1979	*1981*	*1983*	*1985*	*1987*	*1989*	*1991*
1. Corporate							
Downtown	59	54	64	58	57	64	61
Resort	59	61	47	44	47	55	52
Suburban	52	55	47	45	44	44	50
Airport	37	37	24	27	28	29	29
2. Association							
Downtown	61	56	68	70	70	61	64
Resort	35	38	39	40	36	42	42
Suburban	52	52	34	39	34	34	36
Airport	47	46	24	31	29	24	25

Source: *Meetings and Conventions*, May 1990, March 1992.
Other locations mentioned included: private conference centres; suite hotels; condo resorts; and university conference centres.

of variables contribute to whether a city has been able to successfully develop the conference business.

Comparing attendance statistics for the beginning and end of the 1980s decade, it is apparent that there is both stability and change. Inter-regionally, Price Waterhouse (1991) suggest that the convention industry is shifting to the sunbelt. New York and Chicago remain very important, but their dominance has become less. The most notable change is the rise of the resorts, Las Vegas and Anaheim raising their rank, and Orlando having a spectacular period of growth. Some centres well-established at the beginning of the decade, like Houston, Detroit and Kansas City, have stagnated, while a few cities, such as St Louis, have been able to increase their standing. In 1981 the top 20 convention cities received 18 million delegates, nearly 42 per cent of the IACVB total (Table 4.1) for that year. By 1989 the top 20 received 23 million delegates, only 31 per cent of the IACVB total, suggesting that although there was an overall increase in the number of delegates, these were spread more widely, allowing new cities to participate in the market. Surveys of meeting planners show that the downtown area remains the favourite location for conferences in spite of the fact that suburban centres and out-of-season resorts can offer lower prices and also recreational facilities (Table 4.6).

Atlanta: An Example of a Convention City

In order to understand the spatial dynamics of the convention business it is useful to examine the growth of one successful city. From the mid-1970s the convention trade began to grow rapidly in Atlanta and by 1990 Atlanta received almost 1.9 million delegates. This gave it fourth rank in the USA, which compares with its twelfth rank for the population of its metropolitan area. Atlanta has been one of the most rapidly growing metropolitan areas in the country, increasing in population from 1.7 million in 1970 to 2.8 million in 1990. Unlike other top convention centres, it is neither a major population centre like New York nor a resort. Environmentally, its city centre is not very attractive, and although it is attempting to change the situation, the city would not rate highly on either attractions or night life. So how has it become so important for conventions?

Atlanta is a good example of the American urban tradition of boosterism (Rice, 1983). Ever since its foundation, its leaders have looked for ways to make the city more important. In recent years this process has involved slogans such as 'Atlanta: The World's Next Great City'. Its mayors have usually given strong leadership in this area and since 1941 there has been a proactive private sector organization, Central Atlanta Progress, pushing for improvements in the downtown area. Good communications have played a significant role in the city's rise from its beginnings as a railway junction in 1836 to possessing one of America's main hub airports in the postwar period. This nodality has enabled the city to become the dominant metropolis in the south-east of the USA.

One consequence of this position has been the maintenance and enlargement of its marts, permanent exhibition centres for consumer and other goods. Progress in this area is illustrated by the construction of new buildings in the downtown area: the Merchandise Mart in 1961 (extended 1968), the Apparel Mart in 1979, Inforum (for computers) in 1989 and the Gift Mart in 1992 (Figure 4.4). These buildings, designed by the architect–developer John Portman, drew traders from the south-east and created a demand for hotel accommodation. In 1967 John Portman designed the first atrium hotel, the Hyatt Regency, and later in the 1970s, as the convention business expanded, more spectacular hotels were built.

Running parallel with the development of the mart industry, the city also sought to create a convention industry. A civic centre was opened in 1965, but this was clearly inadequate for the growing business. Therefore, the city and its business leaders persuaded the state to establish the Georgia World Congress Center Authority in order to build a convention centre, opened in 1976. This was the first modern convention facility to be owned and operated by a state (Graveline, 1984). In 1984 the exhibit space was increased from 350 000 to 640 000 square feet, and a further extension in 1992 increased it to 952 000 square feet, making it one of the largest facilities in the USA. By 1990 out-of-town attenders alone numbered 650 000 a year. A third strand in Atlanta's tourism industry has been the development of sports facilities and the attraction of sports teams. Following the construction of the Atlanta–Fulton County stadium in 1965, the city attracted the Braves (baseball) team from Milwaukee. The Omni Coliseum was opened in 1976 for use by the Hawkes (basketball) team, which had been attracted to the city in 1968. In 1990 Atlanta won the right to stage the 1996 Olympic Games and the 1994 SuperBowl (American football). To host these events, several new facilities are

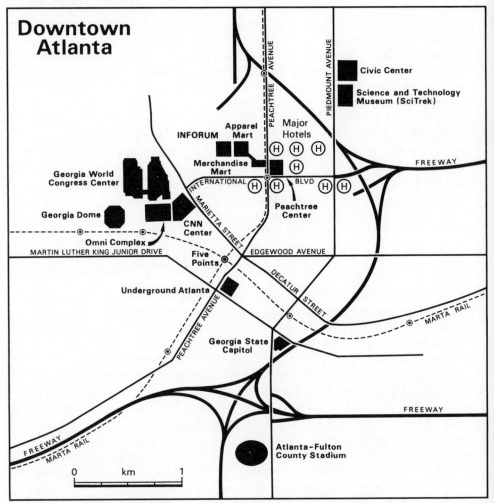

Figure 4.4 Downtown Atlanta.

being constructed, including the Georgia Dome, opened in 1992. The funding
for both the convention and the sports facilities has come from state bond
issues, to be repaid from hotel taxes and the profitable operation of the
facilities. The latter feature of the Atlanta business (so far) distinguishes
the city from many others where the facilities are run at a loss.

Atlanta's success in the convention industry owes much to its early development of facilities and hotels, and dominance within the south-east. For many
years it was the obvious location for a meeting in that part of the country,
although it is now being challenged by centres such Orlando and other cities
in Florida. Early success and profitability meant that the facilities could be
expanded and more hotel accommodation provided. There are now 10 000
hotel bedrooms downtown. City leadership and state backing has also been

an important ingredient. Atlanta also claims that its costs are low and that 'southern hospitality' is an advantage. It is aware that it has some weaknesses (poor downtown environment, few attractions and a poor night life) and has been trying to rectify these disadvantages in recent years. The revival and redevelopment of Underground Atlanta, a festival market-place, is one example of the result of these policies (Sawicki, 1989; Kent and Chestnutt, 1991).

Britain and Continental Europe

Since Britain's population is less than a quarter of that of the USA, it is obvious that not only is the total conference market much smaller in Britain but that the size of association meetings will be reduced, thus making the provision of large convention centres less viable (English Tourist Board, 1984). Unfortunately, there is very little comprehensive and reliable information about the British conference market (Hughes, 1988). Surveys were undertaken in the early 1980s but not continued, the most recent being that for 1985 (RPA, 1985). More recently, Coopers & Lybrand Deloitte Tourism Leisure Consultancy Services (1990) undertook a survey from which it estimated that the entire market consisted of 700 000 conferences and involved 115 million delegate days. These surveys provide little reliable evidence of trends but most observers agree that it is a growing business.

In the popular mind the main providers of conference facilities are the seaside and inland resorts. This is because the high-profile political parties and trade unions have traditionally held their conferences here. Resorts began to develop the conference business in the interwar period in an attempt to extend their short summer season. They had a large quantity of accommodation at a wide range of prices and of different quality and could use their theatres and other halls as conference venues. All these facilities were close together with catering and entertainment on hand. The main resorts where the conference trade is important are Blackpool, Brighton, Bournemouth, Torquay, Eastbourne, Scarborough, Llandudno and the inland spa town of Harrogate. With the continued development of the industry, many resorts have found that the old venues were inadequate and have had to construct purpose-built facilities. This has happened in Brighton (1977), Bournemouth (1984), Harrogate (1982) and Llandudno (1982). Elsewhere, existing facilities have had to be upgraded or extended, as at Eastbourne (1934). In most cases, with the notable exception of Blackpool, these facilities are publicly owned, and the local population have had to bear the cost through local taxation.

Hotels are very important in their own right for conferences and not just as suppliers of accommodation for conferences held elsewhere. Coopers & Lybrand Deloitte Tourism Leisure Consultancy Services (1990) suggested that hotels were responsible for 77 per cent of the venues and 68 per cent of the delegate nights. The main reason for this lies in the importance of the corporate market. Companies mainly use hotels for their meetings, which tend to be small. The corporate sector uses a wide variety of hotel location types from city centre, city periphery near motorway and airport, to rural settings. The main hotel chains, such as Forte, have conference marketing officers, and are designing hotels with the conference market in mind.

Universities and educational institutions are also important providers of conference accommodation. In an effort to boost income they started to market their facilities for use during the vacation. These included main halls, lecture rooms, halls of residence and catering facilities. Where these facilities are all together on one site, as with the campus universities, this can be very convenient. Universities have been successful in gaining academic and scientific conferences, and have advantages in terms of cost. However, in many cases their facilities are now regarded as inferior, particularly the halls of residence, and there is a need to upgrade them. Some institutions have built conference centres for all-year-round use, which can meet the expectations of, say, the industrial market. There are no published figures to show which universities are the most successful, but it is known that places like York, Warwick, Durham and colleges in Oxford and Cambridge do well, suggesting that good facilities plus the ambience of the locality are important. However, some of the large civic universities, like the University of Manchester, also attract much business.

Major cities are also an important location for conferences. Their good stock of hotels and universities enables them to provide the required facilities. In addition, they usually have large halls which are used for meetings and conferences as well as concerts and the performing arts. London is very important for meetings, attracting national events, and in addition many national organizations are based in the capital in buildings which include large rooms where conferences can be held. Provincial cities do attract large meetings but they have found it difficult to win the association market conferences, which have traditionally gone to the resorts. Many of their halls are now dated and the associated facilities (e.g. catering) are inadequate for current expectations. This raises the question as to whether they should construct single-purpose conference centres able to accommodate several thousand participants. Given the limited market in Britain for such events, such an investment could be risky. The 1984 ETB report estimated that there were only 150 conferences a year in Britain with an attendance over 1000. Some cities, such as Cardiff and Nottingham, have built multipurpose halls which can be used for other events like concerts. Glasgow has built an exhibition centre which can be used for conferences (see below). Only Birmingham (1991) so far has built itself an £148 million American-style convention centre, with the intention of gaining national and international meetings (Birmingham City Council, 1991). Edinburgh, already a favourite for international conferences, is planning a conference centre, but has had difficulty in obtaining finance.

The Coopers & Lybrand Deloitte Tourism Leisure Consultancy Services

(1990) survey of the conference market suggested that the most important locations for meetings were southern England and the Midlands. The first area includes London and also the metropolitan region where many companies have their headquarters. Hotels near London Heathrow airport are also able to attract international corporate conferences. The Midlands, as its name suggests, is centrally placed to attract meetings which are bringing participants from all over the country. Other northern cities are probably important for conferences, but of a more regional nature. The examples of Edinburgh and York suggest that conferences can be moved northwards if the locality is sufficiently attractive.

A similar picture emerges of the conference scene in France, Germany and the Benelux countries, although once again there are no statistics (Smith, 1989). Major cities are very important, especially Paris. In Germany the principal cities have large halls, hotels and often facilities within their exhibition centres (see below). Munich hosts over 8700 congresses a year, with more than 700 000 delegates. In France the provincial cities, like Lyon and Nantes (1987), are attempting to develop the conference business. However, the resorts are also attracting trade and some, like Nice (1980), have built modern conference centres.

Exhibitions, Expositions, Trade Shows and Fairs

The word exhibition is used to describe an organized public display of manufactured goods and works of art. Here the word is used to describe the temporary display of sample goods in a specialized exhibition. This chapter will not discuss world fairs or expos which, while including goods, have other elements and will be discussed in Chapter 6 under special events. Neither will this chapter examine North American marts, permanent displays of consumer goods for retailers, which, as was observed earlier, are important in regional centres and therefore attract business visitors.

The advantage of an exhibition is that sellers and buyers are brought together and business can be transacted easily. Firms selling goods can send representatives to potential buyers but it is not always possible to take the goods with them, particularly if they are large. Buyers can visit manufacturers but may be disinclined to do so because of the need to visit several to compare products. Printed material can be sent, but the purchaser may wish to see the product before buying. The exhibition thus serves a very useful purpose for sellers and purchasers, particularly in the area of materials, machinery and goods which firms buy from each other. Contacts made at exhibitions can be followed up by agents. All industries will use a mix of selling techniques, and in some industries and some countries exhibitions may be more important than in others. In 1990, industry in Germany spent 25 per cent of its advertising budget on exhibitions, in France and the USA it spent about 14 per cent, and in Britain it spent only 8 per cent (*The Observer*, 14 April 1991). Figures showing the floorspace leased by exhibitors, which has been increasing in recent years, suggest that exhibitions are becoming a more popular way of selling goods (and services) to other firms.

Exhibitions can be classified into trade only, trade and public, and public. Trade shows are for goods sold to other firms and cover articles such as machinery. Consumer goods may also be displayed for the retail trade. The modern trade show has developed from the trade fairs of the past, which were popular in Germany. These displayed a wide range of goods. In the postwar period these general fairs have evolved into specialist exhibitions covering a particular industry. Some trade fairs which are displaying consumer goods may be open to the general public. Often the first few days are trade only, followed by open days. An example of this type is the Motor Show. Public shows are concerned with consumer goods and services, an example being the Ideal Home Exhibition. Public shows can have very large attendances, while trade shows generally have smaller attendances, although this will depend on the size of the industry which is exhibiting and the area from which the participants are drawn. A very specialist exhibition which is the only one of its type and draws visitors from all over the world might still have a large attendance.

Exhibitions generally last from three to five days, but they can be anything from one day to a month. Many exhibitions are held every year, but some of the more specialist ones may occur in a cycle every two, three, four or five years. In general, the specialist exhibitions will occur on the same site every time, but some rotate between sites, often with different organizers and avoiding each other. Exhibitions are held throughout the year, but there are few over the summer and Christmas holiday periods.

Exhibitions may be organized by a trade association, by a company associated with the exhibition site, or by a company which specializes in organizing exhibitions. Often the trade association works with one of the last two types of company. Firms linked with exhibition centres have been deliberately established to fill the space available and seek industries which are not as yet adequately catered for by the existing calendar of exhibitions. In Germany 80 per cent of the exhibitions are organized by the *messe* (Lawson, 1985b). New industries are clearly targets for these exhibition organizers.

Exhibitions are held in large halls, and an exhibition centre usually consists of a series of linked large halls which can be used either independently or together. Today most exhibition centres are purpose built, but a few have been converted from other uses, such as Manchester's G-Mex, which was a railway terminus. Many exhibition centres also have outdoor space. A specialist type of exhibition centre is the agricultural fair ground, which is mainly outdoor display space. Exhibition centres also require catering facilities and perhaps office space. In recent years exhibition centres have begun to provide rooms for meetings, since conferences often take place in association with exhibitions. Sometimes these conferences take place in hotels which have been built nearby. To be viable, an exhibition centre should be used as much as possible, but, as has been seen, this is difficult during the summer and Christmas holiday periods, and because of the inevitable gaps between shows. To overcome these seasonal lulls, halls may be let out for other events, from concerts to sports events, and private events such as product launches. Even so, it may be difficult to get the usage of exhibition centres above the 200 days a year figure. Very large exhibition centres may have more than one event at the same time.

Many exhibition centres are publicly owned, although often run by an autonomous company. Such companies may have several shareholders. In Germany the *messe* (exhibition centres) are usually owned jointly by the city and provincial (*Land*) government, perhaps with a small shareholding from the trade unions and the Chamber of Commerce. A similar situation occurs in France, while the National Exhibition Centre (NEC) in Birmingham is 99 per cent owned by the city and 1 per cent by the Chamber of Commerce. A few exhibition centres, such as Earls Court and Olympia in London, are privately owned. Manchester's G-Mex is jointly owned by the local authorities and a private company.

While the aim of all exhibition centres is to be profitable, there is widespread public financial support. Those that are publicly owned have obviously benefited from initial funding for the capital cost, and this type of support may continue for extensions and renovation. Even privately owned facilities such as Earls Court and Olympia in London have received grants towards extensions. A few facilities may also require an operational subsidy, at least during their early years. There are several reasons why this subsidy may be given. The most obvious one is that the facility will bring income into the area and thus help create jobs. This will be important where unemployment is high. The German government has helped Berlin and will help Leipzig for these reasons. In Britain, inner city funds have been used to assist exhibition centres. Another reason for subsidizing exhibition centres is the prestige that they bring to an area. Governments may also provide funds in order to develop a national 'shop window', as has happened in Britain and the Netherlands. Even where there are no direct subsidies to the centre itself, the local authority may have to contribute to the surrounding infrastructure.

Like the conference business, the exhibition industry appears to be growing. In the early 1980s Lawson (1985b) estimated a growth rate for Europe of 4 per cent a year, and the figures reproduced below suggest continuous growth. There are no statistics on the international geography of the industry but the information on the industry reported below suggests that the industry is very important in Europe and particularly in Germany. The modern *messe* of Germany evolved at the beginning of the century from centuries-old trade fairs. The Germans have maintained their lead through the development of specialist trade fairs as well as in the continued development of their facilities. Their strength is not in the number of shows, but in their large size and international character. Germany is, of course, an important industrial country and it could be expected that there would be some correlation between exhibitions and industrial development. Frequently, as with Detroit in the USA, there is a link between trade fairs and the industries which are important in the local region. Unlike the case with conferences, there does not appear to be an 'attractiveness' factor affecting the attendance at exhibitions. It is the quality of the exhibition which determines attendance.

Within the urban region there is a debate as to the best location. A central location near the city centre gives the exhibition centre good accessibility by public transport, and access to the varied facilities of the city centre, including hotels and night life, and assists with the revitalization of the inner city. Early twentieth century *messe* such as those of Cologne and Frankfurt are in fact centrally located, but later centres are likely to have found either sites already developed or the ground too expensive. Only where the inner city is in decay, such as in Glasgow, has it been possible to build an exhibition centre in the central area. Inner city sites may have problems with insufficient car parking and congested road access. Generally it has been necessary to choose a site on the periphery where undeveloped land was available with good communications, and at low cost. In the case of the NEC in Birmingham a very advantageous site was found adjacent to the main London railway, near motorways and next to the airport. However, the disadvantage of this type of site is that, at least initially, it is too far away from hotels and other facilities that the visitor wants, and may lack public transport.

Trends in the exhibition industry can be measured in various ways: the number of shows, the number of exhibitors, the amount of space rented (gross or net), the number attending, the foreign component, and figures relating to income and expenditure. Unfortunately, while there is a good collection of statistics for the industry, the figures are not always comparable, some relating to all shows, others just to trade shows, and some covering only shows over a minimum size.

The impact of an exhibition centre can be measured in terms of different components. Firstly, there are the numbers of jobs in the centre itself. Typically, these are not great. Cologne Messe employs 450, while Manchester's G-Mex employs only 40. These comparisons are not as straightforward as they appear, since some centres contract out most of the services that they require. Secondly, there are the jobs in ancillary activities, such as display construction and exhibition organization. These may or may not be near the exhibition centre. Thirdly, there are the jobs created by the visitor – both the exhibitors and the attenders. These people can be divided between those who visit for only one day and those who stay overnight in the locality. As with earlier surveys of expenditure, through these some idea of the income generated can be estimated, and from this some notion of the jobs created. This kind of impact study was undertaken for the NEC in Birmingham (JURUE, 1977) and before the G-Mex centre was built in Manchester. The recent Peat Marwick

(Peat Marwick McLintock, 1989) report on the NEC estimates that in 1988 the centre generated £176 million of expenditure in the West Midlands, of which £63 million was retained income. This resulted in 9481 full-time equivalent jobs or 8534 full-time jobs and 2002 part-time jobs. This compares with 2780 jobs in 1976 and 3922 in 1984. The evolution of the centre since 1976 had encouraged more local hotels and greater local contracting for displays, the number of contractors having increased from 28 in 1984 to 47 in 1988. Of the £3.176 billion income, 79 per cent came from exhibitions and 21 per cent from events. From these kinds of survey it is apparent that the greatest impact comes from those exhibition centres that have a high proportion of international trade shows with a large number of visitors staying overnight. In contrast, an exhibition centre which mainly has public shows, with most attenders travelling from their homes, will have only a small economic impact.

Germany

With the largest exhibition centres and the most well-developed programme of trade fairs, Germany can be considered the leader in the field. Although there is a long tradition of trade fairs, the industry has been greatly affected by two world wars; however, it has been able to restore its fortunes. With a strong industrial base it has been able to develop trade fairs of international importance, with a significant proportion of attendances from abroad. Statistics show that during the 1980s floorspace rented and attendance continued to show an upward trend (Table 4.7). Within the country there are numerous centres with the industry distributed as shown in Table 4.8 and Figure 4.5. As some fairs are not held every year, direct comparisons of one year with another are not valid.

These figures reveal that there are a 'Big Five' in the industry, namely Düsseldorf, Frankfurt, Hanover (Hannover), Cologne (Köln) and Munich (München) (Figure 4.5). Other important centres are Berlin, Essen, Hamburg, Nürnberg (Nuremberg) and Stuttgart. Of these, Berlin is hoping to strengthen its position following the post-1989 political changes. The principal ancient centres of the industry were Frankfurt, Cologne and Leipzig. For Frankfurt and Cologne, modern exhibition grounds were built on the edge of the city centre

Table 4.7 Trade show trends in Germany

	1983	1986	1987	1988	1989	1990
Space rented (net, million m^2)	3.8	4.7	4.4	4.7	5.3	5.1
Exhibitors	83 600	94 442	91 890	99 917	109 380	110 966
Foreign (%)	34.5	39.0	43.0	41.0	44.0	42.0
Visitors (m)	7.7	7.6	8.2	7.9	10.0	8.2
Foreign (%)	6.5				14	

Source: Ausstellungs- und Messe-Ausschuss der Deutschen Wirtschaft.

Table 4.8 The location of German trade shows

City	Floorspace (m²)		Regular fairs	Attendances	
	Halls	Outdoor		1989	1990
Berlin	83 500	10 000	9	1 195 509	982 780
Dortmund	42 000	5 000	1		52 695
Düsseldorf	171 300	42 000	28	1 368 421	1 661 748
Essen	90 000	10 000	8	734 704	279 849
Frankfurt	263 005	48 000	24	1 153 930	879 519
Friedrichshafen	43 160	18 000	3	185 377	137 107
Hamburg	62 500	8 500	4	231 945	291 626
Hanover	461 240	146 420	13	1 512 763	1 234 481
Karlsruhe	20 000	10 000	2	10 324	14 517
Cologne	250 000	52 000	24	829 190	1 108 952
Leipzig	222 174	54 000	2	n/a	545 300
Munich	105 000	250 000	21	1 056 112	895 464
Nuremberg	86 000	80 000	12	156 846	209 566
Offenbach	17 000		3	17 976	17 606
Pirmasens	45 500	11 000	2		19 000
Saarbrücken	24 600	25 410	1	157 564	143 772
Stuttgart	59 500	10 000	10	188 318	252 530
Wiesbaden	20 000	1 000	1		13 204
Total				9 994 054	8 196 474

Trade Fair attendances only, not public shows.
Source: Ausstellungs- und Messe-Ausschuss der Deutschen Wirtschaft, 1991.

in 1907 and 1926 respectively. Leipzig's fortunes suffered as a result of its situation in East Germany within the Communist bloc, although it was given a role as the showcase for COMECON. However, since the political changes of 1989 and reunification in 1990 the federal government has pledged that it will help restore the fortunes of the *messe*, which is to have a new site on the periphery at a cost of DM 1 billion with a grant of DM 300 million. Leipzig is likely to keep its ties with former COMECON members (*Financial Times*, 19 November 1991). Düsseldorf, Hanover and Munich have developed their trade fairs very successfully in modern times.

Britain

The British industry is small compared to the German one, partly, as has been noted, because British firms spend a smaller proportion of their advertising budget on exhibitions, although this has been increasing in recent years. British exhibition costs have also been high, partly because of the lack of government support (Lawson, 1985b). At the end of the nineteenth century many of Britain's cities developed large halls which could be used for exhibitions, mostly public shows. Examples are Bingley Hall in Birmingham, the Kelvin Hall in Glasgow and Belle Vue in Manchester. By the 1950s and 1960s it was apparent that many of these halls were becoming obsolete. At the same time British industry was seeking exhibition space where it could

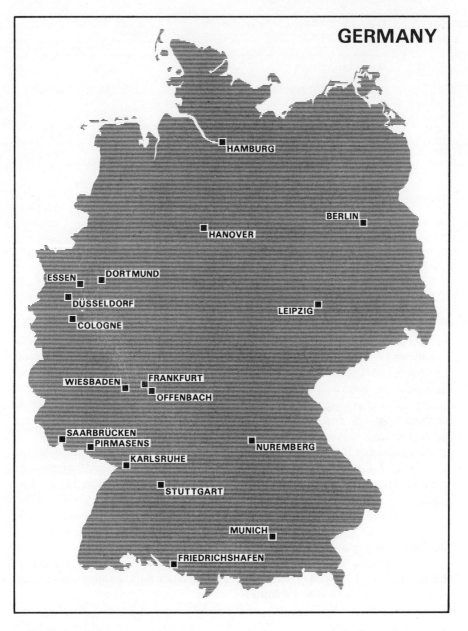

Figure 4.5 German trade fair cities.

Table 4.9 Exhibition centres in the UK

City	1991 Area (m²)
Aberdeen	10 300
Belfast	8 500
Birmingham NEC (1976)	125 000
Brighton Metropole	8 125
Bristol (1978)	7 500
Edinburgh (Ingliston)	7 500
Glasgow (1985)	18 830
Harrogate (1959)	10 000
Kenilworth NAC	6 000
London	
Alexandra Palace	13 070
Earls Court (1887)	59 000
Kensington	6 595
London Arena (1989)	8 000
Olympia (1886)	39 000
Wembley (1987)	17 000
Manchester (1986)	10 000

There are at least 12 smaller centres. Figures in brackets indicate the date of establishment.

display its goods to home and overseas buyers. The Federation of British Industry's Pollitzer Report (1959) suggested that there should be a national exhibition centre, and later in 1962 this organization suggested that it should be located at Crystal Palace in London. In the late 1960s the government accepted the idea and agreed to make a contribution, inviting bids from interested parties. Many assumed that the centre would automatically be in or near London, and were surprised when in 1970 Birmingham's bid was accepted. Even then many predicted that it would be a 'white elephant'.

Birmingham's bid had been made by the city in partnership with the Chamber of Commerce, through which local industrialists had voiced their concern about the lack of exhibition facilities. When opened in 1976 it had an area of 89 000 m², and was located on the edge of the city (see above) rather than in the city centre, which had been the original proposal. The NEC has been a great success and the management are now in the process of doubling the capacity. Table 4.9 lists UK exhibition facilities.

Both Bristol's and Manchester's facilities are in converted buildings. Harrogate's and Wembley's spaces are associated with conference centres, while Glasgow's is a new building.

Figures collected by Lawson and the Exhibition Industries Federation give an indication of the size of the industry and its growth during the 1980s (Table 4.10).

There are some figures to indicate the relative importance of the industry in the different centres (Table 4.11). The NEC is the largest individual centre but overall London has a larger share of the market, with the other provincial centres way behind.

Table 4.10 Exhibition trends in the UK

Category	1982	1983	1984	1988	1989	1990
No. of shows		393	467	651	708	779
Exhibitors		55 300	n/a	45 933	n/a	72 649
Exhibitors–foreign		4 820	n/a	4 769	n/a	7 555
Rented space (net, million m^2)		1.3		2.75	2.79	3.08
Attendance (million)	5.5	5.2		9.55	10.65	9.16
Overseas (000)		169		194	233	n/a
Visitor spend (£ million)		164		4.93	5.37	5.02
Exhibitor spend (£ million)		183			800	901

Source: Lawson (1985a), Lawson and Wilkie (1985), Wilkie and Lawson (1983), Exhibition Industries Federation (1989, 1990, 1991).

Table 4.11 Location of exhibitions in the UK (%)

	1984	1988	1990
London	44	43	44
Rest of South East	10	5	4
South West	9	10	
West Midlands	10	13	35
North West	7	8	
Yorkshire	14	8	
Scotland	4	8.5	
Other	2	12.5	

Source: Exhibition Industries Federation (1989, 1990, 1991).

The Rest of Europe and the USA

Most countries in Europe have followed the German lead and constructed exhibition centres. Often these 'national showcases' are in the capital city, but another popular location is in a major industrial centre. Within France, Paris is by far the most important centre. According to Wilkie (1988), Paris in 1983 had 74 per cent of business and attracted 420 000 delegates. Because most French companies have their headquarters in Paris, it is the obvious place to have exhibitions, a fact which makes it difficult for the provincial cities to compete with the capital. In Italy Milan is dominant.

In the USA, as mentioned above, the convention centre has a series of large halls and can take trade shows. With the exception of Cleveland and Houston, all the largest exhibit halls are convention centres (Figure 4.6). In recent years there has been a great expansion in specialized exhibition centres. One example is the Bayside Exposition Hall in Boston, built in 1982 with an area of 180 000 square feet. The largest exhibition centre is McCormick Place in Chicago, with 1 625 360 square feet. The number of trade shows increased from 4500 in 1972 to 9000 in 1982 (*British Business*, September, 1984).

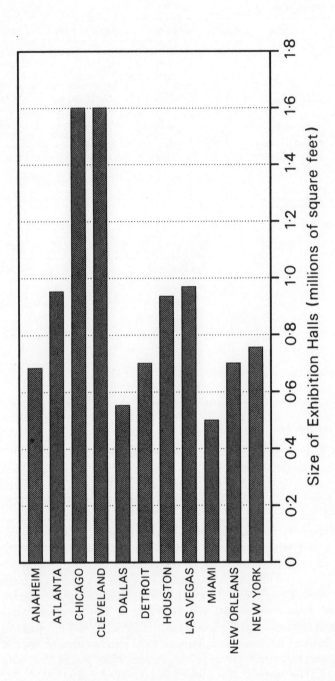

Figure 4.6 Major exhibition centres in the USA.
Source: Chicago Convention and Tourism Bureau.

Conclusion

The conference and exhibition industry has evolved rapidly during the 1960s, 1970s and 1980s with a growth of business and much new stock, in the form of convention centres and hotels, having been put in place. When all types of activity are considered, including corporate meetings, the industry is widely dispersed, but most attention has focused on the large conference and exhibition which takes place in a specially constructed facility or purpose-built hotel. It is useful to recap the features which explain why particular cities have become successful before examining the prospects for new entrants.

A critical factor in the success of cities has been a supply of facilities and accommodation. This can be a chicken and egg situation. Business will come only when these are available, but investment will occur only when there is a proven demand. Those cities where there is already a demand for hotel accommodation therefore have a good basis on which to develop the conference and exhibition industry. Such cities are either resorts or large commercial centres which attract many business visitors. Initially, a multipurpose hall may be used for meetings and exhibitions. Once the business has been developed, then investment can take place in a dedicated building such as a convention centre. As trade grows, further investment can take place in the modernization and extension of the convention centre, and/or in the construction of further hotel capacity. The latter should cover the various sections of the market from luxury to budget price (see Chapter 7).

There are several other factors which have been seen to be important in the rise of convention cities. An early interest in the industry, as in the case of Atlanta, gives the benefit of initial advantage. Trade can be built up before too many other cities become involved and the competition becomes stiff, and out of this situation good facilities and accommodation can be created. A location in a part of a country where there are not too many rivals is another advantage since, as we have seen, conferences tend to rotate around the regions. Some cities in the north-east part of the USA may find it difficult to compete because there are too many nearby rivals. Other advantages include: having an attractive physical environment; having a range of attractions; having good evening facilities; and having good accessibility, particularly via an airport. None of these may be critical, but being strong in at least some of these areas is important. Perception is also important. Many older industrial cities have a poor image which may make the attraction of delegates difficult. Finally, not to be forgotten in assessing the success of particular cities is the quality of the management (Petersen, 1989).

These points are relevant when considering the possibility of new cities attempting to enter the market. As in other areas of the economy, there are barriers to entry. Existing cities have a well-developed product. It is costly to invest in the necessary infrastructure when there is no certainty of a return on investment and success in the endeavour. In the case of trade shows, some cities have captured a particular market through the organization of specialized industrial exhibitions.

Against this, it can be posited that in a growing market there is usually room for new entrants. New industries are developing and trade shows can be developed for them. The conference organizer or attender is often looking for something different so that existing centres cannot be assured of maintaining their position. A city that wished to enter the industry should be able to capture a share of the market, provided it has a rounded and well thought out strategy, and the determination to pursue it over a number of years. Atlanta is one example of a successful city and several references have already been made to Birmingham. In the late 1960s this British city, with a long industrial tradition, decided to become an important exhibition centre. Its NEC, opened in 1976, has been successful, profitable and is continuously expanding. In the mid-1980s it decided to expand its business tourism and develop the conference business through the construction of an American-style convention centre. In part, the construction of this facility, opened in 1991, was made possible because of the profitability of the NEC. It is too early to say whether this will be successful. Birmingham is also improving the environment and developing the arts in its city centre, partly as an aid to its convention business.

5

Urban attractions

A basic question that must be asked is why people do or should visit cities. As suggested earlier, people may visit cities for business, including conferences and exhibitions, and also to see friends and relatives. However, they may come because of the reputation and qualities of the city, which might include the attractions, to be discussed below, or the entertainments which are available. A survey by Longwoods International entitled 'Travel USA' asked Americans, 'What makes a city an exciting place to visit?'. Figure 5.1 contains the salient features of the results, suggesting that visitors want something that is unique and interesting, is popular, is entertaining and includes cultural attractions and sightseeing. These categories are not clear-cut, as further details show. Within 'unique and interesting' the two main responses were 'lots to see and do' and 'an interesting place'. Under 'entertainment' the chief responses were 'exciting night life' and 'shopping'. For 'cultural attractions and sightseeing' the main headings were 'well-known landmarks', 'interesting architecture', 'noted for history' and 'excellent museums and galleries'.

When visiting a city many people might ask – what is there to see? In other words, what are the attractions? These might include museums and art galleries, historic buildings, theatres and concerts, sport, and the 'sights', the general landscape of buildings. These last two topics will be considered in Chapters 7 and 8. The aim of this chapter is to concentrate on those attractions which fall under the general heading of museums, using this term fairly broadly. It will seek to understand how these facilities can and do attract people to cities and what cities have to do if they are to be more successful. To achieve this, some background to the nature, purpose and history of museums will be provided.

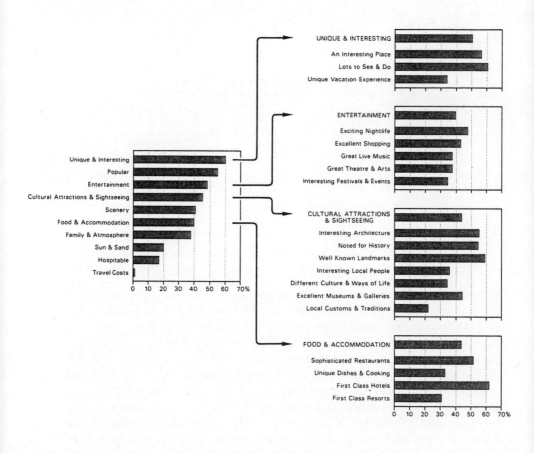

Figure 5.1 Why people visit cities.
Source: Denver Convention and Visitors Bureau 1991 Annual Report.

Museums

A museum has been defined as 'a permanent establishment administered in the public interest with a view to conserve, study, exploit by various means, and basically to exhibit for the pleasure and education of the public objects of cultural value' (International Council of Museums, quoted by Hudson (1975)). Establishments which call themselves museums or art galleries will clearly fall within this category but there may be other facilities which are on the borderline. The American Association of Museums (1992) has a broader definition which embraces historic houses and sites as well as living collections, but excludes profit-making organizations. In Britain the confusion about definition can be illustrated by reference to historic buildings. These are usually classified under a different heading, but often they contain within them collections of art, furniture and other objects which are similar to what a museum or art gallery might display. However, historic buildings owned by local authorities are more likely to be called museums. In recent years the range of urban attractions has widened to include industrial establishments which provide public tours, television studios, waxworks and theme parks. While these would not generally be classified as museums, they may have some similar characteristics. Thus a visit to an industrial establishment might include not only a factory tour but also a display of articles relating to the company's history. So when statistics are collected about museums, there may be some fuzziness at the edges, with some facilities having the possibility of being classified in different ways.

The traditional museum was very much concerned with scholarship, the collection and preservation of cultural objects, and their display for educational purposes. The old museums obtained a reputation for being dull and dreary and consisting of boring objects in glass cases. Since the late 1960s there has been a great change in museums, in the way articles are presented and in the general facilities of museums (Cossens, 1991). In part this reflects greater public interest in museums, itself a consequence of a more educated public, and also the professionalism of curators, who naturally want to use the latest methods of presentation. However, it also reflects the fact that museums must increasingly justify themselves (Hewison, 1989). Public funds will be forthcoming only if museums are seen to be attracting large numbers of visitors, performing an educational role and being a part of the life of the community, which may include being a significant part of the tourism resource base. Increasingly, many museums have been forced to charge for entry, and to win patrons they must show that they have an appealing product. Additionally, to gain the finance they need, many museums have resorted to commercial sponsorship, and once again this will be forthcoming only if the sponsors can see a large number of visitors. These factors have forced museums into the market-place to compete for visitors. Hewison (1989) has written, 'a visit becomes a day out, one of a number of options where museums must compete with sporting events, the seaside, funfairs, and so forth, for the necessary number of visitors to justify their existence'. In this situation it is easy to see how 'museums have become part of the leisure and tourism industry' and how 'entertainment has become an over-riding factor in their presentation'.

In the contemporary museum, curators have attempted to make their collections more interesting, often by telling a story which is illustrated by the objects. There is much more interaction with the objects, such as in science museums, and museums are seeking to re-establish their links with the community and perform an educational role in collaboration with schools. Entertainment is being introduced, as actors perform in heritage museums, and there are more audiovisual presentations. These are sometimes called 'anti-museums'. Museums are becoming more commercial, attempting to make money from catering, conferences, sales and special temporary exhibitions for which an entrance fee can be charged. These temporary exhibitions may bring together objects either from other collections or from the museum's own store, and it is hoped that they will encourage return visits. Such exhibitions may also be linked with other special events in the city (see Chapter 6). This commercial role is also seen in the fact that museums are being encouraged to make themselves tourist attractions and actively market themselves, not just locally but over a wide area. To some curators this shift of emphasis is a retrograde step and they would like to return to a more scholarly public service ethos.

Modern museums and art galleries date back to the end of the eighteenth century and the beginning of the nineteenth century. In some cases wealthy patrons gave their collections to either the state or a city and this formed the basis of a new museum or gallery. In other cases local groups established museums for educational purposes. Thus in Britain in the early nineteenth century many philosophical (scientific) societies were founded which created collections, later to be handed over to local authorities. Wealthy industrialists also gave funds to establish art galleries and some donated their own collections. The 1845 Museums of Art in Corporate Towns Act gave British municipalities the powers to fund museums and art galleries. Thereafter new facilities were established as cities and towns mushroomed following the industrial revolution. In 1860 there were about 90 museums in Britain. By 1887 the number had grown to 217, by 1963 to 876 and by 1984 to 2131. The Museums and Galleries Commission estimated that in 1989 there were 2500 museums and art galleries and that a new one opened every two weeks (but also some were closing). Many local authorities began with a general museum, and this has subsequently been divided into specialized facilities such as industry, science, art, archaeology, transport, heritage, etc. In the USA in the 1960s a new museum opened every 3.3 days and by the early 1980s there were 6000 museums, of which 2000 were funded by some level of government (Glaser, 1986). A 1989 survey by the American Association of Museums recorded over 8000 organizations using its broad definition, of which nearly two-thirds had opened since 1960 (American Association of Museums, 1992). In the world, it has been estimated that there are over 25 000 museums.

Museums continue to be provided for traditional reasons, to conserve materials and to have an educational role, but in addition museums may be built to make a statement about the importance and role of culture, to express confidence in the future of a place, and to be part of the tourism resource base (Cossens, 1991). At every level from the local to the national, an authority may think that a museum will demonstrate to the world its importance and status. This may be achieved by employing an architect of international renown to design a spectacular new museum building. Examples include

Fort Worth (Texas), Paris (the Pompidou Centre) and Stuttgart. While both national and local government museums have increased in number, there has also been a growth of private and independent museums. Private museums may either be run for profit, or be linked to a commercial organization but not necessarily run for profit, as with company museums. Independent museums may be organized by a non-profit-making trust, established to further a particular interest, such as the preservation of an historic site.

The growth of museums this century reflects a public interest in and a desire to preserve the best of the past and to display our culture. Much activity has been funded by the public sector, and even the private and independent museums often receive grants for capital works. In a few cases, financially insolvent independent museums have been taken over by public bodies. Thus the public cost of providing museums has continued to increase, often faster than inflation because of the high labour component and the fact that many museums are in historic buildings which need costly repairs. However, in the 1980s in Britain and the USA at least, there has been an attempt to cap both national and local government finance, with consequences for the funding of museums. This has forced them to turn to other sources of finance from private sponsorship, entrance charges and sales. The possibility of private sponsorship varies from place to place and is clearly greater in capital cities. Entrance charges may depress the number of visitors and this in turn may have other consequences, not least in suggesting a reduced role for the museum.

Museums may be administered by the state, by a local authority, by a non-profit-making trust and by a private company. National museums and art galleries tend to be among the largest in the world, benefiting from generous financing, arising from a feeling that they must match the status (or desired status) of the country, and from private donations. They usually not only have large collections but also perform research with large staffs. National galleries tend to be located in capital cities, which thus benefit from having these attractions, but smaller cities can benefit, as with Cardiff and Edinburgh in the UK, and when branch establishments are opened. Paris illustrates the benefits of having national galleries. During the 1980s the French government was determined to make the city the cultural capital of Europe and was prepared to spend large sums of money on the Louvre, the Pompidou Centre, La Villette (the Cité des Sciences et de l'Industrie, a science and industry museum) and the Muśee d' Orsay. In contrast, the finance available to local authorities is much less and depends on their size and wealth. In the past, cities with strong locally based companies have benefited from this wealth via donations, but today, with large companies more globally based, this support may be weaker. Once again some cities have been prepared to invest strongly in museums, to raise their status in the eyes of the outside world and/or to provide a tourist attraction. Public spending in Britain in 1988–1989 on museums was £301.1 million, of which 60 per cent was spent by the central government and 40 per cent by local authorities (*Cultural Trends*, No. 8, 1990,

p. 5). Many of the new independent museums have struggled into existence strong only in the enthusiasm of their founding group. However, a few have become large, with a good product imaginatively displayed, and helped by public and private grants. A final category that may be mentioned is the private commercial venture, although these are rarely museums in the strict sense. They are usually large, well financed, strongly marketed and often strategically located.

Museum Attendances

Attendance figures can be used to illustrate the general popularity of museums, trends and the importance of different types of museum. Not all museums record attendances and of those that do not all release the figures. Further, the methods of recording the numbers of visitors varies, including entrance fee records, manual counts, and electronic eye counts, which may have different degrees of accuracy, and changes in method may invalidate historical comparisons. Nevertheless, the figures do give a rough indication of trends. In the USA, museum attendance grew rapidly from 300 million in 1975 to 565 million in 1988. By contrast, in England the number of visitors to museums increased from 57 million in 1977 to 61.7 million in 1990, a growth of only 8 per cent. This small increase either reflects the imposition of charges in many museums or suggests that the market for museums is saturated and that the increasing number of museums may merely dilute attendances at existing museums and increase competition overall (Middleton, 1990a). In this situation some museums may close and those that can create a competitive product will either grow or maintain their position. Overall, in the whole of the UK in 1990 attendance was 74.2 million.

Figures for the main sectors are available for 1984 (Myerscough, 1988a). In that year UK attendance was 72.8 million of which 25.1 million or 34.5 per cent was in the national museums, 22.6 million or 32.0 per cent in local authority museums, 19.7 million or 27.0 per cent in other museums, and 5.4 million in temporary exhibitions. According to Victor Middleton (*Museums Journal*, November 1989), 95 per cent of local authority museums had an attendance of less than 100 000 a year, and 75 per cent had less than 50 000 a year. From these and other figures, a picture emerges of the distribution of attendances at museums and similar attractions (Table 5.1). Within a large stock a small number of establishments have the bulk of the attendances, each having at least 100 000 a year and in some cases up to 3 million a year. In 1990 the top 11 museums had 25 per cent of the total attendances at museums and art galleries in the UK, and the top 60 facilities, each with an attendance of over 200 000, had 50 per cent of all visits. These facilities include the national museums and the major municipal museums. In the USA the top 595 museums, accounting for 7.3 per cent of the total number, attracted 266 million visitors in 1988 or 47.1 per cent of all attendance. By contrast,

Table 5.1 Distribution of visits to museums by total attendances in the UK

Annual attendances	Percentage of museum sample				
	1978	*1982*	*1986*	*1988*	*1989*
1000 or less	5	8	9	9	9
1001–10 000	34	34	37	37	36
100 001–50 000	38	39	37	38	40
50 001–100 000	13	10	8	7	7
100 001–200 000	5	4	4	4	4
200 001–500 000	2	3	3	3	3
500 001+	2	2	2	2	1
All	100	100	100	100	100
Sample number	716	832	1118	1222	1560

Source: Middleton (1990b); *Cultural Trends*, No. 8, 1990, p. 22.

the 6591 small museums, 80.6 per cent of the total, attracted 168 million visitors or 29.7 per cent of the total (American Association of Museums, 1992). The situation is likely to be similar in other major Western countries.

During the year there are distinct trends in visitor numbers. These are greatest in summer and least in the winter, with the exception of school holidays. Visitor numbers also peak at the weekend and are often low during the week outside the summer (Greater Manchester Visitor and Convention Bureau, 1992).

The regional distribution of visitors to museums in Britain is shown in Table 5.2, where it is seen that London has a very high share, far greater than its population would suggest. The importance of London is clearly due to the role of national museums in the capital.

Museum Visitors

The last section has introduced the topic of visitors to museums, and in this section the question is asked – who visits museums and why? Several surveys have been conducted both among the general population and among museum visitors to discover their characteristics (Table 5.3). When they were asked if they have visited a museum in the last year the answers varied between 29 and 39 per cent for museums and 11 and 28 per cent for art galleries (Myerscough, 1988a, pp. 26–28). A survey by the Henley Centre for Forecasting in Britain in the early 1980s found that 45 per cent of the population visited museums. Merriman's postal survey of 1985 indicated that 58 per cent of his respondents had visited a museum or art gallery in the previous year (Merriman, 1991). On the basis of his results he was able to divide the population into five groups:

Type of visitor	Percentage of sample
Frequent: Visit three or more times a year	17
Regular: Visits once or twice a year	37
Occasional: Last visited between one and four years ago	14
Rare: Last visited five or more years ago	14
Non-visitor: Never visited a museum	18

Table 5.2 Regional distribution of visitors to museums in the UK in 1990

Region *	Visitors (000s)	Share (%)	Population share (%)
Cumbria	696	0.9	0.9
Northumbria	2 796	3.8	4.5
North West	5 667	7.6	11.1
Yorkshire/Humberside	7 694	10.3	8.6
Heart of England	4 428	6.0	10.0
East Midlands	3 161	4.3	7.0
Thames/Chiltern	1 695	2.3	6.1
East Anglia	3 091	4.2	6.3
London	22 639	30.5	11.8
West Country	4 273	5.8	6.4
Southern	3 124	4.2	3.7
South East	2 443	3.3	6.8
Scotland	9 422	12.7	8.9
Wales	2 269	3.1	5.0
N. Ireland	786	1.1	2.8
Total	74 184	100.0	100.0

*Tourist Board regions.
Source: British Tourist Authority and English Tourist Board.

In the USA in 1985 22 per cent of the adult population had visited a museum in the previous 12 months (quoted in *Statistical Abstract of the United States*), although the Association for Arts survey suggested a figure nearer 50 per cent (quoted in Merriman, 1991).

British surveys have found that, by age, attendance is highest in the 35–44 age group, and for class the higher socio-economic groups have a greater tendency to visit museums and art galleries. Overall, men make more visits than women, although there is hardly any difference for art galleries. However, the characteristics of visitors do vary between one type of museum and another, as the art gallery figures show. Not surprisingly, science and industry museums attract a higher proportion of men and also a wider social class spectrum. They are often visited as part of a family day out, so that children form an important part of the visitor numbers. Merriman (1991) found that 51 per cent of his respondents had visited a museum while on holiday or on a day trip. In contrast to science and industry museums, art galleries attract more women, and more people on their own, and they have a more middle-class clientele (Harvey, 1987; Heady, 1984). These figures relate to the whole

Table 5.3 Museum and art gallery visiting in the UK 1989–1990

	Percentage attending at least once a year	
	Museums	*Art gallery/Exhibition*
All	29	21
Male	31	22
Female	27	21
Age		
15–24	28	22
25–34	31	22
35–44	36	25
45–54	31	23
55–64	27	21
65+	21	16
Social grade		
AB	46	41
C1	35	26
C2	24	15
D	22	13
E	16	10

Source: *Cultural Trends* No. 8, 1990, p. 24 (see also Merriman, 1991, p. 50).

population. For tourists who are willing to travel a long distance to visit a city attendance at museums is likely to be much higher. In 1981–1982 a survey of overseas visitors to Britain found that more than 75 per cent had visited a museum or art gallery (quoted in Capstick, 1985).

In a study of visitors to museums in Toledo (USA), Hood (quoted in Greenhill, 1988) examined the factors affecting adult use of leisure time. These were:

1 Being with people
2 Doing something worthwhile
3 Feeling comfortable and at ease with one's surroundings
4 Having the challenge of new experiences
5 Having the opportunity to learn
6 Participating actively

He then classified his respondents in a household survey on the basis of frequency of visiting museums into:

(a) Frequent visitors
(b) Occasional visitors
(c) Non-participants

The frequent visitors (a) formed only 14 per cent of the total but were responsible for 40–50 per cent of all visits and were influenced by factors 2, 4 and 5, all favouring them to go and do things. The non-participants, who formed 46 per cent of the total, were influenced by factors 1, 3 and 6, which tended to make them less explorative. The occasional visitors, who represented 46 per cent of the sample and accounted for 50–60 per cent of the visits, were affected more by factors which influenced the non-participants than the frequent visitors but they could be influenced to make more visits. This analysis suggests that a person's approach to museums will be affected by education, general approach to life and emotional stability. In practice, income and other personal factors will also influence how often a person visits a museum.

Other surveys have asked visitors why they had come to the museum (Harvey, 1987; Heady, 1984; Smyth and Ayton, 1985). Some, of course, came because they were interested in the subject of the museum, but only a minority of all visitors fell into this category, although interest in the subject is more important among frequent attenders (Merriman, 1991). Others came because they had heard of the reputation of the museum, a situation which may apply only to the large and famous establishments. A survey of visitors to the British Museum found that many did not have a clear idea of what they had come to see (Capstick, 1985). Others came because they were on holiday and had free time and wanted something to do, and finally some came because they were with a group. The proportion giving an answer to each of these choices will clearly vary from place to place, but in general there are likely to be more reasons for visiting the large museum in the big city than for visiting museums elsewhere.

Museums and Urban Tourism

In order to increase their appeal to tourists, cities must expand their attractions so as to draw in more visitors. This must be done in such a manner that the attractions are complementary and add pulling power to the city, and do not result in a redistribution of the same number of visitors over a larger number of facilities (i.e. displacement). In the main, this will be the responsibility of local authorities and other public sector bodies since it is they who own and administer most museums. However, some of the new-type attractions are commercial operations (see below) and so there could be an important role for the private sector.

In Britain several cities have policies to expand the number of attractions. Most cities already have museums, but as a result of the growth of their collections there is not always enough space to display the articles. Many cities have decided to split their collections and create new specialized museums. Often these are in topics like industry and transport. In Glasgow the Burrell Collection (art and cultural objects) was removed from the main art gallery to create a new gallery, opened in 1983, with considerable success. Attendance has been between 500 000 and 1 million a year. Sometimes a small museum can be expanded if the resources are available. In Manchester a small science museum was relocated to the historic 1830 terminus of the pioneer Manchester to Liverpool railway, partly to provide a new use for the site and enable it to be preserved, and subsequently greatly enlarged. This was largely made possible by funding from the Greater Manchester Council on its demise in 1986. Other cities have competed to attract new branches of national museums. In the early 1980s Bradford (in Yorkshire) attracted a branch of the Science Museum in London specializing in photography and film, and subsequently the city has won a branch of the Victoria and Albert Museum, which will display its Indian collection. Elsewhere, Liverpool has obtained a branch of the Tate (art) Gallery and Leeds is to have a branch of the Royal Armouries (headquartered in the Tower of London). Many cities have established new museums and the most common theme relates to heritage. A list of the most popular attractions in Britain shows that many of the most successful have only been opened in the past 15 year (Law, 1991b).

The location of existing and new attractions within the city is important. The clustering of attractions enables the visitor to move easily from one to the other, and if this is known in advance it is more likely to encourage the tourist to visit the city. A complex of museums enables a city to project a clear image of itself and obtain a high profile, even though most tourists will visit only a few of the total number of establishments. Coordinated events and special exhibitions within the museums can be used to boost attendance with greater effect than for a single institution. Clustering will also accelerate external impacts in the form of souvenir and craft shops, and restaurants, as thresholds will be reached sooner.

Many cities have therefore adopted policies of grouping attractions, although clearly this is not always possible when some of the major existing ones are scattered and in historic buildings and could be moved only at great cost. One of the earliest examples of museum grouping is to be found in South Kensington in London, and perhaps the best known example is Washington DC, where the Smithsonian Institution has 13 museums. More recently, cities in Germany, like Cologne and Frankfurt, have followed a similar policy. Frankfurt has used the southern bank of the Main as the location for seven of its 24 museums, 11 of which were established in the 1980s. These museums attract about 2 million visitors a year. This policy of creating new museums has arisen because of Frankfurt's desire to prove that it is one of Europe's leading cultural cities with a mix of facilities providing a high-quality lifestyle for its inhabitants, and that it is not just prominent in banking. The South Bank (Museumsufer) is near the historic Romer Square and some other museums and so provides a compact tourist area (Figure 5.2). In Britain, Liverpool has the opportunity to group its new attractions in the regenerated docklands around the Albert Dock, where already there is a maritime museum and the branch of the Tate Gallery (Figure 5.3). Similarly, Manchester is hoping to have a concentration of attractions in the Castlefield area of the city centre (Figure 5.4) (Law and Tuppen, 1986; Law, 1991a).

The success of these policies can be measured in terms of how many visitors are attracted, but any evaluation must be placed in the context of existing patterns (see Table 5.2). The regional figures do not show the strength of

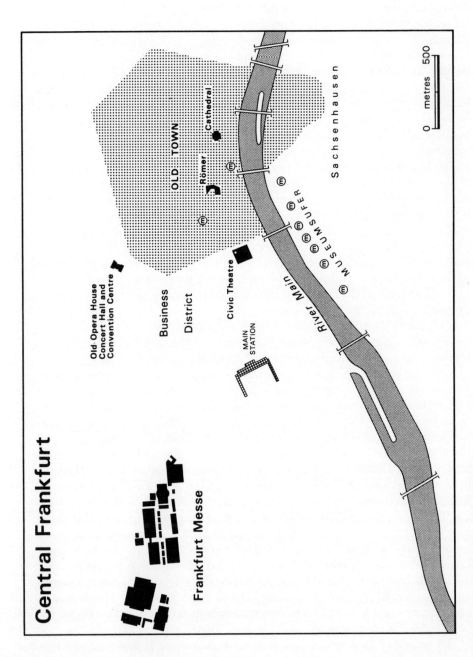

Figure 5.2 Frankfurt city centre and museums.

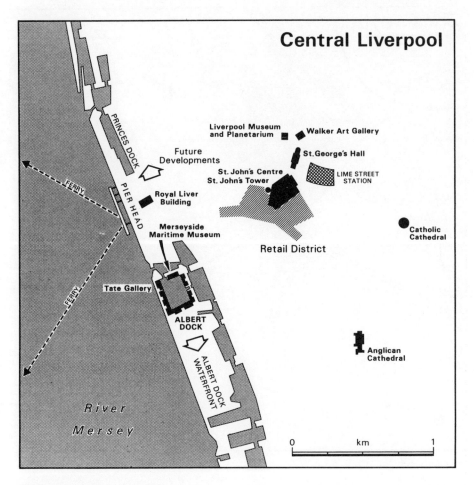

Figure 5.3 Liverpool city centre.

cities but Table 5.4 shows that cities are very important as far as museum visitors are concerned. The top ten cities had 20.6 per cent of all UK attendances to museums and art galleries. Figure 5.5 shows that those cities that have invested in new attractions have gained increasing attendances without any displacement. Bradford, Glasgow, Liverpool and Manchester increased the number of attractions in the 1980s, whereas Birmingham and Bristol did not, the latter having level attendances.

A crucial question for urban tourism is how many of these visitors to museums came from outside the local area, and thus brought income into the local economy. Many surveys ask visitors for their home area so that they can be classified into locals (those within a 10–20-mile radius), day trippers and tourists (i.e. those staying overnight). Table 5.5 gives the results of

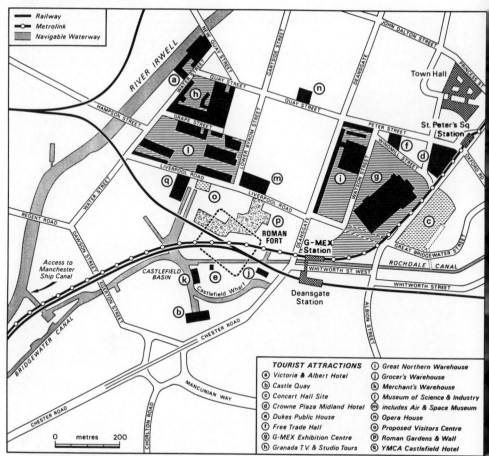

Figure 5.4 Manchester's Castlefield area.

some of these enquiries. Within Britain, London has the highest proportion of tourists, with all other centres having a much lower share. Edinburgh and Glasgow do well, but most other cities have only a small share. However, if day trippers are taken into account it can be seen that many cities have up to about 25 per cent visitors coming from outside the local area, and thus making a significant contribution to visitor numbers. As a general summary of this point it can be suggested that the larger the museum in terms of attendance, then the greater its share of tourists is likely to be. Perhaps this is obvious, since to attract large numbers a museum will have to draw people from well outside its local area.

A second crucial question concerns how many of these non-locals have come to the city because of the attraction. Replies are usually classified into: (a) sole reason; (b) one among a mixture of reasons; and (c) of no importance. This enables some estimate to be made of the importance of the attractions

Table 5.4 Visits to museums in British cities outside London ranked by attendance 1991 (000s)

Rank	City	Museum visits only	All attractions
1	Edinburgh	2695	5320
2	Glasgow	2395	3010
3	York	2097	2271*
4	Liverpool	1750	2251
5	Birmingham	1246	1356
6	Nottingham	1241	1647
7	Manchester	1040	1699
8	Bradford	947	988
9	Portsmouth	827	1401
10	Bristol	747	1235
11	Sheffield	630	675
12	Cardiff	553	746

*Not including York Minister.
Source: British Tourist Authority and English Tourist Board, *Visits to Tourist Attractions*, 1992.

Table 5.5 Museum visitors by origin: selected British cities

Area	Percentage of total		
	Local resident	Day tripper	Tourist
London	29	27	44
Glasgow (1985)	56	19	25
Merseyside	65	20	15
Ipswich	36	34	30
Glasgow (1990)	50	23	27

Source: Myerscough (1988a, 1991).

Table 5.6 Glasgow museum and art gallery attendances 1986: main reason for visiting area or city (%)

Reason	Residents	Day visitor	Tourist*
To visit this venue	48	56	11
To visit arts in general	14	10	5
General sightseeing	11	11	16
Work	8	6	8
Shopping	4	3	—
Visiting friends/relatives	3	11	59
Personal business	8	3	1
Other	3	—	—

*Overnight stayers.
Source: Myerscough (1988a).

and how many tourists can be said to have come because of them. Surprisingly few people give these attractions as the sole reason for visiting a city, but it is usually important as one of the reasons for visiting the city (Table 5.6). This applies even in the case of London, suggesting that except for specialists a city often sells itself on the basis of a range of appeals, including cityscape,

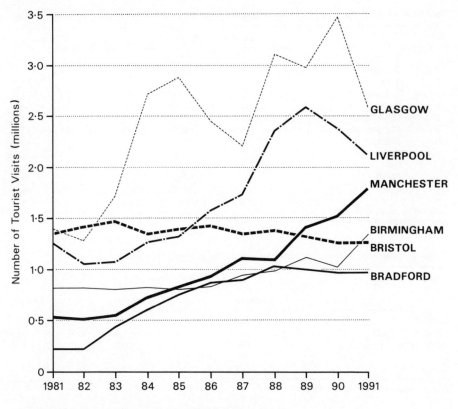

Figure 5.5 Museum attendance in selected British cities.
Source: British Tourist Authority and English Tourist Board (1992).

attractions and entertainment. Visitor surveys usually ask museum visitors
how much they have spent and will spend on the trip, and thereby attempt
to calculate the economic impact of an attraction. The greatest impact will
obviously be made by visitors who stay overnight in serviced accommodation,
while day trippers and those staying with friends and relatives may only make
a small impact. Since this is a topic that will be discussed in another chapter,
it will not be pursued now.

New Types of Attraction

Mention has already been made of the fact that new types of attractions
are being developed in cities and elsewhere. Among these is the factory tour,
or as it is sometimes called, industrial tourism. Can these new attractions
become a big draw for cities? This kind of visit is in fact nothing new, for
as MacCannell (1976) points out, Baedeker's guide to Paris in 1900 listed
workplaces open to the public, including the morgue! Factories have for a

long time shown people around, and what is happening now may be no more than a formalization of this process with advertised times for the general public. In some cases these tours represent a goodwill gesture to the community and involve link-ups with schools to provide for the education of children. However, in some industries there is very clearly an opportunity for advertising of the product, and the possibility of sales to the consumer. For this reason glass and pottery firms have long arranged tours and had shops (Ball and Metcalfe, 1992). With stringent health and safety regulations, factory tours are often more difficult today and special areas may have to be provided for the public. In the late 1980s the British government encouraged industrial tourism, suggesting that this could be of real economic importance to industrial districts. A few cities, such as Sheffield, have attempted to develop a coordinated programme of factory visits (Speakman and Bramwell, 1992). Unfortunately there is little information about the impact of industrial tourism, but it seems unlikely that most tourists would travel far to go on a factory tour. A few industries, such as china and glass, might be an important draw which together with other attractions would bring tourists into an area.

Another new type of attraction is the theme park, first developed in its present form by Disney in California in 1955, and subsequently diffused around the world. These parks are large-scale entertainment complexes attracting millions of visitors from a very wide area. Because of the area required, they can usually be built only on the edge of cities and therefore appear to have few links with the rest of urban tourism. However, where they have been built, such as by Disney on the edge of Paris (1992) and Tokyo and by other companies elsewhere, they may help to attract people to the area (Boggs and Wall, 1984).

Other Attractions

Zoos have been a traditional attraction in urban areas. In recent years in Britain a number of urban zoos have closed and now even London zoo has recently been threatened with closure in spite of receiving over 1 million visitors a year. Some of these zoos had constricted sites and were in need of modernization which forecast revenues could not justify. They were in competition with newer zoos with more space located in rural areas. Like other attractions, zoos have to modernize themselves. The modern family visiting a zoo expect more information presented in an interesting way and also information about endangered species. They also expect a zoo to provide entertainment. In this, zoos are very much competing against other attractions which offer an alternative day out. Given the widespread availability of zoos it is unlikely that they are or were a major attraction drawing visitors to cities from outside the region.

In recent years there has been a growth of other types of wildlife attraction.

In the USA marine (or sealife) museums have appeared, and they can take two forms. The larger attractions in terms of space include marine life parks like Marineland developed in Florida in the 1960s, and followed by the Sea Worlds at San Diego (1964), Aurora, Ohio (1970), Orlando (1973) and San Antonio (1988) (Brown, 1992). The more compact type of facility includes aquariums, some of which, like the Shedd in Chicago, date back to the interwar period. Boston's New England Aquarium opened in 1969 and quickly attracted over 1 million visitors a year, showing how this type of facility could be a phwerful attraction in bringing people back downtown. Subsequently, aquariums were built in Baltimore (1981), Monterey Bay (1984), New Orleans (1990) and Camden (Philadelphia) (1991), and again showed that they could attract visitors. During the 1980s many cities in the USA and Britain examined the feasibility of constructing an aquarium, but few have been built as yet. One reason for this is that most of the aquariums recently built have required a large public subsidy and in fact many are publicly owned (Guskind, 1990). The main justification for this has been that they have been the anchors for downtown revitalization schemes. Aquariums were also seen as being both educational and entertaining. While only a few cities have an aquarium, those aquariums can obviously appeal to visitors from a wide area, but if they were to be found in most cities this attraction would cease. Already the new aquariums being built are attempting to have a distinctive theme to give them appeal (Guskind, 1990).

Many cities are attempting to establish heritage centres. This is often in spite of the fact that most cities already have museums which deal with local history, and also that there may be displays of local history in historic buildings. In some cases the new heritage centre will bring together the different collections into one place. In other cases the centre will act as an entry point for tourists into the city, perhaps using a historic building at a central location, and also functioning as a tourist information centre. Since local history might be thought to have little appeal to the visitor, it is often necessary to dress it up in some way, possibly making it a form of entertainment or visitor experience. In Britain this innovative approach was pioneered by the highly successful Jorvik (1984) in York, and subsequently other cities such as Canterbury, Dover, Nottingham, Oxford and Plymouth have introduced variations on this theme. In the case of Nottingham the historical theme has used the city's most famous mythical son, Robin Hood.

Other types of attractions (some old) include waxworks, planetariums and various forms of entertainment. Some of these have an educational component, but this is overlaid by their portrayal as places of fun. This type of project is likely to become more important in the future. In Manchester the regional television company, Granada, opened its studios to the public in 1988, to exploit the popularity of its thrice-weekly soap opera, *Coronation Street*, and attracted 600 000 visitors in the first year.

A few cities still have major permanent funfairs which attract large attendances. Copenhagen's Tivoli Gardens has over 4 million visitors a year. However, many such funfairs have been closed in cities in recent years, and most surviving funfairs are found in seaside resorts or as part of theme parks.

Impact

The direct impact of museums and these other attractions is fairly small. Employment in museums is not large. Glasgow, which has one of the largest municipal museum services in the country, employed only 367 people in 1986. Of these, 11 per cent were in management, 26 per cent in curatorial and education, 56 per cent in technical and security and the rest were not classified. Many museums employ part-time labour, some of which is seasonal, corresponding with rising visitor attendance. Many small independent museums rely on unpaid volunteers without whom they could not function. Museums may have additional impact if they are responsible for attracting visitors to the city, but, as has been seen, it is difficult to attribute a single motive to many of those who visit museums. A cluster of attractions in a tourist quarter may persuade visitors to stay longer and spend more money. The greatest impact is likely to occur when tourists are persuaded to stay overnight in serviced accommodation and patronize numerous facilities.

Conclusion

This chapter has attempted to review the role of museums and other attractions in bringing tourists to the city. They are clearly important but for most people seldom function on their own. Cities that wish to develop tourism as part of their economic strategy will need to develop attractions, but these will need to be large and of high quality. There is a hierarchy of attractions and it is only those that rank high that will be able to pull in visitors from a distance. They will face competition from capital cities with their well-financed national museums, and from the fact that potential visitors are likely to allocate only a limited amount of time to this activity. Given this, cities will need to have distinctive products on offer. Another problem is in obtaining finance for these facilities at a time when local government finance is stretched to its limit. Finally, cities will need continually to update their attractions so that they remain competitive in the market-place.

6
Culture, sport and special events

The cultural and sporting activities of cities have not traditionally been regarded as part of the tourist industry. Theatres, concert halls and sports grounds were all built to meet the needs of the resident population, and probably until at least recently a very high percentage of their patrons would have been local. After many years of neglect, much investment is going into these areas, including a significant amount from the public sector. Among the various reasons for this, three are worth mentioning here. Firstly, they are perceived to bring prestige to a city and raise its profile in the outside world. As cities are desperate to attract inward investment and the first stage in this process is to gain attention, having a high profile in the arts and sport is a good starting point. Secondly, related to this is the perceived importance of quality of life factors, which are believed to be significant to management when investment location decisions are made. Thirdly, they are perceived as having tourism potential. If the events are of a sufficiently high quality then people will be prepared to travel some distance to attend. There is clearly some validity in this idea, since places like Aldeburgh (in Suffolk, UK) and Stratford-upon-Avon (UK) have traded on arts tourism for many years. But could this phenomenon become more widespread and be a significant component in the tourism industry of many cities?

The term 'special events' covers many activities, as will be seen later. However, one important component is the festival. As with culture and sport, many cities have had festivals for many years and they were primarily created to meet the needs of the local population. But as with these two other topics, the reasons for holding festivals are now being perceived differently, and once again the motives of high-status profile and tourism potential are coming to the fore. In discussing these topics it is important to be aware of the multipurpose objectives behind the development of these activities, and that it is not always easy to separate out the pure tourism element.

The Arts

The terms 'arts industry' and 'cultural industry' are sometimes used in a comprehensive way to include not only the performing arts but also museums and art galleries, cultural heritage, special events such as arts festivals, and the producing arts, as in some of the studies of the economic importance of the arts (Myerscough, 1988a; McNulty, 1985; Tighe, 1985). Here the use of the terms will be limited to the performing arts, and in particular to the role of theatres and concert halls. Because of their size and thus high threshold population, cities have always been important for drama, concerts, ballet, opera and other arts (Blau and Hall, 1986). Patrons living in smaller places have to travel to big cities to experience live performances and in the process become tourists (Hughes, 1986). Even if a city has an orchestra it cannot perform more than a limited repertoire in any one season, and also the quality of its performance may be judged inferior. Thus some patrons, albeit small in number, may be prepared to travel to other cities to extend their experience.

Any economic impact that the arts can have is constrained by the fact that only a small percentage of the population attend performances. A survey of participation in the USA found that only 17 per cent of adults had attended a musical in the previous 12 months, 13 per cent a classical musical performance, 12 per cent a play and 10 per cent a jazz performance, with much less for ballet and opera (Table 6.1). Attendance was greatly affected by the level of income and education. It is likely that the position in Britain and continental Europe is similar (Myerscough, 1988a). Apart from inclination, accessibility to performances is probably a major factor affecting participation, with higher rates in cities.

However, until recently these cultural resources of cities were perceived as purely local amenities and not part of the tourism resource base. Starting in the USA and now, increasingly, in Britain, the arts are considered to have an economic importance – a tendency which some believe will result in their devaluation – and also in a focus on providing for the more affluent (Hughes, 1989a). The reasons why the arts are thought to have an economic importance is that they have a high profile, a 'quality' label which gives and will give prestige, a positive image and the potential to bring publicity to cities (Whitt, 1988). Their presence suggests that a city has a level of civility and culture, and is progressive and resourceful (Shanahan, 1980). In the USA it has been argued that they have become the centrepiece of growth strategies (Whitt, 1987). With sports and special events, they will offer a high-quality lifestyle which will attract professionals, who are important in the new industries which cities must attract, to live in the city and in turn persuade major companies that the city concerned is a good place in which to locate an

Table 6.1 Participation rates for various arts performances in the USA in 1985

	Percentage attending at least once in last year					
	Jazz	Classical music	Opera	Musical	Play	Ballet
All	10	13	3	17	12	4
Household income						
Under $5000	8	9	2	10	8	3
$5000–9999	7	7	1	8	4	2
$10 000–14 999	6	8	1	11	8	3
$15 000–24 999	8	11	2	12	9	4
$25 000–49 999	11	15	3	22	14	5
Over $50 000	19	30	6	37	28	11
Education						
Grade school	1	3	1	3	1	1
Some high school	3	3	1	6	4	1
High school grad	7	7	1	12	6	2
Some college	13	15	3	21	15	6
College grad	18	29	6	34	26	9
Grad school	24	41	11	40	36	15

Source: US National Endowment for the Arts, 1985 Survey of Public Participation in the Arts, quoted in *Statistical Abstract of the United States*.

establishment (Hendon and Shaw, 1987). They may also attract tourists and help bring life and variety back to city centres, thus assisting with revitalization (Bianchini et al., 1988; Bianchini, 1991). The arts have traditionally been located in the urban core, and as Perloff (1979) has written, 'The arts serve to increase the element of excitement and variety which is the key to urbanity. Government and the private sector need to recognise the role of the artist as dynamic city builders.' In Britain, several cities have adopted cultural policies during the 1980s, including Birmingham, Coventry, Glasgow (see below), Liverpool, Newcastle and Sheffield (Bianchini, 1991; Comedia Consultants, 1989; Parkinson and Bianchini, 1990). In France since the decentralization reforms of 1982, large cities have had more funds and greater freedom to pursue cultural policies (Renucci, 1992).

The physical manifestation of these policies is seen in the renovation of old facilities, the construction of new concert halls and theatres, and the evolution of cultural districts (Wynne, 1992; Chapter 2). The latter are often located on the edge of the city centre in order to assist regeneration, but in some cities in North America they are a little removed in districts that are sometimes referred to as mid-town. In the USA, arts districts are found in Boston, Dallas, Pittsburgh and St Paul (British American Arts Association, 1989). Interestingly, finance for these facilities has often come from the private sector and private foundations, which partly reflects the role of business elites in growth coalitions and their perception of the arts as having high status (Whitt, 1988).

Table 6.2 Tourism and visits to theatres and concerts in Britain in 1984 (%)

Place	Residents	Day visitors	Tourists	
			British	Other
London	39	21	5	35
Elsewhere	82	10	8	0

Source: Myerscough (1988a), Table 5.1.

In Britain many city theatres have been refurbished since the early 1980s, often through a mix of finance from the public sector, private donation and commercial investment. The influx of commercial investment reflects the increasing affluence of the local population and the fact that with easier car travel because of the construction of better roads the hinterlands of theatres have increased. Concert halls have also been built or are planned, sometimes as single-purpose facilities (Glasgow 1990, and Manchester 1994), sometimes as part of a conference centre (Birmingham, opened 1991), and sometimes for joints use as a conference centre (Cardiff 1983, and Nottingham 1982). Once again, cultural or arts districts are being planned in British cities, notably in Birmingham, Bradford, Newcastle and Sheffield. Another advantage seen in developing the arts is that they help keep the city centre alive at night so that with more people it is perceived as a safer place (Comedia, 1991). It is also argued that a policy of clustering enables a critical mass of cultural facilities to evolve.

Only a small amount of research on tourism and the arts has been conducted. Cwi (1980), in a study of the impact of the arts in cities, concluded that it was overwhelmingly through tourists that the performing arts could generate additional income for the urban region. Probably in most cities only a small percentage of the patrons at any performance could be classified as tourists, i.e. coming from outside the immediate region. The share will obviously be related to the importance of tourism in the local economy and the amount of performing arts available, and is therefore likely to be high in capital cities, Tighe (1985) suggests that tourists represented 37 per cent of the audiences in New York in 1983–1984. In Britain the situation has been studied by the Policy Studies Institute, which confirms the importance of visitors in London's theatres and concert halls (Myerscough, 1988a) (Table 6.2). These figures show the combined share, but in fact most visitors attend theatres and only a few go to concerts. The situation for the different types of theatre in London is shown in Table 6.3, where it is seen that visitors prefer musicals, thrillers and to a lesser extent comedy and drama. One would expect the share of visitors to vary from place to place. In a few special places the share of non-residents is very high, as in Aldeburgh (77 per cent), Stratford (60 per cent) and Bath (53 per cent). Another special case is that of seaside resorts, where in the short summer season the proportion of tourists is very

Table 6.3 London West End theatre audiences by origin

Performance type	Percentage of respondents in survey		
	London resident	Other UK resident	Foreign
Modern drama	39	28	33
Comedy	37	35	28
Modern musical	20	45	34
Traditional musical	14	26	60
Revue/variety	42	47	11
Opera	59	31	10
Dance	63	24	13
Classical plays	43	32	25
Children's shows	47	44	9
Thrillers	22	18	60

Source: C. Gardiner (1991), The West End Theatre Audience 1990/1, City University. Quoted in *Cultural Trends*, No. 11, 1991, p. 18.

Table 6.4 Attendance at Glasgow theatres and concerts

	Numbers (000)		Change	Percentage		Difference
	1986	1990	(%)	1986	1990	
Residents						
Glasgow City	484	800	+66	41	46	+5
Outer Glasgow	524	420	−19	44	24	−20
Day visitors	149	330	+125	13	19	+6
Tourists	27	188	+596	2	10	+8
All	1184	1738	+47	100	100	—

Source: Myerscough (1991), Tables 45 and 47.

high. However, in most British cities the share of non-residents is likely to be less than 20 per cent, and only in London do they form the majority. A survey of theatre-goers in Manchester in 1985 found that 70 per cent lived in Greater Manchester, a further 12 per cent lived outside but had travelled from home, and 18 per cent had stayed overnight, with just under a half using serviced accommodation (Manchester Polytechnic, 1985). This compares with a 1986 survey in Glasgow, which found that 85 per cent of the patrons were Greater Glasgow residents, 13 per cent were day visitors, and only 2 per cent were staying overnight (Myerscough, 1988b). For the day visitors attending the theatre or concert, the overwhelming main reason for coming to Glasgow was the performance, while for tourists this was not a significant reason for two-thirds. During the 1990 European Year of Culture, Glasgow greatly increased the number of visitors attending theatres and concerts, although they still only formed 29 per cent of audiences (Table 6.4). In North America only about 5–10 per cent of theatre patrons stay overnight and so consequently they have a low economic impact (Petersen, 1989).

These statistics have only recently been collected and are often hard to come by. Even more difficult to obtain is information on the role these arts play in attracting people to cities, whether as a prime draw, as one of a bundle of attractions, or as mere entertainment when they are there (Hughes, 1989b). It is likely that the numbers of people for whom the arts are a prime draw is very small, and that for most people the possibility of attending a theatre or concert is a bonus after they have made the decision to visit the city. Many may in fact be primarily visiting friends and relatives. A third research question concerns the ancillary activities engaged in by the arts tourist and the pattern of expenditure. The arts tourist is likely to be more affluent and therefore a relatively high spender (Whitt, 1988). This should help support restaurants and perhaps specialty shops. There is not enough space to discuss the wider issue of the role of the arts in influencing economic development, but it is always likely to be difficult to prove the arts a strong influence, given the multiplicity of factors involved.

In addition to these 'high arts', cities are also the location for pop music events. Much pop music takes place in clubs, which may attract young people from a wide area on a regular basis. Cities are also the location for pop concerts held in major multipurpose venues such as arenas, discussed below, and which again may attract patrons from a wide area.

Sport

As with the arts, large cities, because of their large populations, have developed major sports facilities and are the home bases of prestigious teams. In recent years there has been a tendency to see sport as more than simply a local amenity. Major sporting activities, whether regular fixtures or special events (see next section), are perceived to project a high-status image of the city via media coverage which may help attract economic development, persuade senior executives to live in the city, and attract visitors (Baade and Dye, 1988a, 1990). It may also increase civic pride, community spirit ('social bonding') and collective self-image. Since the Los Angeles Olympic Games in 1984 it has also been believed that the profits from hosting a mega-event could pay for high-quality facilities which would be of permanent value to the community. In this section attention is focused on professional team sports and their facilities.

In the USA, professional sports teams are privately owned and can move from one city to another, and from the central city to the suburb (Johnson, 1986; Knack, 1986; Rosentraub, 1988; Rosentraub and Nunn, 1978). The number of teams in the top leagues is also limited. To keep teams in the city and in the downtown area, and to attract them from elsewhere, municipalities have been prepared to offer inducements, including building and retaining ownership of a stadium which is then let to the team, sometimes on an uneconomic basis (Petersen, 1989). Of the 29 stadiums constructed in the

USA between 1960 and 1990, 25 were publicly built (Baade and Dye, 1990), and of the 94 stadiums used by professional teams between 1953 and 1988, 67 were publicly owned (Baade and Dye, 1988b). This process has produced an oversupply of facilities so that teams are in a buyers' market. The rent for these stadiums rarely pays for all the costs, particularly debt service or loan repayments, but they are justified on the basis of the indirect benefits (i.e. general visitor spending), of the role they play in the physical and economic regeneration of the downtown area, or of the presumed general economic benefits to the area. Included in the latter is the enhanced image which a major sports team gives a city which will help it attract firms to the area and produce intangible benefits. Baade and Dye (1988a) could find no evidence to support these claims and concluded that in the final analysis the building of a stadium was based on non-measurable intangible benefits. To support this view they quoted the mayor of New Orleans: 'the Superdome is an exercise in optimism. A statement of faith. It is the very building of it which is important, not how much it is used or its economics.'

The various team sports have different demand schedules and may require special facilities. A major baseball team will occupy a stadium for about 81 days in the year and require a special oval pitch. In contrast, an American football team occupies its stadium for only about 8–11 days in the year (although attendances are likely to be greater), and the game requires a rectangular pitch. Basketball teams play about 41 home matches and use indoor arenas. In recent years the open baseball and football stadiums have been replaced by enclosed domes; examples include the Astra Dome in Houston (1965), the Superdome in New Orleans (1975) and the SkyDome in Toronto (1989) with a retractable roof. Covered facilities, whether arenas or domes, have greater flexibility and can be used for many different purposes, from sport and pop concerts to conventions (Petersen, 1989). Accordingly, in many cities, such as Atlanta and Indianapolis, the same authority has built the convention and sports facility; they are adjacent to each other and are run jointly.

Another key feature of North American urban development is that central cities have located these sports facilities on the edge of the downtown area, and have used them as part of their revitalization strategy, of which tourism is a central element. In many cities the stadium has traditionally been near the city centre and municipalities have fought to keep it there, particularly when a new, more modern facility was proposed for the suburbs. In other cities without a long-standing stadium, the first one has been constructed in this area (see Atlanta). In a few cities, such as Baltimore, an old stadium in a middle suburb has been replaced by a modern one adjacent to the downtown area. There are several advantages to this strategy, not least in its reinforcement of the tourism role of the city centre. Another advantage found in cities such as New Orleans is that the multistorey car parks built next to the sports facility can be used in the daytime by office workers and in the evening and at weekends by the spectators (Miestchovich and Ragas, 1986; Ragas *et al.*, 1987).

In Britain the dominant spectator sport is football, which has a high density of teams and facilities. Consequently a spectator is unlikely to have to travel far to find a match, unless it be as a fan to an away game, and so the tourist share of attendance is likely to be low (Collins, 1991).

The role of sport in tourism and urban regeneration in Britain has only recently begun to be considered. Sheffield attracted much attention through its successful bid for the World Student Games held in the city in July 1991 (Foley, 1991), and both Birmingham and Manchester have bid unsuccessfully for the Olympic Games. Cardiff and Edinburgh have hosted the Commonwealth Games and gained improved facilities. London (1989), Sheffield (1991) and Birmingham (1991) have recently constructed indoor arenas which can be used for sports events, and Manchester is building one as part of its preparations to bid for the 2000 Olympics. Liverpool and Manchester have sought to use football to assist tourism through sports weekend breaks involving game and entertainment tickets as well as hotel accommodation. However, in Britain there are only about half a dozen sports museums, whereas in North America there are over 400 'halls of fame' which are overwhelmingly in honour of sportsmen and sportswomen (Redmond, 1991). On the continent of Europe, many cities have invested heavily in sports facilities in order to host major events, including Barcelona and Duisberg.

Most of the research on sport and local economic development has been undertaken in the USA, where many reports (usually unpublished) have been commissioned by both municipalities and teams as part of the case for the public subsidy of stadiums (Baade and Dye, 1988a). These studies can focus either on the costs and benefits to the public sector (Johnson, 1986) or on the wider economic benefits to the area. When the public sector is in deficit, justification is usually sought in these wider benefits. Figures are often calculated to show how much the spectators spend inside and outside the ground at regular fixtures. However, since most of the spectators are locals, a large share of the expenditure cannot be counted as additional income to the region, being merely displaced from other activities, unless it can be shown that in the absence of a local stadium the participants would have visited stadiums outside the region ('import substitution'). Given the large distances between North American cities, it is likely that games attract some spectators for a short-break vacation, although research shows that for ordinary games only 5–10 per cent of spectators stay overnight. However, for bigger events like the Super Bowl this may rise to 90 per cent (Petersen, 1989). A study for the subsidized Louisiana Superdome in New Orleans found that when all the benefits were considered, the benefit to cost ratio was 12.4 to 1 (Ragas *et al.*, 1987). In contrast, in Britain, with its small distances, it is likely that nearly all spectators are either locals or day visitors. Unfortunately, in Britain there does not appear to be any research on the economic impact of regular sports programmes (Bale, 1991). The American evidence would suggest that sports programmes can have their greatest economic impact when they are linked with other tourist attractions and when they are family leisure activities.

As regards the impact of sport on general economic development, this relationship is likely to be very difficult to disentangle since this is only one factor among several which will affect the growth performance of an urban area. Baade and Dye (1990) found no relationship between assistance to teams and the building of stadiums, and the growth of personal incomes in nine US metropolitan areas. At a very local (site) level, sports facilities may have both positive and negative effects; positive because the prospect of large numbers of people may encourage investment in other activities (e.g. catering), and negative because crowds and congestion may discourage investment. Much may depend on the characteristics of the spectators. Baade and Dye (1988b) suggest that the maximum impact of a stadium is likely to be felt when it is close to other tourist attractions and hotels.

Indianapolis

Many cities have included sport as part of their economic development strategy but few have put it at the forefront. One exception is Indianapolis in the Midwest of the USA, sometimes called 'Sports City USA'. In the 1960s and 1970s the city experienced economic stagnation and was unable to attract new economic activities and was apparently not benefiting from its central location and low cost of living. Then the public and private sectors joined together to forge a regeneration strategy which included downtown rejuvenation, infrastructure improvement, tourism and world-class sport (Bamberger and Parham, 1984). In the late 1970s, under the leadership of the mayor, the concept of 'development through sport' was evolved; this contained within it the idea that specialization in sport would enable the city to carve out a separate identity (Wilkinson, 1990). At this time the city was known only for the Indianapolis 500 motor race. A convention centre was opened in 1972, the Market Street Arena in 1974, and the Indianapolis (White River) Sports Center in 1979. However, a bid for the World Student Games failed and the ensuing post-mortem suggested that it was because the city had insufficient facilities. To remedy deficiencies, a not-for-profit Indiana Sports Corporation was established in 1980 to stimulate the development of sports facilities and the attraction of events. By 1982 a natatorium and velodrome had been built, and in 1984 the $77.5 million, 60 000-seat Hoosier Dome was opened, linked to an enlarged convention centre. This was partly financed by $30 million of private grants and partly by bonds covered by a 1 per cent food and beverage tax (Petersen, 1989). The dome is used for sports, other events such as concerts, and conventions. The city used the facility to attract the Colts (American) football team from Baltimore (Johnson, 1986). Since 1984 other facilities have been added, including a regatta course, soccer complex and skating rink. In addition, hall of fame museums have been attached to the motor racing circuit and the Hoosier Dome, and a National Art Museum of Sport opened in 1991.

As a consequence of having spent $168 million on these facilities, the city has been able to win 230 national and international sports meetings between 1981 and 1991, including the Pan-American Games in 1987. For the 1991 World Gymnastic Championships held in the Hoosier Dome, an impact study was undertaken by Herron Associates Inc. (1991). Herron found that of the 70 000 spectators, two-thirds came from outside the state, and that there were were a further 1600 competitors, officials and press personnel. These visitors spent $37.2 million in the area. Another type of impact has been that two dozen sports organizations have located their headquarters in the city. The city has also been able to attract many non-sports companies, which have created many thousands of jobs and brought growth to the metropolitan area. Of course, it is difficult to evaluate the extent to which these firms have moved to the city because of the impact of sports, either in enhancing the lifestyle or changing image.

Special Event Tourism

The term 'special event' is used to describe themed events which occur infrequently or are one-off (Getz, 1991a). While a football match or a concert could be described as an event, these are often part of regular programmes. Typical special events are ones that occur only on an annual basis in the same locality (e.g. the Edinburgh Festival), or move from one place to another (e.g the Commonwealth Games). Another type of special event is the one-off celebration (e.g. bicentenaries). Special events may have almost any theme and take any form. A special event could be as simple as an annual street parade. Munich's Oktoberfest consists of parades and beer drinking. The arrival of the Tall Ships Race at an Atlantic port is an event which can attract millions of visitors. Many special events are related to existing attractions. An art gallery may have a special exhibition, perhaps of pictures on loan from elsewhere. A cathedral may be the setting for a choir festival. The terms mega-event or hallmark event describe large events of world importance and high profile which have a major impact on the image of the host city (Syme *et al.*, 1989). This definition is mainly psychological, as it is difficult to specify a quantitative one that would be widely applicable (Witt, 1988). Special events can therefore be anything from the annual village carnival to the Olympic Games. Often, special events involve a considerable amount of spectacle which acts as a visitor draw. Most special events are only of short duration, lasting either a few days or a few weeks, but some last several months and even up to a year.

Many special events have a long history but new ones are constantly being created, and Getz (1991a, 1992) provides evidence of their expansion.

This increase in special events is not unconnected with the fact that they are increasingly being used as a means of attracting tourists, and raising the profiles and changing the images of places. The large special event, whether it be a festival, a sports competition or a political convention, gains tremendous television coverage which can give more effective publicity than any other method (Guskind, 1988). In the past, most special events were conceived as purely local celebrations, but today the tourism motivation is often being added, and sometimes events are deliberately being created to attract tourists. Getz (1991a, p. 6) lists six reasons for special events:

1   To attract people into the area
2   To attract people outside the main season
3   To create media attention and raise the profile of the area
4   To add animation and life to existing attractions
5   To encourage repeat visits
6   To assist regeneration

The current inflation in special events is a consequence of the competition which exists between places; no city can afford to miss out on this type of attraction. Getz (1992) notes that the use of theme years is increasing. The advantage of special events is that they can be used by cities with few other attractions and that they appeal to the short-break market (Getz, 1991b).

Given the great variety of special events, it is imphssible to generalize about the impacts they have. Studies attempt to measure the number of people attending, their origins and characteristics, and their expenditure patterns. From these statistics an estimate can be made of the net income generated and the number of jobs created (Myerscough, 1991). In addition, an attempt may be made to measure the level of knowledge of the event in other parts of the country and how this has changed the perceptions of the area. Finally, an assessment can be made of the long-term effects, including the amount of inward investment and the growth of tourism. Because of the wide diversity of special events it is not possible to cover all of them and attention will be concentrated on arts festivals, sports events, world fairs and garden festivals (see Getz (1991a) for a comprehensive treatment).

Arts Festivals

Getz (1991b) defines a festival as a themed public celebration which extends leisure and cultural opportunities beyond everyday experiences and choices. Arts festivals may cover several arts or focus on a single art such as classical music, jazz, literature, drama, film, etc. In the UK there were 557 arts festivals in 1991, most of them having been founded since the mid-1970s (Rolfe, 1992). However, five festivals accounted for more than half of all receipts. By far the majority of festivals were held in the May to October period, with those in cities occurring in mid-season, when other activities fall away, and those in resorts in the early or late season, to boost trade. Local government support was important in most cases. Arts festivals attract mainly the middle class, and only the largest or most specialized attract a majority of attenders from outside the locality.

Many cities have attempted to introduce arts festivals in recent years. To attract attention and so be able to draw people from a distance they have increasingly been focused on a particular art form, such as film or jazz, but in a world awash with festivals late arrivals on the scene have found all the main themes taken. A recent innovation has been the introduction of year-long arts events which move from one city to another. In western Europe there is now a European City of Culture in which one city is given the title for a year and attempts to project itself across the continent (see Glasgow below). In Britain there is now a similar arts year for cities, except that each year has a specific theme. Cities bid for the title and the small amount of financial assistance that goes with it. Birmingham's 1992 Year of Music was the first, and in 1994 Manchester will have the Year of Drama. Once again, these festivals have multiple objectives of extending the arts experience of the residents, of raising the profile of the area and attracting visitors (Manchester City Council, 1991).

The success of an arts festival in terms of drawing an audience from outside its local area will probably depend on having a clear theme and achieving high quality. This is certainly true of British festivals such as Aldeburgh and Edinburgh (Myerscough, 1988a) and the well-known European ones of Bayreuth and Salzburg (Frey and Pommenehne, 1989). It is also likely that the more attractive the setting, the easier it is to draw an audience, and perhaps this is why older industrial cities may find it difficult to create a hugely popular event.

Some of the major arts festivals have been the subject of economic impact studies. The Edinburgh International Festival was established in 1947 and by the late 1980s, together with four other festivals and the Military Tattoo, was attracting 600 000 visitors for a three-week-long programme, generating income of between £30 million and £40 million. A study of 1990–1991 found that the arts festivals attracted a predominantly middle-class audience, whereas the Military Tattoo attracted a wider cross-section of the population (Scotinform Ltd and Leisure Research Services, 1991; Scottish Tourist Board, 1992). However, whereas between 30 and 50 per cent of festival-goers visited another festival, there was little multiple visiting between the festivals and the Tattoo. Direct expenditure was estimated at £43.8 million, producing a net income to the area of £9.2 million, and creating 2043 jobs or 1319 full-time equivalents. An earlier pioneering study by Vaughan of the 1976 festival found that it attracted 33 200 overnight staying visitors and 100 000 day trips (Vaughan, 1977, 1979, 1980). In that year the Lothian Regional Council gave a subsidy of £206 000. Vaughan found that visitors spent £3.7 million and generated a net impact of £960 000, yielding a benefit–cost ratio of nearly 5 to 1. In the context of Edinburgh's full year of tourism, the festival was responsible for 19 per cent of income generated, and the creation of the equivalent of 250 full-time jobs. As Vaughan points out, these are only the easily quantifiable benefits. The publicity surrounding the festival may have encouraged people to visit the city at other times of the year, and possibly firms may have been attracted to the area. However, arts festivals may also have negative impacts in the form of congestion during the event and the underutilization of facilities during the rest of the year.

The Olympic Games

The four-yearly, 16-day summer Olympic Games is the world's greatest mega-event. Each time the event is held it gets bigger, with more countries represented and more sports. At the twenty-fifth summer Olympics in Barcelona in 1992, 172 countries were involved and 28 sports. This compares with only 59 countries at the London games in 1948. The competitive national element plus the various spectacles associated with the event ensure an interest well beyond the relatively few that follow sports. For the 1992 Barcelona games up to 3.5 billion viewers worldwide were expected to watch the event. With television networks outbidding each other to have the rights to broadcast the event in their own country, and, similarly, companies competing to obtain the commercial sponsorship rights, the event has been transformed from loss making before 1984 to profit making since (Gratton and Taylor, 1988a, b). It is this income which sets the Olympic Games apart from other large events such as the World Student Games and the continental games, where TV interest and commercial sponsorship are much less (Collins, 1991). As a result, of this income the Los Angeles games in 1984 made a profit of $250 million and the Seoul games in 1988 made $350 million.

This transformation of the economics of the games persuaded many cities of the benefits of hosting them. These cities hope that the profits to be made can be used to pay for the facilities that are required and which will be left behind after the event. Given also the national prestige that goes with the Olympiad, host cities also hope that governments will pour money into the facilities and general infrastructure of the area. The act of winning the games is a catalyst for bringing forward general infrastructure investments that have been pending for years. In the case of the Barcelona games in 1992, a ring road was built, a new airport constructed, and a derelict waterfront area cleared and redeveloped for an Olympic village. For the host city, winning the games offers the prospect of worldwide publicity as well as investment in permanent facilities and infrastructure, which should enable it to attract further general investment, future events and more tourists. Accordingly, since the Los Angeles games of 1984 there has been fierce competition between cities to win the games and the prizes that go with it. Even to fail to win the games, having been the national champion, can be perceived as a good thing with several benefits. During the bidding process public money may have been provided to build some facilities and infrastructure, since bidding cities must show a significant degree of preparedness. Private finance may also have been levered, both for the bid and for facilities, which would not have been forthcoming without the city having made its claim. Perhaps of greatest importance is the element of unity which the bid engenders. Politicians of different parties, leaders of the private sector and voluntary groups are able to come together around the bid and perhaps agree not only on the proposal itself, but also on the general direction in which the city should be moving. Almost certainly included in this will be a role for the tourist industry in the city, how it should be developed, and how the city should be marketed.

The economic impact studies that have been made of sports events like the Olympic Games involve two elements, namely the costs and revenues to the organizers themselves, and the impact of the event on the area. Post-event impact studies have been made most recently of the Los Angeles games (Economic Research Associates, 1984) and of the Seoul games (Kim *et al.*, 1989). The results of these studies have been used by cities making pre-event evaluations (for Manchester, see Hague *et al.* (1990)). The costs of the games involve direct expenditures on sports facilities, indirect expenditures on infrastructure from transport to hotels, the operating costs of the games themselves, and the consequent expenditures of all visitors, including competitors, team officials and the media. At Barcelona in 1992 there were 10 500 athletes and probably half that number again of officials. These figures compare with only 4700 competitors at the London games in 1948. However, it was estimated that the number of media visitors at Barcelona would exceed 15 000. The US NBC (TV) network alone brought 1300 staff – more than the 925 in the US team. Overall, Barcelona expected 600 000 visitors, and if this is achieved it will have been one of the most successful Olympiads as regards attracting tourists (Pyo *et al.*, 1988). The larger the injection of funds into the area, from whatever source, the greater the impact of the event on the area. In the case of Los Angeles there was very little expenditure on direct and indirect infrastructure, so that the impact was much less than in Seoul, where this figure was greater. At Barcelona in 1992, £3.8 billion was invested, but only 10 per cent of this was on sports facilities (Stevens, 1992).

Of course, there are also long-term tangible and intangible benefits such as improved infrastructure, the ability to host further sports events, improved image and the attraction of economic development, and civic pride. Very little research has been undertaken in these areas but for enhanced image in an elementary survey, Ritchie and Smith (1991) found that Calgary's visibility had increased in Europe and the USA as a result of hosting the 1988 Winter Olympic Games. However, awareness of the city had decreased after two years. In another (annual) survey of 500 of Europe's leading businessmen, familiarity with Manchester, which is bidding for the Olympic Games, increased from 32 per cent in 1990 to 42 per cent in 1992 (Healey & Baker, 1990, 1991, 1992).

World Fairs and Expos

The Great Exhibition held in London in 1851 was probably the first show that could be called a world fair. Since then many cities have sought to have a world fair, and in 1928 the International Bureau of Expositions was founded in Paris to coordinate these events and ensure that there is only one each year. There are various and interlinked objectives for holding a world fair which have been listed by Ley and Olds (1988). The stated objectives include encouraging trade, increasing the visibility of a city and country, developing tourism, attracting economic development and thus promoting employment, stimulating land redevelopment and infrastructure improvement, the celebration of a past event, and the entertainment of the masses, as well as the often unstated one of obtaining extra funds from higher levels of government. Ley and Olds (1988) suggest that the prime motive for holding a world fair is to boost the city, but as well as selling the city there is also the selling of ideas. Most expos link themselves in some way to the notion of the progress of civilization or modernity (Bennett, 1991). Not surprisingly, Expo 92 in Seville had the theme of discovery. The host city usually prepares a special site for the event where new buildings and structures of hoped-for architectural distinction are erected. Early examples were London's Crystal Palace and Paris's Eiffel Tower and a more recent one is Seattle's Space Needle. These will remain as a permanent legacy to the area, as will any general infrastructure put in place. The fair itself usually contains exhibitions of both arts and manufactures, with pavilions being provided by foreign countries. World fairs usually last between five and seven months, but sometimes they may last for a whole year. At Expo 92 in Seville, the pavilions had an area of $650\,000\,m^2$, of which one-third was permanent; 110 nations were represented, and there were 50 000 cultural events. Total investment was put at £5.4 billion of which only 20 per cent was on the fair itself, the remainder being on general infrastructure. Among the benefits to the city have been new roads, an airport and a high-speed railway. These, with the fair ground, should have a long-lasting effect on the development of the city and region. The organizers hope for 20 million visitors, most of whom would be tourists. To cope with this influx, the number of hotel beds in the city was increased from 12 000 to 24 000.

Historical Celebrations

It has become commonplace for countries and cities to celebrate the anniversary of some landmark achievement in their history. In recent years, the USA (1976), France (1989) and Australia (1988) have all had bicentennial celebrations. Cities may celebrate the anniversary of their foundation or some event of national and international significance, such as a sailor leaving to discover the New World. Once again, the motives are various, from pure celebration to the idea of promotion and visibility, including the attraction of tourists. The celebration can take various forms, including festivals, firework and other outdoor spectacles, new buildings and infrastructure, possibly including museums and arts venues, and world fairs. The event or events may last from a few days to a whole year. In the case of national celebrations the events are likely to take place either in the national capital or in a city with a historical connection. The outcome of the historical celebrations has not always been as positive as the organizers expected. In Australia and the Americas indigenous peoples have objected to the idea that they were 'discovered', and have used the event to air their grievances, while Spain has found that 1492 was not only the year that Christopher Columbus set sail for America, but also the year in which the Jews and Muslims were expelled. Elsewhere the local populace have shown so little interest in the celebration that it has been shown to be false and merely a contrived event as a pretext for commercial promotion or political propaganda (Getz, 1992). There are few impact studies of these celebratory events but the impact is likely to be similar to that of other events.

Garden Festivals

Garden festivals are a new type of special event in Britain, introduced from Germany in the 1980s, although possibly with antecedents in the great exhibitions of the nineteenth century, which had extensive gardens (Chetwynd, 1984; PA Cambridge Economic Consultants, 1990). The aim of the garden festival is to accelerate the reclamation of derelict land, to bring short-term benefits to a locality in the form of tourists, to bring longer-term benefits in the form of image enhancement, and to provide sites for new urban land uses, including the provision of jobs to replace those lost on the site when the industries closed down. Compared to continental Europe, the British model has more emphasis on the after-uses, and less on the involvement of the horticultural sector and the provision of parkland. It was intended that the government would pay for the costs of reclamation, while the festival would pay for itself. Subsequently some costs would be recovered through the sale of land. A programme of festivals was planned for Liverpool (1984), Stoke-on-Trent (1986), Glasgow (1988), Gateshead (1990) and Ebbw Vale (1992). In the event, many of the festivals have made a small loss, met by the local council, or a development corporation in the case of Liverpool. Various accounts and impact studies have been made for each of the garden festivals (Lawrence and Rosenthal, 1990; NOP Market Research, 1985, 1987; O'Connell, 1986). The government also commissioned a study which examined the first three garden festivals (PA Cambridge Economic Consultants, 1990), and an independent study has also been written by O'Toole and Robinson (1990) which, in particular, examined the impact of the festivals on the local community.

Garden festivals use a tourism event to support a specific piece of urban regeneration. There are short-term benefits in the form of extra income to the area and resultant employment. These benefits can be increased by an associated promotion of local attractions so that the tourists are encouraged to stay longer in the area. Provided the after-use of the site has been carefully considered, there can be long-term environmental and economic benefits. However, if the government had been willing to allocate funds without the impetus of a garden festival, these could have been achieved without an event. There are wider benefits to the area in the form of a high profile and enhanced image, which might result in more tourists and general economic gains, but these gains are likely to be only short term unless they form part of a long-term strategy of events and developments, as in Glasgow. In many cases the after-use of the site does not provide for a tourist attraction or facility, and even where it does there may be problems in exploiting it because of remoteness from the main tourism sites. Overall, it would appear that garden festivals have only a limited role in urban regeneration and the long-term development of tourism (Kerslake, 1988). Nevertheless, it should be noted that garden festivals have often acted as a catalyst, persuading local authorities to increase funding for tourism promotion and development.

Glasgow

The city of Glasgow illustrates how a city can use the arts and special events to assist regeneration. Although Glasgow is an ancient town, its rise in importance came in the nineteenth century with the growth of industries like shipbuilding and engineering. By the early twentieth century the population of the conurbation had reached 1.6 million, and it had become a major commercial city with many fine building, large companies and strong institutions. Although Glasgow is much larger than Edinburgh, this latter city retained the title of capital of Scotland, with many associated administrative, legal and financial institutions.

Since World War I Glasgow has faced economic decline as many of its staple industries have bled away. Notwithstanding assistance from regional policy, new activities have not compensated for the decline; the population has been falling since 1961 and unemployment has remained high. Apart from its relative remoteness, the city has suffered from a poor image involving low-quality housing, militant labour and an industrial character.

Since the early 1980s the city has been fighting back in a number of ways. It has benefited from proactive leaderships in both the public and private sectors who have been prepared to work together. It has also benefited from government assistance, which from 1975 to 1991 was mainly channelled through the Scottish Development Agency. To the outsider the revitalization of Glasgow began in 1983 when the Lord Provost (Scottish equivalent of mayor) launched a marketing campaign with the slogan 'Glasgow's Miles

Better'. In the same year a long-planned project to build a new museum for the Burrell art collection was completed and an annual arts festival, Mayfest, was launched. By 1985 a public–private partnership organization, Glasgow Action, one of whose aims was to encourage tourism, had been founded to promote the city centre. Also in this year an exhibition and conference centre was opened, and festivals of choral, folk and jazz music and dance were started to enliven the summer months. In 1987 a festivals unit was established by the city council. Plans made at this time resulted in Glasgow hosting a Garden Festival in 1988 (see above), and in a large transport museum relocating to a site opposite Glasgow's impressive art gallery, thus helping to create a cluster of tourist attractions.

The momentum was kept going in 1990 when Glasgow became the European City of Culture, resulting in even wider publicity (Wishart, 1991). This was conceived both as a celebration of achievement and as an exercise in development. The year-long event used the existing extensive resource base and built on it with enhanced programming involving world-famous artists and high-profile performances. Museums and galleries had special displays and there were additional exhibitions. Buildings were cleaned and floodlit at night, a new £28.5 million concert hall was opened, the McLellan art gallery was refurbished for special touring and loan shows, and several parts of the city, such as the cathedral precinct, experienced physical improvements. In many ways this year was the culmination of several years of change which had included inner city revitalization programmes such as GEAR (Donnison and Middleton, 1987), and the opening of two new city centre covered shopping centres. Glasgow was able to bid for the title of European City of Culture because it had many cultural resources, including Scottish Opera, Scottish Ballet, the Scottish National Orchestra and the Royal Academy of Music.

Since several reports have been published about Glasgow, it is possible to measure the progress that has been made (Myerscough, 1988b, 1991). During the 1990 European Year of Culture the number of attendances at the events and attractions reached 6.59 million, 74 per cent attending museums and galleries and 26 per cent attending theatres and concerts. This was an increase of 40 per cent over 1989; this increase was broken down into 40 per cent visiting new sites, 34 per cent visiting existing sites, and 26 per cent attending special events not associated with existing or new sites. The distribution of this increase varied considerably and was more pronounced at high-profile facilities and events such as the Burrell Collection, and at high-quality performances. Compared with the findings of an earlier (1986) study, the number of visitors from outside Glasgow had increased by 85 per cent, and there was an estimated increase of 72 per cent over 1989. Visitors were particularly drawn to the high-profile events and attractions. About 80 per cent of the visitors were drawn from classes ABC1. Visits to the main attractions increased from 1.4 million in 1981 to peak at 3.2 million in 1990 (the Year

Table 6.5 Perceptions of British cities, February 1990

	Percentages agreeing*				
	Glasgow	Birmingham	Bristol	Edinburgh	Munich
Increasingly important fhr arts	45	13	7	42	9
Rapidly changing for the better	48	18	11	11	17
Is rough and depressing	40	45	9	3	29
Has interesting museums	31	6	14	57	10
Has wide variety of theatres and music	26	17	14	60	18
Has good pubs/restaurants and night life	23	17	20	27	31
Would like to visit	36	12	32	67	19
Would be happy to live and work there	11	6	30	31	8

*Among ABC1 residents in London and the South East.
Source: Saatchi and Saatchi, quoted in Myerscough (1991), Table 132.

of Culture) and then fall back to 2.2 million in 1991 (Figure 5.5). The Year of Culture is estimated to have generated a net income to the city of £10–14 million and created around 5500 jobs for the year.

During 1990 the city received much publicity across Britain, and this appears to have changed the image held by many people. A survey of residents of classes ABC1 in London and South East England enquired about the perceptions held of British cities (Table 6.5). Before the Year of Culture it could be presumed that the standing of Glasgow would have been similar to that of the other main provincial industrial cities such as Birmingham and Manchester, shown in Table 6.5. However, within a few weeks of the beginning of the event, with its attendant publicity, the perceptions held of Glasgow appear to be noticeably better than for these other cities. This change of image has been regarded as a precondition for recovery. While there was no significant improvement in the amount of inward industrial movement, the city has been able to attract, between 1986 and 1991, 18 service organizations, creating 7340 jobs. Civic pride has been restored and in 1992 the city adopted a new slogan, 'Glasgow's Alive'. It is too early to assess the longer-term impact of the Year of Culture but one early indicator is that 12 large conferences, each of over 2000 delegates, were booked in 1990 to be held during the 1990s.

Conclusion

While the topics of arts, sport and special events have been treated separately, there is a high degree of interrelatedness, and of course also links with the other topics dealt with in this book. They are being developed by cities for a mixture of reasons, including raising the profile of a place, changing its image and attracting tourists. The mega-event is becoming a key part of this strategy, as it acts as a catalyst for change by persuading people to work together around a common objective and as fast track for obtaining extra finance and getting building projects off the drawing board. This is not without problems, since some would argue that it gives priority to development issues over those of welfare. The physical aspect of this strategy is that it has frequently been linked with inner city regeneration and in particular with that of the city centre. This is reinforcing the role of the downtown area as entertainment centre.

Given the mixed motives and the intangibility of some of them, as with changing the image, it is often difficult to evaluate these policies. Sometimes success or failure can be measured in accountancy terms. Mega-events may make a profit or leave behind debts which the community will have to pick up for years to come. But good or bad publicity is more difficult to evaluate, particularly in terms of its effect on economic development. One consequence of the inflation of special events is that no city can afford to rest on past achievements. Success one year is soon forgotten, particularly as other cities come along with their special events. Each special event is thus only part of a long-term campaign which must be repeated in some way if the progress made is not to be wasted. In this competition between cities, a continuing inflow of tourists and economic development are the ultimate prizes to be won. For most major cities tourists will usually represent only a small percentage of patrons of regular arts and sports activities. For the occasional high-profile special event the share of visitors may rise. In the context of the whole of the city's tourism market, arts, sport and special events visitors are likely to form only a small percentage of the total. However, such a quantification of their role in urban tourism would underestimate their significance, since, as has been seen, a key aspect of their purpose is to raise the visibility of the city and so stimulate the attraction of tourists, and also to provide additional benefits for visitors. They are also important in bringing back people to the urban core from the wider urban region.

Surveys of audiences have found that arts events, including arts festivals, attract mainly middle-class participants, whereas spectacles such as sports, parades and carnivals attract a broader cross-section of the population. In terms of the economic impact of tourism there may be a trade-off here. A smaller number of high-income middle-class tourists may spend as much as a larger number of average-income visitors. Whether a city goes for the middle-class market or the broader market will depend on its tourism strategy, and this may in turn depend on how it sees itself positioned in the marketplace.

7

Secondary elements: hotels, shopping and evening activities

In this chapter those elements of a city's tourism resource which, while not primary in the sense of being the main attractors of visitors, can be critical in whether it is successful or not as a tourist centre are considered. These elements include hotels, shopping facilities, restaurants, clubs, pubs and other forms of entertainment. Other elements that might be considered under this heading include transport and car parking.

Relatively few visitors would travel a long distance because a city has good hotels, interesting shops and a varied and exciting range of activities for the evening and night. However, they might be deterred from visiting a city if there is a shortage of hotel rooms and it is known that it is a very expensive place. On the other hand, knowing that these elements are easily available, of good quality and not too expensive may provide an additional reason for visiting the city or tip the balance between one city and another when a decision is being made. Thus the provision of these elements is essential if a city is to become a successful tourist centre.

Another reason for considering them is that these are the principal forms of expenditure and therefore have the most economic impact. Table 7.1 provides a breakdown of tourist expenditure in the UK in 1991, from which it can be seen that accommodation, eating and drinking, shopping and entertainment account for 83 per cent of all spending.

The importance of these activities is not only that they are the principal forms of expenditure and therefore have an economic impact, but also that the nature of these activities will determine the type of employment created. In the main, these activities tend to employ a significant proportion of low-skilled and low-paid jobs.

The aim of this chapter is to understand how these activities develop, how

Table 7.1 Spending by UK tourists* 1991

	Percentage of expenditure
Accommodation	34.9
Eating and drinking	24.1
Travel in UK	14.0
Shopping	18.9
Entertainment	5.5
Other	2.6

*Overseas and domestic overnight-staying tourists.
Source: *Tourism Intelligence Quarterly* (1992), No. 3.

they are located in cities, and the consequences they have for the tourism industry and its impact.

Hotels

Any large city which aspires to be an important tourist centre will require a substantial stock of hotel rooms. Not all tourists will stay in hotels. Some will be day visitors, others will be staying with friends and relatives, and some may choose to stay in bed and breakfast or unserviced accommodation. Compared with resorts, camping and self-catering are not very important as tourist accommodation in cities. It is likely that the more important a city is as a tourist centre, the higher the proportion who will require some type of hotel (inn, motel etc.). It is the visitor who stays in a hotel who has the greatest economic impact. As Table 4.1 showed, up to 60 per cent of expenditure may be accounted for by the cost of accommodation and meals bought in hotel restaurants. It is therefore pertinent to examine the factors behind the growth of hotels in cities, what type of hotels are required, where they should be located and the employment implications.

As mentioned above, for most hotel users staying in a hotel is a means to an end, not an end in itself. Thus the demand for hotels is a derived demand (Medlik, 1980; Goodall, 1989). The demand for hotel services can be broken down by market type into business, tourist, conferences and other (Table 7.2).

The exact composition will vary greatly from one hotel to another and particularly with location. City hotels depend much more on business travel and less on the leisure market, whereas for resorts it would be the reverse. The business market consists of executives travelling to visit other company establishments to transact business, salesmen visiting clients, as well as many other activities such as artistes working at theatres and official government business. The size of the business market will depend on the nature of activities undertaken in the city and the role of the city in the urban system, and is unlikely to be simply correlated with size. Industrial cities with high proportions of manual jobs are likely to require less hotel stock than an important financial centre. The conference and leisure markets will also vary in size

Table 7.2 Composition of hotel markets, 1989

Type	Percentage of total			
	USA	Canada	UK	Continental Europe
Government officials	0.0	10.1	1.7	2.0
Business travellers	39.6	30.8	39.9	40.0
Conference	21.6	16.8	13.0	12.0
Tourist (individual)	31.6	18.6	18.4	19.9
Group tour	0.0	13.7	9.9	16.1
Other	7.2	10.0	17.2	10.0

Survey covers properties with more than 25 bedrooms.
Source: Horwath International (1990).

from one city to another. Although most cities are attempting to develop these markets, as described in earlier chapters, there have been differing degrees of success. As regards conferences, a supply of hotel rooms is an essential ingredient in attracting the business, but, as was shown in Chapter 4, there can be a chicken and egg situation here. Without the trade, hotels will not be built, but without the hotels, the trade will not be attracted. Under 'other markets' are included people travelling for personal reasons, such as to attend a wedding. A growing market is the traveller in transit where the demand is likely to be either on the edge of cities or between cities. The world's first motel was built in the USA in 1926, but it was not until the postwar period that demand grew rapidly. Hotels also derive business from non-staying clients through providing meals in restaurants and space for receptions.

Hotels can be classified by size, tariff, ownership and location. The quality and price of services provided is sometimes indicated by a star system. Other terms used include luxury, first class, upscale and budget (Lundberg, 1984, p. 43). Much business travel is at the upper end of the market, while the leisure traveller is often looking for the cheaper, budget-priced hotel. The nature of the market in any city will usually be reflected in the types of hotel, but an aspiring tourist city should attempt to offer accommodation of varying quality and price.

The demand for hotel accommodation would appear to have been growing steadily since the 1950s, arising from the expansion of the various component markets discussed above, and in particular because of general economic growth (Laventhol and Horwath, 1984). During this period it is likely that the composition of the market has changed, with certain sectors, like conferences, becoming more important. This increased demand is shown in the growing supply (see below) and occupancy figures. The latter are collected by tourist organizations and consultants such as Pannell Kerr Forster, and Horwath International. Occupancy figures in cities vary from 50 to 80 per cent, and reflect current market conditions. Because tourism is less seasonal in cities,

Table 7.3 English hotel occupancy 1990 by area type

Type of area	Occupancy (%)	Average length of stay (days)
London	69	2.9
Large towns	60	2.0
Small towns	59	1.9
Countryside	55	2.1
Seaside	52	3.0

Source: British Tourist Authority (1991).

Table 7.4 Hotel occupancy in Manchester city centre 1991

	Percentage occupancy	
	Weekday	Weekend
January	59.0	38.6
February	66.0	38.1
March	70.6	49.0
April	67.4	44.7
May	69.0	43.9
June	65.8	43.5
July	67.2	51.8
August	52.8	45.0
September	70.7	54.3
October	81.3	52.5
November	79.6	50.5
December	57.5	40.8
Average	67.2	46.0

Source: Greater Manchester Visitor and Convention Bureau (1992).

occupancy rates are higher than in other types of area (Table 7.3). Recessions affect all the markets for hotel services, and obviously the state of the local economy will be another factor affecting occupancy rates.

The demand for hotel accommodation varies over the week and over the year. Business travel tends to be concentrated into weekdays, leaving the weekend with low demand. In contrast, leisure travel is concentrated towards the weekend. Ideally, a city would fill its hotels during the week with business travellers and at the weekend with the short break leisure market. However, because these markets are rarely nicely balanced, it is often necessary for hotels to offer cut-price rates at the weekend to attract visitors. Table 7.4 shows the weekday and weekend occupancy rates in the recession year of 1991 for Manchester, a city where as yet the weekend leisure market is only weakly developed. Unlike the market in seaside resorts, hotels in cities experience only minor seasonal variations in demand, as can be seen from the statistics for Frankfurt and London (Figure 7.1).

The business and conference markets decrease around Christmas–New Year and in the summer holidays, while the short break market peaks in the

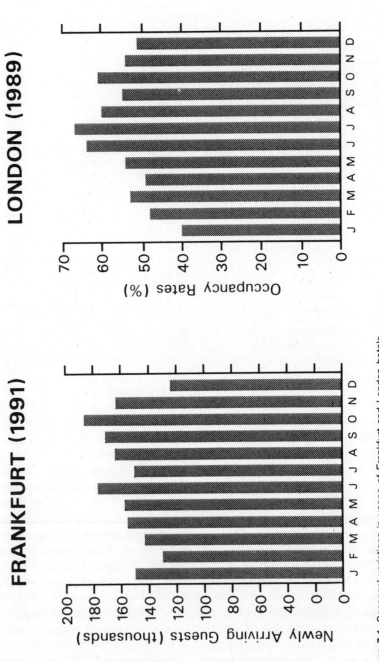

Figure 7.1 Seasonal variations in usage of Frankfurt and London hotels.
Source: Frankfurt Tourism Office (personal communication) and the British Tourist Authority's *Digest of Tourism Statistics*.

Table 7.5 Hotel income and costs 1982

Income		Costs	
Rooms	60.5%	Employees	28.1%
Food	23.5%	Cost of goods	12.1%
Beverages	8.9%	Operating costs	30.7%
Other	7.1%	Tax	5.5%
		Interest/profits depreciation	23.6%

Source: Pannell Kerr Forster (1983), quoted in Lundberg (1984).

spring–early summer and autumn periods. Major tourist cities like London and Paris have a summer peak. Some compensation at Christmas may be found through offering parties and special meals. However, at any time of the year there can be peaks and troughs. A large conference or exhibition can fully use all the capacity in a metropolitan area, while in between events there can be low occupancy.

Hotels can be built by either a hotel company or an independent developer and then leased to a hotel chain. In either case the investor will have to decide whether there is sufficient demand and of what type. With the redevelopment of city centres it is becoming quite common for hotels to be planned as part of a multi-use structure, and therefore built by a developer rather than a hotel company. Developers are also building hotels elsewhere, as these are seen as a profitable investment and many hotel chains do not want to have their capital locked up in property. However, many free-standing hotels are still being built by hotel companies.

The basic economics of hotels are shown in Table 7.5, where it is seen that the prime income will come from the letting of rooms and probably the selling of food and beverages to guests. Another reason why the letting of rooms is of prime importance is that the profits on rooms are higher than those on meals and other services (Kotas, 1975). On the cost side a significant proportion goes on interest and depreciation. The greater the capital cost of the facility, the higher these overheads will be, and hence there will be a need for high occupancy rates. For this reason the break-even occupancy rate is usually lower for budget-price hotels than for luxury ones. Land and capital costs may be high in prosperous city centres and this may deter the construction of hotels. In the late 1980s the cost of a hotel bedroom in London was £175 000 (Business Ratios, 1989). Employee costs may also be higher in city centres. Given these factors it is not surprising that the cost of hotel accommodation varies around the world, from one city to another, and from inner city areas to urban fringe zones. Figures for city hotel prices in the USA are shown in Table 7.6.

The physical requirements for a hotel building have been increasingly affected by the rising expectations of customers and higher safety standards. Most customers now expect an *en suite* bathroom even in low-price

Table 7.6 Hotel price and occupancy in US cities 1987

City	Average daily rate ($)	Occupancy (%)
New York	107.62	74.4
Boston	93.49	67.9
San Francisco	91.90	72.0
Washington, DC	91.80	72.0
Chicago	86.19	67.0
New Orleans	73.70	64.2
Los Angeles	70.99	73.2
Philadelphia	69.66	70.5
Atlanta	65.64	62.6
Detroit	64.05	68.7
Dallas/Fort Worth	61.34	55.7
Seattle	60.09	62.6
Minneapolis	56.43	62.1
St Louis	55.72	64.2
Denver	50.62	54.5

Source: Pannell Kerr Forster (1987).

accommodation. In the 1980s new types of hotel have been developed, such as the all-suite hotel, where the accommodation may consist of a bedroom, living room and kitchenette. At the luxury end of the market, patrons expect a very high standard of design, both inside and outsdle the building. Since 1967, when John Portman opened an atrium hotel in Atlanta with its open lobby soaring to the top of the hotel, architects have attempted to make hotels spectacular and dramatic in some way, often through having towers and wall-climbing lifts (Frieden and Sagalyn, 1989). These are sometimes known, irreverently, as JC hotels, because when many people enter the building and look up they exclaim 'Je-sus Christ!' Inside the building more facilities are required, such as swimming pools and gymnasiums. Because of the increasing importance of conferences, suitable rooms for meetings must be provided and also display areas. The convention hotel is a specialized type of hotel which, since the late 1960s, has been built in major cities and resorts and may have up to 2000 bedrooms. The super or mega hotel may be ideal for a conference but is often regarded as impersonal by the leisure tourist.

Many city centre hotels were built at the end of the last century or the beginning of the twentieth century. There appears to have been very little hotel building in the period between 1929 and 1959 (Laventhol & Horwath, 1984). Most of these older hotels were built without *en suite* facilities and do not meet modern safety regulations. The cost of adapting these hotels to current conditions is high, and in many cases the return on investment would not justify modernization. Not surprisingly, therefore, many of these old downtown hotels have been demolished, often to make way for office blocks. Some cities, such as Boston, found that in the 1950s and 1960s their hotel stock was declining. Some of these old hotels were found in architecturally fine buildings, and cities have been willing to give grants towards the cost of modernization in order to protect historic and attractive urban landscapes. These old hotels also rarely had conference facilities and this is another reason for their demolition. Outside city centres, many hotels have been situated in converted large houses. These again have needed modernization. Failure to modernize has meant that many hotels have had to go down-market, but this probably only delays the time when they will be closed and demolished. While some hotels will survive these temporal changes, it is likely that the hotel building life cycle is an important factor in the supply of hotels in urban areas.

Another factor affecting supply is the hotel development cycle, akin to the office development cycle and other economic cycles. As demand grows for hotel accommodation, occupancy rates and profits increase. This encourages developers and hotel chains to invest in new properties, thus increasing the stock of hotel rooms. However, because the economy is cyclical it often happens that just as this extra capacity comes on stream there is an economic downturn, and demand for hotel accommodation falls. With more capacity and lower throughput, occupancy rates and profits fall. During a recession some of the older, less profitable hotels may close. Low occupancy and low profits discourage any further building of hotels. It may then take several years of recovery before occupancy rates and profits reach former levels and even further time before increased demand encourages further building. During the 1980s hotel building in the USA and Britain went through a cycle from recession to boom and back to recession. Another feature of the cycle is that during the upturn new types of hotel and new locations may emerge.

The supply of hotel accommodation has also been greatly affected by the rise in importance of the large company. In the past the industry was characterized by the fact that most hotels were independently owned and often family run. If all hotels are counted in all locations, then the small firm is still seen to be important, although less so than in previous years. However, when the number of rooms and turnover are taken into considera-tion, the increasing importance of the large firm can be seen. In Britain in 1988 the corporate sector owned 15 per cent of the hotels but had 35 per cent of the bedrooms. This is true within the major Western countries and increasingly across the world as the major chains become multinational (Table 7.7). At the luxury end of the market, important chains are Hilton, Sheraton, Hyatt, Omni, Holiday Inn, Marriott, Inter-Continental, Forte and Maritim. At the budget end of the market are firms such as Howard Johnson, Days Inn, Comfort Inn, Accor, Campanile and Travel Lodge (Forte). Some of the major chains attempt to cover the whole market but with a different brand name for each sector. In some cases the chain is only a franchise, with hotels inde-pendently owned and operated. Many hotel companies are part of larger corporations. Historically, hotels have been linked with transport (railways and now air), breweries, leisure and property via holding companies.

Large firms have been able to develop because of certain advantages. They

Table 7.7 The 20 largest corporate hotel chains in the world

Rank (1989)	Organization (country)	Rooms	Hotels
1	Holiday Corporation (USA)	370 081	1900
2	Marriott Hotels (USA)	135 901	542
3	ITT Sheraton Corp (USA)	134 400	454
4	Days Inn (USA)	120 725	951
5	Quality International (USA)	120 352	1082
6	New World/Ramada (Hong Kong)	108 134	591
7	Accor (France)	100 000	850
8	Hilton Hotels (USA)	94 752	271
9	Howard Johnson/Rodeway	73 850	610
10	Hyatt Hotels (USA)	71 047	150
11	Trusthouse Forte (UK)	67 065	751
12	Club Mediterranée (France)	62 996	251
13	Motels 6 (USA)	60 000	522
14	Balkantourist (Bulgaria)	56 250	386
15	Econo Lodges/Friendship (USA)	51 216	690
16	Carlson/Radison (USA)	49 586	223
17	Hilton International (UK)	47 350	142
18	Super 8 Motels (USA)	42 188	672
19	Inter-Continental (USA)	40 608	102
20	Sol Group (Spain)	37 787	142

Source: Waters (1991).

are able to use marketing techniques effectively in order to reach potential customers, and can make use of central reservation systems. They can agree special terms with major clients. They know of major firms that need conference facilities and can offer these in a wide range of locations. They offer the same formula around the world so that customers know what to expect and come back to them. Because of their size they can extract good terms from suppliers. All these factors give them an advantage over the independent firm. Having established themselves, they seek to have a presence in all the major markets, whether these be seen in national terms or as cities and resorts. As such they may be courted by cities that are revitalizing inner city areas and may even be given grants as an incentive to invest.

Overall it would seem that the supply of hotel rooms around the world has been steadily increasing in the past 30 years. Problems of definition and coverage make comparisons over time and space difficult and imprecise. Not all countries require the registration of hotels and in some cases only those over a certain size are counted. Further, some countries count bedrooms and others bedspaces. However, in 1979 it was estimated that there were 7.5 million hotel rooms in the world, a figure which had increased to 11.1 million by 1989. The loss of some older hotels has been more than compensated for by the opening of new hotels, not always of course in the same location. In the USA the number of hotel bedrooms increased between 1959 and the mid-1970s, when growth was interrupted by the oil crisis (Laventhol and Horwath, 1984). The stock then grew from 2.1 million in 1979 to 3.0 million

Table 7.8 US hotel location 1988

Location	Percentage of total	
	Property	Rooms
Urban/city centre	8.6	16.8
Suburban	30.0	31.6
Airports	4.2	7.5
Highway	50.8	32.5
Resorts	6.5	11.7

Source: Waters (1991).

in 1989. After the 1973 recession the growth rate for 1975–1978 averaged 1 per cent a year, but in the period 1982–1986 it averaged 2.7 per cent a year, with higher rates for the economy/budget and all-suite hotels. The 1990 recession has reduced the growth rate again (Waters, 1991).

The location of hotels in cities is also an important topic. Guests will want hotels close to the places they wish to visit and so cut down intermediate transport as much as possible, while developers will be looking for sites which are proven generators of patronage (Karver, 1982). The traditional location for hotels was in the city centre, with many being built in the nineteenth century near railway stations (Ritter, 1985). Other hotels in the city centre tend to be located on the fringe of the retail and business zones away from the highest land values. These city centre hotels have nearly always included the most expensive and luxurious. In British cities cheaper hotels are often found along the main radial routes not far from the city centre whe re large Victorian houses could be converted and extended. Taken together these two groups of hotels provide a range of choice and location. In the world's largest cities, like London and Paris, there is often a distinct clustering of hotels, such as on the western side (Pearce, 1987, p. 180–189).

In recent years hotels have been constructed on the edge of the built-up area, either near the main roads which connect with other parts of the country or near airports (Wall *et al.*, 1985). Often the newer budget-priced hotel/motels are found here, or on highways (Table 7.8). Nevertheless, the city centre still remains an important location for hotels.

These new locations are distant from the downtown area where the main tourist attractions are likely to be found and also convention/conference facilities. While some visitors may be willing to trade off convenience against cheaper lodging costs, many will not (Arbel and Pizam, 1977). It is clearly desirable to have modern budget-priced hotels downtown even if they are more expensive to construct and operate.

The size of the hotel stock downtown as measured by the number of bedrooms together with the range in the price of accommodation is an important indicator of the success of the city as a tourist destination. It is a critical factor in determining whether the city can function as a conference and

Table 7.9 UK hotel employment 1989

	Employment (000s)	Share (%)
All jobs	238.1	100.0
Women		
Full-time	68.4	28.7
Part-time	81.1	34.1
All women	149.5	62.8
Men		
Full-time	62.6	26.3
Part-time	26.0	10.9
All men	88.6	37.2

Source: Department of Employment.

exhibition centre (see Chapter 4), and its size will also reflect the importance of business and leisure tourism. Table 4.5 gave statistics for US cities, from which it can be seen that urban tourist destinations will generally have at least 5000 hotel bedrooms downtown, with some centres having up to 20 000. The position is similar for German cities, where there is a large stock downtown, but less so in British cities, other than London, which have yet to develop the tourist industry in a big way. Manchester city centre had only 1300 hotel bedrooms in the early 1980s. Following the opening of an exhibition centre and business growth this number had increased to 2300 by 1992.

Many cities are attempting to encourage the building of hotels in the downtown area so as to assist the development of the tourist industry. This may initially take the form of designating areas for hotels in locations near the main convention centre, as at Boston (see Figure 4.1), or near other attractions. To encourage the building of hotels, grants may be given, as with the urban developmer t action grants in the USA, or the city grant in Britain. In the USA, cities may also grant exemption of the payment of property taxes for a number of years to stimulate development, a policy used in St Louis to encourage hotel construction near the riverfront. Hotel development may also be encouraged on the edge of the city centre where land prices are lower and where budget-priced hotels could operate profitably.

Hotels have a distinctive employment structure. A small management staff is complemented by a catering and cleaning staff. Many of the latter are unskilled, female and lowly paid (Bagguley, 1990; Wood, 1992). While some may be part-time, many have full-time jobs. The employment structure for the UK hotel industry is shown in Table 7.9, where it is seen that 45 per cent of all workers are part-time, and that for women this figure rises to 56 per cent. Hotel work in cities is available throughout the year, since, as mentioned above, the industry is not subject to seasonal variations. Although some decry these types of job, they are suitable for many inner city residents. Overall, hotels employ about one person per bedroom; this is higher for the luxury end of the market, and lower for the budget-priced sector.

Shopping

In the general mind, tourism and retailing are not associated, but any analysis of the behaviour of tourists will show that a significant amount of time and money is spent on shopping. As Kent *et al.* (1983) have pointed out, surveys of tourists which ask the purpose of the trip rarely find shopping mentioned, but when asked what they did, visitors list shopping as one of the most important activities. This is not shopping for essential (convenience) goods, for with the exception of those who go self-catering this is not required. For many people, shopping is a pleasurable experience and something they like to do when they have time. Increasingly, people are spending their leisure time shopping and so it is not surprising that they should wish to do so on holiday (Jansen-Verbeke, 1990). There is also the desire to see if different goods will be found in another place. A survey of festival market-places in the USA found that 60 per cent of the patrons came with no specific purchase in mind (quoted in Jones Lang Wootton, 1989). A pleasant environment may make shopping more enjoyable, and also many people like to take gifts back for friends and relatives when they return. So whether it is a day out, a short break, a long holiday or even a business trip, there is nearly always an element of shopping. Consequently it is not surprising that retail premises are nearly always found within, adjacent to or near the principal tourist attractions (Pearce, 1987, p. 193). These may vary from the simple gift/souvenir shop to outlets selling a wide range of specialty goods. When there are many shops of this type they become part of the attraction of the place. Thus in Britain the historic cities of Bath, Chester and York, through the large numbers of visitors they receive, have all become important retailing centres, far greater than could be expected from the size of their population. Accordingly it can be suggested that the right kind of retail facilities can enhance the attractiveness of a city to tourists.

Very large and specialized retail centres may be able to attract tourists. Many people visit London or Paris because of their shops. Similarly, it is reported that the West Edmonton Mall in Alberta, Canada, which has a large leisure component, attracts many tourists (Butler, 1991). The developers of a comparable facility, the Mall of America opened in Minneapolis in 1992, also hope that it will attract tourists, defined as those travelling more than 150 miles. However, these are likely to be rare examples, and in general retailing complements other attractions and is not the main draw.

Major cities are already important retail centres because of their large populations. In most European cities the city centre retains its importance, but in many American cities downtown retailing has gone into serious decline (Law, 1988a). This is because the decentralization of population has been followed by that of retailing and the downtown area has been left serving a shrinking and relatively poor inner city population. Even if it survives, it is likely to be dominated by mass market goods of the type that tourists are accustomed to, and so have little appeal. There will a familiar look to the

'High Street', dominated as it is so often by national retail chains. In most European cities there is still usually an upmarket quarter and other specialist shops, and here the tourist may find something of interest.

Tourists are particularly attracted by what is now termed 'specialty' retailing. These are types of goods which are not found everywhere (Pysarchik, 1989). They are not mass produced, and in some cases are genuine craft goods. They could be described as luxuries in the sense that they are not goods which are essential for living. Among the goods sold are arts and crafts, including pottery, unusual and designer clothes, books (both new and high-quality second hand), perfumes and unusual household articles. This type of retailing has always existed but it is only recently that it has been categorized as a distinctive market sector. With this recognition, more developers are attempting to bring the various elements together to create specialty shopping areas.

One model which takes this idea and extends it is the concept of the 'festival market-place', which combines specialty shopping, eating and drinking, and entertainment. This formula was pioneered in the USA by James Rouse, a developer of shopping malls (Rouse, 1984). He was brought in to develop the Faneuil Hall–Quincy Market area of Boston in the early 1970s after the old vegetable market had closed down. The city had sought to find a new use for the fine old buildings which Rouse restored and in which he installed the new functions (Whitehall, 1977). Opened in 1976, it became an immediate success, attracting office workers, suburbanites and tourists in large numbers. Part of its appeal was that it remained open all evening and at the weekends.

The success of the project resulted in a spate of imitations across the USA and later in Canada, Britain and Australia. Rouse was asked to develop schemes in New York (Seaport Street), Baltimore (Harborplace), Milwaukee (Grand Avenue), St Louis (Union Station) and Atlanta (Underground Atlanta). Most of these projects received large public subsidies. Similar schemes were undertaken in San Francisco (Ghiraldi Square) and Toronto (Queens Quay). In Britain the model of Quincy Market was used for London's Covent Garden, and later festival market-places were constructed at the Albert Dock, Liverpool, and Ocean Village, Southampton. Murray Darling Harbour in Sydney, Australia is another example of a festival market-place. Not all festival market-places have been successful (Guskind and Pierce, 1988). On its own a festival market-place is unlikely to be a sufficient draw for tourists, but if it is set within a wider visitor attraction and city centre revitalization strategy then it can enhance the amenity (Frieden and Sagalyn, 1989; Sawicki, 1989). Close attention must also be given to the quality of the shops, the tenant mix, their environment, and security, as the example of the first Underground Atlanta shows (Kent, 1984). Successful festival market-places are usually found in a thriving city centre where there are a large number of office workers, and within a populous metropolitan area (Jones Lang Wootton, 1989).

There are few examples of festival market-places on the continent of Europe. Perhaps this is because in many ways the historic streets of many European cities provide a themed background for retailing, as do the examples of Bath, Chester and York.

Restaurants

The visitor to the city will require food and drink. This may be to meet an essential need or to be a pleasurable experience in itself, part of the enjoyment of going somewhere different. The potential or existing tourist city must therefore ensure that the right kind of catering facilities are provided. We have already seen that the festival market-place combines retailing, eating and drinking, and entertainment, but this is likely to be only part of a much wider scene of restaurants. A successful tourist city should have a wide array of restaurants in or near the city centre. In order to understand why this occurs in some cities and not others, it is useful to discuss the general development of restaurants in urban areas.

In recent years there has been a very great growth in the demand for restaurants, here defined very broadly as any establishment which serves food and drink which can be consumed on the premises. There are many reasons for this, but most importantly it arises from greater affluence and changing lifestyles (Smith, 1983). More people are travelling further away from home whether for work, to shop or for leisure activities, and while away will need food and drink. More women are working and are often less willing to prepare meals on their return home, and as an alternative they and their families are eating out. There are also more one-person households, including young adults, some of which have arisen because of divorce, and this group is more likely to eat out. Finally, more people are eating out as a leisure activity. The trend is particularly strong among the more educated.

Statistics confirm the growing importance of eating out. In the USA in the late 1980s the average adult ate out 192 times a year. Another way of stating this is that on average people had 3.7 meals away from home each week, with a figure of 4.2 for men and 3.4 for women (Waters, 1989). By 1990, 43 per cent of a household's food expenditure was spent on meals outside the home, compared to only 25 per cent in 1955. In Britain the number of adults eating out for leisure grew from 18 million in 1979 to 25 million in 1989. Obviously, eating in restaurants is more common when people are away from home.

The market for restaurants can be classified in various ways. There is a business market for meals arising from hospitality as part of the business transaction and from meals provided for conferences. Individuals buy meals when they are out at work, shopping or leisure activities, and on these occasions they may want either a snack or a full meal, and usually fairly quickly. People also, as we have seen, eat out as a leisure activity in itself, and here the meal is more substantial and taken at a more leisurely pace.

Pillsbury (1987, 1990) has classified eating out into two types, described as body food and soul food. Body food is consumed to keep the body going. It may be simple, taken quickly and relatively cheap. While soul food does satisfy basic needs, it is sought after as an enjoyable experience. The food will be more sophisticated, the cost greater, the surroundings more important, and time taken much longer. It is also a social event, rarely undertaken alone, and often undertaken as part of an important personal relationship, or as a special family or group occasion. As standards of living rise, individuals want to experience life to the full. Eating in good restaurants is perceived to be one of the experiences of life. Dining in upmarket surroundings may also improve the self-esteem of an individual (Lundberg, 1984, p. 211).

Restaurants can also obviously be classified by the type of cuisine. Compared to the past, there is an enormous range of foods available, from the ethnic, such as Chinese, Indian and Italian, to the traditional, seafood, the gourmet, to the menu of the fast food chain such as burgers or chicken. This new range of cuisine is perhaps why dining out has become a leisure activity.

Not surprisingly, restaurants can also be classified by price. Snacks can be provided not only in fast food restaurants or cafes, but also in more upmarket surroundings. Full meals can be provided at a range of prices, at different levels of quality, and in different settings. At the cheaper levels the food is tending to be mass produced or produced to a tight formula, a trend that reaches its ultimate in the fast food restaurants such as McDonald's.

The demand for restaurant facilities obviously varies throughout the day, and may vary throughout the week and from one season to another, depending on location. Restaurants are busy around lunchtime and also in the evening. In the daytime the customers are more likely to be shoppers, local workers and perhaps business people. In the early evening the patrons are more likely to be people on their way to other activities such as the cinema, concert or theatre, while from mid-evening they are more likely to be making an enjoyable night out by having a meal. The latter, whether local or a visitor, may or may not be aware of the choice on offer. Some will therefore be in the position of searching for a good restaurant with the type of meal they want and at a price they can afford. There may still be business people and perhaps conference attenders and tourists. This weekday pattern may change at the weekend, when the business element disappears. Seasonal factors may reflect several influences, such as business fluctuations, tourist flows and special events such as Christmas and New Year when many people eat out.

These comments suggest that the market for restaurants can be classified in various ways into different components and that particular establishments will tend to specialize, serving a distinctive market niche. Thus some restaurants will primarily cater for the business market, others the gourmet market, others the quick snack for office workers and shoppers, and so on. The richness of the gastronomy of a city may not simply depend on whether it has some highly rated upscale restaurants, but may lie in the range of experience and type of eatery which it can offer to the visitor.

As the demand for restaurant meals has increased, so has the supply of establishments. In the USA in the late 1970s there was one restaurant for every 7000 persons, and by the late 1980s this had increased to one for every 2700 (Waters, 1989). The number of outlets increased from 560 000 in 1983 to 657 000 in 1990. Of these about 120 000 were classified as fast food stores.

Like other sectors of the economy, the restaurant business is increasingly dominated by large corporations. By the late 1980s in the USA, corporatihns controlled 56 per cent of the outlets, and this of course was very important at the cheaper end of the market and in the fast food sector. These corporations gain economies of scale in purchasing and marketing. Some of these corporation-controlled businesses form only part of a much larger enterprise, perhaps specializing in the drink or leisure industries. Restaurants are also found within hotels, department stores and other places. At the high-quality end of the market there are many independent businesses, and here there is a considerable entry and exit rate. In the USA, 50 per cent of these businesses fail in the first year and 65 per cent within two years (Lundberg, 1989). Many of these businesses have been founded by chefs who have poor management abilities and find it difficult to hold and recruit staff.

Turning to the spatial distribution of restaurants, an adage states (as for other retail activities) that the three most important factors for success are location, location and location (Farrell, 1980). However, Smith (1983) and Pillsbury (1987) found this to be too simple to be of great use when they sought to understand the distribution of restaurants in Kitchener-Waterloo and Atlanta respectively. Two important ideas in understanding restaurant location are accessibility and visibility. The former may mean that a large number of pedestrians are passing by, or that it is well located along a busy highway. In 1980 P. T. Smale, a director of the UK fast food chain Wimpey International, described how the location of an outlet was chosen. 'At present we consider such things as customer counts, other multiple retailers, car parking, entertainment, etc. Once the sales potential is established we will search for a site that is the right rent at about 5–7% of the sales projected'. The concept of visibility describes the fact that restaurants often cluster, not simply because they all choose the same accessible locations. Customers who are going out for a meal and who do not know the reputation of individual restaurants are attracted to clusters of establishments where they feel confident that they will find an outlet to their liking. This may even apply to fast food outlets which line main roads. Customers can head for the cluster without the need to decide which store they are going to patronize (Smith, 1985).

Pillsbury (1987) found his division of restaurants into those providing body food and those providing soul food to be helpful in his search for an explanation of the pattern of restaurants in Atlanta. Body food establishments, and particularly fast food ones, sought accessibility. They were located in the city centre, in malls and office parks, near where people worked, shopped and attended leisure activities, and also along the main arterial roads, described as 'Hamburger alleys'. Soul food establishments were found in the city centre, usually on the fringe of the retail and business quarters, accessible for business people and conventioneers, and elsewhere in what were described as 'ambient clusters'. These were often found in upmarket housing areas or gentrified neighbourhoods, but Pillsbury maintained that while there was a local market base, they attracted patrons from all over the city. These areas had developed elite restaurants, and had a certain ambience which patrons found attractive. Once established, these districts obtained visibility, which enabled them to continue to attract both new customers and entrepreneurs. These ambient clusters will develop only in parts of the city where the market conditions are right, and will not be found in the poorer and deprived parts of the city.

Using this analysis, it can be seen why in many cities the downtown area contains the largest and most varied cluster of restaurants. For body food, an essentially derived form of demand, there are shoppers, office workers and patrons of leisure facilities such as theatres to maintain a stock of establishments. For soul food there are business people, conference attenders and often a historical legacy which has helped maintain a stock of quality restaurants. This has traditionally been the place to come out to for a good meal. Many cities, particularly in Europe, have historic quarters which have become the location for outlets, having the right ambience. In Cologne, in Germany, the riverfront district south of the cathedral is an example of this phenomenon. Elsewhere, immigrant quarters have developed, providing ethnic food. An example is Manchester's Chinatown.

From this analysis it might be thought that most cities are well resourced to supply the gastronomic needs of visitors, but this is not always so. The decline of American downtown areas has weakened the base of restaurants. Upmarket retailing has often decentralized to the suburbs. Entertainment functions have often been reduced. There may be only a weak convention business. For many white people the area may be associated with the black population and therefore be a place to be avoided, particularly in the evening. Accordingly, the number of restaurants, and particularly high-quality ones open in the evening, may have greatly diminished. It is a distinct disadvantage to have to tell visitors staying downtown that if they want a good meal in the evening they will have to travel to a restaurant cluster in the suburbs. In this situation many American cities which are attempting to develop their tourism industry have given consideration to this topic. The festival marketplace, which has eateries and stays open all evening, has been one answer to this problem. Baltimore's Harborplace (1980) and Atlanta's Underground (1989) are examples of this type of response. Another has been to encourage the development of a restaurant (and perhaps retailing) quarter in an historic part of the downtown area. In St Louis, the last remaining built-up part of the waterfront in the downtown area, Lacledes Landing, has been so designated and supported with improvement grants. In many cities the redeveloped waterfront area has become the location for restaurants.

Given the increase in eating out and the growth in the number of restaurants, it is not surprising that employment has grown rapidly. Many of these jobs are low paid, part-time and on a casual basis. There has been an increase in the share of women and young people in the labour force as employers seek to cut costs (Wood, 1992). In the USA in particular, many young people take jobs in catering as a means of working their way through college, so that the spatial coincidence of educational establishments and tourism in cities is beneficial. Similar links may increasingly be forged in countries like Britain as public grants for student maintenance are either withdrawn or reduced.

Entertainment

Many tourists staying overnight in a city will want some form of entertainment. This could take the form of a visit to a theatre or concert hall for music, opera, ballet or drama, or possibly a visit to a club for music and dancing. Most city centres have been well equipped with these facilities in the past, and if they retain these then supply should be no problem. Only if there has been some decline or decentralization, as in some American cities, might there be a need to stimulate their revival. The topic of the arts and culture has already been discussed in Chapter 6. A more difficult topic concerns what in American cities are referred to as 'adult entertainment' quarters. These attract both locals and tourists and could even be described as a tourism resource. Most city councils are keen to reduce the visibility of these areas, in case they offend, and they are likely to be confined to one part of the city centre fringe.

Transport

Cities attract tourists from a wide range of distances, from the surrounding region to the intercontinental, and different forms of transport will be required. Most cities will have good transport systems, but differences in quality and cost could influence tourist flows. In the USA it is suggested that having a hub airport is an important factor influencing some tourists, since they may be deterred if they have to make changes at airports. Having a hub airport may mean having not only more direct flights, but also more flights, and perhaps cheaper flights as spare seats are off-loaded. Within Europe, railway travel is still important, and having a station which is nodal in the network, and also one which is central to the city, is important. Once again it is suggested that visitors do not want to have to make too many connections when they arrive at a city. Many visitors will arrive by car, and having a good circulatory system, a lack of congestion and ample car parking is regarded as important by them. Overall these would appear to be marginal factors in determining whether tourists visit cities, but they could tip the balance in a few cases. When organizers are deciding where to hold a conference, exhibition or special event, ease of transport is certainly a factor considered (see Chapters 4 and 6). Cities certainly think that this is a consideration, as they make every effort to improve transport and advertise its availability.

Conclusion

The topics examined in this chapter are all very important for tourism in cities. Just because they are not the main reasons why people visit cities does not mean that they cannot influence tourist flows. Very importantly, they will influence the quality of the experience had by the urban tourist. This in turn may affect whether a return visit is made and whether it is recommended to others. Accordingly, cities wishing to develop their tourist industry should give attention to these topics, the existing situation and the planning for improvements. Insofar as jobs are provided and investment made in hotels, shops and restaurants because of tourists, the contribution of tourism to urban regeneration can once again be seen.

8

Environment and planning

The discussion of urban tourism so far has been primarily concerned with activities and only secondarily with their location and setting. In this chapter the focus will be reversed and one question that will be asked is whether tourism facilities should be clustered and whether specialized districts should be developed. This discussion needs to be placed in the context of the urban regeneration process (see Chapter 2) as tourism is being used for both the economic and physical revitalization of cities. In many cases new tourism facilities are likely to be placed away from the heart of the city, where land is fully occupied and expensive, and to be steered to districts where regeneration is being encouraged. In this respect it is crucial to understand the inner city planning process. However, the construction of tourism facilities and districts should be more than just the placing of buildings. The appearance of the urban landscape is part of the attraction of cities, and a memorable architecture and setting is itself a critical tourism resource. At the same time, as MacCannell (1976) points out, the placing of 'attractions' within a 'stage set' acts as a marker for the tourist and assists in the production of 'touristic space'. These three components, the location of facilities, the link with urban regeneration, and the creation of a townscape, therefore need to be woven together. Initially in this chapter they will be taken separately, but at the end of the chapter they will be brought together and illustrated with examples.

The Location of Tourism Resources

In many cities the prime tourism elements have developed over many decades, perhaps centuries, and their location was determined by specific and unrelated factors, so that their scatter rather than concentration is not unexpected. Some tourism attractions are at the very heart of the city, a legacy of a long history, while others, more recently constructed, were located according to diverse factors. Many facilities were built to meet the needs of the local community, some were placed in parks, and others were linked to institutions such as universities. In this section the main question is whether the concentration or scatter of tourism resources is desirable, and whether tourism districts should be planned and constructed.

The argument for concentration is that tourists prefer a compact, walking city, and that a clustering of facilities makes a city more attractive to potential visitors because the total is perceived to be greater than the sum of the parts. With a critical mass of facilities and therefore tourists, higher thresholds will be reached to support secondary activities like hotels, catering and retailing. The concentration of tourism activity into one district will create a clear focus with benefits for visitors, locals and planners. This belief in concentration, in the creation of honeypots, is derived intuitively from personal experience, rather than the results of mass surveys and their analysis. When facilities are close together, visitors can walk from one attraction to another without the inconvenience of returning to a car and then finding another place to park, or of the need to use public transport. This ease of movement will encourage them to come, heighten their enjoyment when they have come, maybe encourage them to come again, and also help them to recommend the city to others. This clustering of facilities includes both the primary and secondary elements.

The clustering of tourism resources is sometimes referred to as the development of honeypots or tourism complexes, and will obviously result in the creation of districts in which tourism is a very important component (Jansen-Verbeke, 1988, p. 115). In earlier chapters mention was made of the way in which cities have brought together museums, cultural facilities and convention facilities. These might be in separate districts, together or in adjacent districts. They could also be associated with historic buildings and quarters. In Cologne a tourist area has been created near the cathedral and railway bridge, with a cluster of museums recently located adjacent, and the *messe* (exhibition centre), hotels, retailing and night life districts nearby (Figure 8.1).

Not all cities are so fortunate in being able to bring all their tourism resources together in this way. Often museums, which have been developed over many decades, are in scattered locations and it would be expensive, although not impossible, to bring them together in one location. If this is the case, then the only realistic strategy may be to develop several, albeit smaller, tourism districts. Methods will then be needed to facilitate movement between these zones, either marked trails, special (vehicle) bus routes, or distinctively signposted public transport routes. This is the situation in Glasgow, with museums in parks outside the city centre (Figure 8.2). Here the policy has been to maintain the Kelvingrove cluster, through the relocation of the Transport Museum to the vacated Kelvin Hall. At the same time,

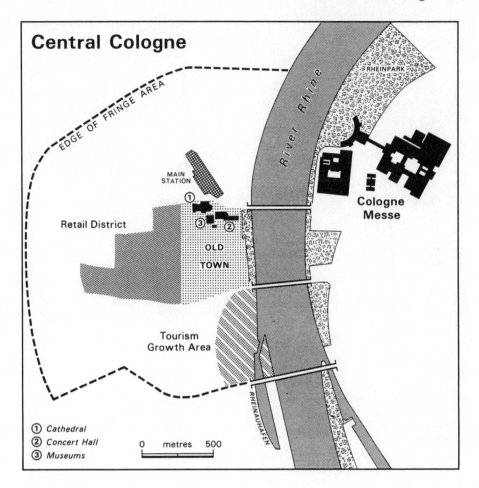

Figure 8.1 Cologne city centre.

tourism resources are being maintained and enhanced on the other (eastern) side of the city centre.

There may be disadvantages to concentration in the form of saturation and congestion. Great crowds of tourists could themselves be unpleasant, create problems of litter, and through overuse damage historic structures. At the same time the local population may feel crowded out and come to resent the invasion. The demand for car parks may be very great and difficult to meet, either because of problems in finding sites, or because car parks (multistorey) are usually expensive to build and sometimes uneconomic. Too high prices could drive tourists away. However, sometimes tourist attractions which operate mainly in the evening may be complementary to other activities of

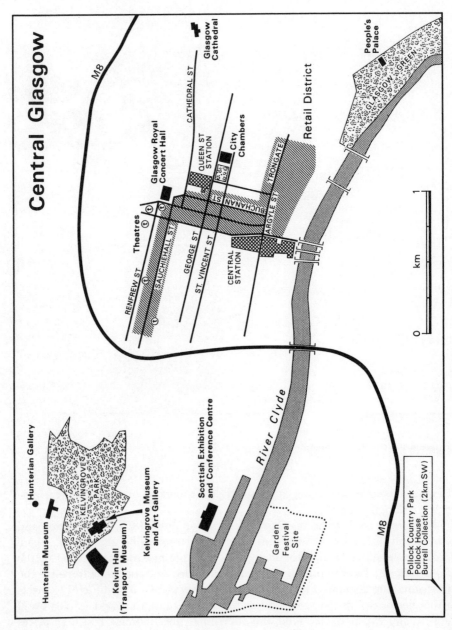

Figure 8.2 Glasgow city centre.

the city centre. The New Orleans Superdome provides daytime cheap car parking and has attracted office development to a rundown area of the city (Miestchovich and Ragas, 1986).

Physical Regeneration

In Chapter 2 the topic of urban regeneration was discussed. It was observed that many cities are concentrating their new investment in the city centre rather than in the surrounding inner city neighbourhoods, where there is great need, because of the potential of this district. This potential is also seen with respect to tourism, since many of the facilities are found in or near the city centre. At the same time the fringe of the city centre is often in decay as transport facilities, warehouses and small industries close down. There is an urgent need for the physical and economic regeneration of these areas, to clear away the derelict land and buildings. The availability of space in this area so close to the heart of the city offers opportunities for the siting of new tourism resources and the creation of tourism and cultural districts. These may use as a basis an existing tourist facility or an historic building.

There are very few cities in which the reuse of transport lands has not been important. Examples include railway stations at St Louis (Union Station festival market-place) and Manchester (G-Mex exhibition centre), railway sidings at Toronto (CN Tower and SkyDome), railway goods depots at Manchester (museum), or canals, ports and docks at Liverpool. Waterfront developments were a key feature of urban redevelopment in the 1980s as the revolution in shipping connected with containerization left much port land redundant (Hoyle *et al.*, 1988). Many of these lands were previously cut off from public access and dock walls and buildings obscured the view of the water, but they can be reclaimed for the community. As will be discussed below, the juxtaposition of land and water is appealing to most people and these waterside zones have been reused for a variety of purposes, including prestige offices, upmarket housing involving gentrification, and tourism activities.

The reclamation of these areas on the fringe of the city centre has often primarily been planned and managed by the public sector. Compulsory purchase of land is required in order to assemble land for new activities, as the old geographical pattern of land ownership often presents a problem for its reuse. At the same time, reclamation is costly and is often possible only with public subsidy. Investment is needed in the infrastructure, and the redevelopment of old sites is usually more expensive than that of greenfield land. Fortunately, public subsidies became available in these areas in the 1970s. For many years in the USA there were the community development block grants and urban development action grants available to central cities. In Britain since 1978 there has been a plethora of policies, including inner city partnerships, city grants and urban development corporations. The policies have ranged in their purpose from infrastructure development to specific projects, which can include tourism schemes. With the upsurge of interest in urban tourism in the 1980s these inner city policy funds have proved very useful for pump priming (Central London Polytechnic, Leisureworks and DRV Research, 1990). In Britain these funds are usually limited to the inner city areas, thus reinforcing the concentration of tourism development in this area. Many of the major tourism projects in British cities have benefited from these funds: the urban programme, including the Albert Dock in Liverpool, Castlefield and G-Mex in Manchester, the convention district in Birmingham and the exhibition complex in Glasgow. Without this money most of the schemes would not have been possible, and the continued development of tourism in these older industrial cities requires that these funds are available.

The Urban Landscape

The architecture of buildings, the arrangement of open spaces, and the vistas over the urban area constitute an important attraction and reason for visiting cities, as the examples of historic and capital cities show. Margaret Drabble (1991) has written:

> Who can forget the first vision of Venice, of Rome, of Istanbul, of Marekesh, of Carthage, of Tangiers, of Paris, of Rio de Janeiro, of Moscow, of Sydney, of Cape Town? Who can fail to be stirred by the grandeur of New York and Chicago? All these cities have burst upon me with an extraordinary impact, far outstripping even representations by Guardi, Turner and Whistler. Cities are beautiful. Cities are powerful. They are our largest, our most diverse and complex and passionate works of art, assembled from many interlocking visions and with many intricate moving parts. Visitors to London . . . may receive the impression of a grand and beautiful city. One can still cross Westminster Bridge and feel something of what even that profoundly rural northerner Wordsworth felt as he stood there. Dull would we be of soul not to respond to the river at night or early morning, the view of the city from Parliament Hill, the South Bank, the Lloyds building, the window display of Liberty's, the Mall, the Henry Moores' by the Serpentine and at Spring Gardens, the squares of Kensington, the dome of St Paul's, and curve of Regent Street.

J. Wijnberg has written, 'Buildings are not merely constructions of functional utility. They exist as powerful symbols of the environment, a medium where man made marks have become as important as natural geography' (*South China Morning Post Property Review*, October 1985). Buildings are symbols of success for the city and for the wider world. Cities become known because of their buildings and structures: the Eiffel Tower in Paris, the Statue of Liberty in New York, Tower Bridge in London, the Opera House in Sydney, and many other examples. A city that does not have memorable buildings and vistas lacks a way to publicize itself. What picture does Birmingham conjure up? And how fortunate is Liverpool to have a waterfront backed by fine buildings?

The skyscraper has become the typical feature of American cities, creating an impressive skyline, and is now spreading to cities around the world (Ford, 1992). It can be used for offices, hotels and apartments. Its role as a visual landmark has been strengthened in recent years through postmodern architecture, with its distinctive shapes and pointed roofs (Urry, 1990, p. 120). Towers and skyscrapers are not only powerful symbols but they often provide a public vantage point from where a bird's eye view of the city can be obtained, creating another tourist attraction. New York has its World Trade Center, Chicago its Sears building, Rotterdam its Euromast and Toronto its CN Tower. In some cities a natural feature such as a hill provides a viewpoint.

The aspiring tourist city will therefore wish to consider very carefully its physical environment. It must be of high quality. It must have some memorable buildings. It must have some spectacular vistas. It must have some distinctive physical features which can be used to project an image of the city in order to gain attention from the rest of the world, both to attract visitors and to persuade the decision makers to locate economic activities there. Given this background it is not surprising that urban design has become an important component of economic development and tourism strategies. A firm like LDR (Landscape, Design Research), which first made its name in Baltimore, has been contracted to prepare urban design plans for cities around the world. Similarly, many cities have sought world-famous architects, such as I.M. Pei, Richard Johnson, Richard Rogers and James Stirling, to design striking landmark (signature or trophy) buildings, which not only enhance the aesthetics of the environment, but give them the high-profile image which they desire. Examples include the Grand Arch in Paris, the Gateway Arch in St Louis, and art galleries in cities such as Fort Worth and Stuttgart. This type of architecture, often postmodern in style, is of course not unique to urban tourism facilities, but, given the need to project an image and the large number of projects in the 1980s, it is not surprising that it is so well represented.

While the interiors of buildings cannot be used in the same way to project an image, from the point of view of the tourist experience they are equally important. Atriums, glass wall-climbing lifts and glass-vaulted roofs were first developed in the USA (in contemporary times) for hotels and shopping malls, and have subsequently diffused to western Europe and many other parts of the world.

The problem for older industrial cities attempting to put themselves on the tourist map in a big way is that they lack in quantity the really memorable architecture that is found in capital and historic cities. Unfortunately for them, their high-quality Victorian architecture is often underrated and undervalued. Until a few years ago it was often barely visible beneath the soot and grime of several decades. However, from the 1970s onwards most of the good buildings have been cleaned and restored to their pristine glory, often with great effect. In recent years their night-time appearance has often been greatly improved with lighting, creating a 'festival of light'. Many of Britain's older industrial cities have very fine town halls, exchange buildings, and headquarter-type office blocks. Since the 1960s, conservation areas have been created to preserve these buildings, the most important of which have listed status. However, it is difficult to maintain these buildings if their former use has disappeared. Sometimes one aspect of a development strategy for the tourism and leisure industries is to find new uses for these buildings. In Manchester the old Royal Exchange (cotton) has been reused as a theatre, a fine old warehouse as a hotel (the Britannia), and the original historic 1830 railway station as a science and industry museum. The conversion of old buildings and the introduction of new uses is, of course, not unproblematic. The new uses may be completely out of character and destroy the integrity of the building. However, if they are sympathetic they can be an aesthetic and a financial success. Notwithstanding the achievements of cities like Glasgow and Manchester in preserving the best of their past, they have still found it difficult to create a truly memorable urban landscape. Further, much of their central area has been blighted by the cheap, low-quality, characterless architecture of the 1950s, 1960s and 1970s. Most North American cities have also suffered from the extensive demolition of historic properties, but once again there are widespread efforts now to preserve the best of the past that is still left (Ford, 1979). In contrast, many Continental cities have old quarters near the city centre which can be renovated. The historic Le Vieux Lyon was rehabilitated in the late 1970s and early 1980s and has become important for shops, restaurants, night clubs and gentrification, and is of interest to the tourist (Renucci, 1992).

The opportunity to create memorable landscapes in newly created tourism districts will obviously vary from one city to another, depending on factors such as imagination, determination, resources both of the public and private sectors, and not least the opportunities afforded by the physical environment. It is here that cities with waterfronts have significant advantages and opportunities. Water can be used to offset urban landscapes as well as be the setting for boats and events. Many of the famous city landscape paintings have involved water, notably in the work of Canaletto on Venice and other cities. Because of the public regard for this type of vista, attempts to create similar views win ready approval. With the decline of port activities in old districts and their transference downstream, one of the most promising areas for redevelopment near the city centre is often the waterfront zone, where tourist activities may be developed. Examples include Baltimore, Boston, Toronto, Liverpool and Southampton. Other cities, like Birmingham and Manchester, with only small rivers and canals, have a more difficult task. It is important that the waterfront is open for pedestrian access. Several cities have destroyed their opportunities by constructing main roads along the waterfront, which not only create a barrier to access, but result in noise pollution. Others, like Cologne, have put roads in tunnels and thus created a green, quiet and pleasant pedestrian area.

Conclusion and Examples

One of the main themes of this book is the attempt by many older industrial cities to substantially increase their tourist industry through the development of new attractions and the expansion of the conference and exhibition industry. It has been suggested in this chapter that there are advantages in clustering these activities into distinct districts. While this idea appears intuitively sensible, further research might usefully explore the movement patterns and experience of tourists in a number of cities to affirm the conviction that clustering is beneficial. In line with urban regeneration policies and public subsidies it is likely that these new tourist districts will be on the fringe of the city centre in the run-down industrial periphery. The new and still evolving urban morphology consists of a central business district with offices and retailing surrounded by two or three tourist/recreation clusters plus, in some cities, gentrified quarters. As well as planning these areas in the most efficient manner possible, it is desirable to create high-quality environments, which in themselves will be attractive to tourists and provide a reason for visiting the city, and also give a high profile to the city by providing a symbol of its success. In order to illustrate these ideas, an account of Baltimore, hailed as a success and exemplar, will be given, and also of Manchester, which is still in the early stages of its strategy.

Baltimore

The city of Baltimore lies on the north-east coast of the USA between Philadelphia and Washington. It was founded as a port in 1729 around what is now known as the Inner Harbor, and for most of its history its economy has been dominated by the port and industry. The city's regional role has been limited because of the neighbouring cities of Washington and Philadelphia, and for many decades its higher-order service industries were also small in size. However, the metropolitan area remains prosperous and is growing, benefiting from its location in the important corridor along the north-east coast and from an overflow of federal government and linked activities from Washington. Within the metropolitan area the population is about 2.25 million. Because of its port and industrial character, Baltimore was never regarded as an attractive city, but one to be avoided rather than visited.

The modern problems of Baltimore are typical of those of American cities, and concern the decentralization of activities and consequent problems for the core (Law, 1988a), and the movement downstream of its port activities and the consequent redundancy of the old harbours. Population and employment have shifted to the suburban areas, with the central city of Baltimore losing people so that by 1991 its population was only 750 000. In the city centre the greatest impact of this decentralization has been felt by retailing, which has been in decline since the early 1950s. The inner city neighbourhoods have also lost population, and there are serious problems of poverty and housing decay. As elsewhere, the increase in the size of ships and the change to containerization has resulted in a movement downstream of port activities and abandonment of old harbours, including the Inner Harbor. Many of the old waterfront industries near the Inner Harbor have also closed down.

The city of Baltimore has tackled these problems with determination over a long period and achieved some dramatic successes which have earned it a high reputation in the outside world (Lyall, 1982). Politicians, planners and academics have flocked to Baltimore to look at the spectacular transformation of the Inner Harbor, and glowing accounts have been written by these visitors, who have only spent a few days in the city. In reality, urban regeneration has been less successful than claimed (Levine, 1987). The city has failed to halt the decline of the traditional downtown retailing district, and poverty and housing problems remain in the inner city. Baltimore's success around the Inner Harbor is in reality only skin deep. This account will concentrate on the physical planning of the city centre since the mid-1950s, and the role of tourism.

By the mid-1950s the decay of the downtown area was already apparent, to the alarm of the retailers in particular. This group, together with the newly formed Greater Baltimore Committee, consisting of the leading business people in the area, commissioned a plan for the central area. Because it was felt that the whole area could not be tackled at once, a detailed plan was prepared for the small zone lying at the junction of the retail and office quarters, later named the Charles Center project. This plan was put to the mayor and city council; they accepted the proposal in 1959 and work commenced. In the event the city was able to receive federal government grants and a federal government office. Most of the space was occupied by offices, but there was also a theatre, civic centre, hotel, and residential block. Although the scheme was not completed until the late 1960s, its success was assured by the middle of the decade and this gave confidence to the city and the business leaders to think about further projects.

During the 1950s trade had been departing from the Inner Harbor, leaving an empty, derelict and often unsafe area which was located immediately south of the business district (Figure 8.3). This therefore provided an opportunity for another project. In 1965 a plan was drawn up which provided for improvements to the waterfront, a park around the waterfront, housing and some offices next to the business quarter. The cost of the project was high, mainly because of the investment needed in the infrastructure, but also because the housing was to be subsidized, and it was obvious that federal government grants would be required. At this stage tourism was not seen as a major component of the project. As discussions proceeded with the federal government, it became apparent that while grants would be available for the infrastructure, they would not be given for housing. During the 1970s work began on the remodelling of the Inner Harbor; this was largely complete by

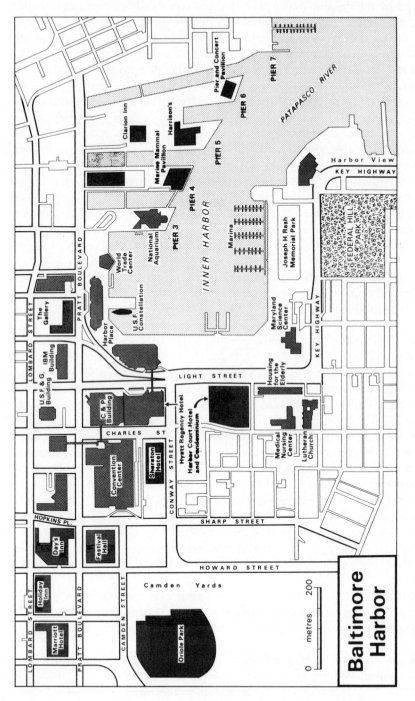

Figure 8.3 Baltimore's Inner Harbor.

the end of the decade. Both the Charles Center and Inner Harbor projects were managed by a quasi-autonomous development agency of the city.

At the same time as these works were proceeding, many cities in the USA were considering initiatives in tourism, and so it was not surprising that the plans for the Inner Harbor should move in this direction. Already the City Fair and other ethnic festivals had been moved to the waterfront, but the new plans envisaged more permanent structures. In 1976 a museum, the Maryland Science Center, was opened, followed by a convention centre in 1979, a festival market-place (Harborplace) in 1980, and the National Aquarium and Hyatt Hotel in 1981. These were either built by the public sector or received substantial urban development action grants. In 1972 the US *Constellation*, built in 1797, was moored in the harbour and later other ships were brought in to create a maritime museum. By 1981 the first stage of the remodelling of the Inner Harbor was complete and it was beginning to look like a success, although this had been achieved at great public cost. Private investment had occurred on the north side in the form of office blocks, and one of these, the World Trade Center, built in 1977, had a public viewing platform.

By the early 1980s the success of the project was attested by the growing number of visitors, whether from the suburbs or from outside the metropolitan region, and whether for pleasure or for conventions. This inflow encouraged further investment, this time predominantly privately financed, in the form of hotels, the Gallery specialty shopping centre, and other entertainments. The success of the project also encouraged the city to extend the project area in both an eastward and westward direction. To the west around the old railway yards two stadiums were planned (Petersen, 1988). The first one, Oriole Park, Camden Yard was opened in April 1992, and is the base for the relocated Oriole baseball team. In the east, development will proceed along the waterfront as more land is vacated by port and industrial activities. On the north side a marina, offices, hotel and housing are planned together with a waterfront pedestrian promenade. On the south side an old shipyard is being transformed into a marina and apartment area. Both here and around the Inner Harbor expensive high-rise apartments are being built, evidence that the middle classes are returning to the city centre. The management company, now merged into the Baltimore City Development Corporation, aims to continue the tourist theme with at least two new developments a year. A marine life museum (and research centre) is one such project which is planned.

This account shows that within the space of about 15 years Baltimore created a new urban landscape around a waterfront, itself an attraction, and also implanted a number of primary tourism elements which attracted people to the area, which in turn brought investment in the secondary elements as higher thresholds were reached. Baltimore has other museums and attractions outside the immediate area of the Inner Harbor and since 1985 these have been linked by a trolley system so that they can form an integrated tourist system. The city claims that over 20 million visits are made to the Inner Harbor area each year.

The success of Baltimore owes much to the fact that there has been strong leadership over many years and that the regeneration has been spearheaded by a proactive development agency. It is now beginning to deal with the problems that come with success. The convention centre is too small and needs to be expanded. Possibly it also needs a convention hotel and an improved evening entertainment area.

Manchester

Like Baltimore, Manchester is an older industrial city, but its interest in developing tourism is more recent, and it has yet to achieve success. Manchester was one of the world's first industrial cities, the terminus for the pioneering Bridgwater Canal, completed in 1763, and the world's first successful passenger railway in 1830. Its early interest in industry, particularly cotton textiles, enabled it to become the commercial capital of the North-West region of England and the focus of a conurbation with a population of 2.5 million. Although Manchester is situated inland, a ship canal was constructed and opened in 1894 with a port about a mile to the west of the city centre. With the containerization of traffic and shifts in trade this port became empty by the early 1980s and has subsequently been redeveloped as Salford Quays (Law, 1988b; Law and Grime, 1993). The decline of the textile and other industries since World War I has meant that the region has struggled to maintain its level of employment, and is in need of new economic activities.

Manchester, like Baltimore, has suffered from decentralization. The outer parts of the conurbation already contained significant urban centres in places like Bolton, Oldham and Stockport, and as the population shifted outwards these centres gained trade and activities. The city centre has suffered some retail loss but not nearly as much as Baltimore. City centre campaigns have attempted to boost shopping and it is hoped that a new tram system, Metrolink, which opened in 1992 and links the north and south railway systems, enabling people to reach the heart of the city, will give a further boost to retailing. As the commercial heart of the region, the city centre contained many warehouses, but as the textile industry declined and as wholesale distribution moved to the periphery, large parts of the city centre fringe became derelict. This was exacerbated by the the decline of other industries, including clothing, printing and transport. Between 1961 and 1981 the number of jobs in the city centre declined from 167 000 to 108 000. There is thus a need to find new activities for the city centre and to have new investment to reclaim these fringe areas. As with Baltimore, the surrounding inner city neighbourhoods have experienced population decline and in spite of redevelopment there are severe housing difficulties, and also much poverty.

The movement to develop tourism arose from the desire not only to participate in a growth industry, but also to preserve historic buildings (Law, 1991a). In the late 1970s industrial archaeologists and transport enthusiasts were concerned about the state of the Castlefield area south-west of the city centre, which contained the historic canal and railway termini (Figure 5.4). The 1830 railway station, which had latterly been used as a goods depot, closed in 1975, and was unused. Nearby, the Central Station, closed in 1969, was also vacant, being used only as a car park. When some factories had closed in Castlefield the opportunity was taken to excavate the Roman remains of the precursor city and subsequently the site was turned into gardens. As a result of the growing interest in the area it was made a conservation area in 1978. Later in 1982 a heritage park was established, followed by a plan in 1983 to turn it into a tourist area. This visionary plan was incomprehensible to most local people at the time since most of the area was either industrial, or derelict, without any appeal except to the most intrepid industrial archaeologist.

Subsequent rehabilitation work has significantly improved the Castlefield district but there is still a long way to go before the area would be recognized as a tourist quarter by most people. The main actors in the transformation so far have been the city council, the Greater Manchester Council until its demise in 1986 and the Central Manchester Development Corporation since its establishment in 1988. Much money has been spent on the physical appearance of the area through the renovation of the canal basins, including the re-excavation of old arms, the reclamation of derelict industrial sites, and new paving and the planting of trees along roadsides. A science and industry museum has been relocated to the 1830 railway station site, and greatly enlarged, while the Central Station has been converted into an exhibition centre, G-Mex. The regional television station, Granada, located on the edge of the district, opened its studios to the public in 1988 and attracts 600 000 visitors a year. Two hotels have also been opened, one associated with Granada Studios Tours.

There is still much to achieve. A proposal to convert the Great Northern warehouse, another disused railway depot, into a festival market-place had to be shelved in 1991 because of the recession. Another proposal for a concert hall next to G-Mex has also been delayed because of the recession. In both cases the tourism element of the project would have been cross-subsidized by office schemes, and the downturn in the office market has made them, temporarily at least, unviable. There are still a number of sites in the Castlefield area and it is hoped to develop one or two large attractions. If all these proposals go ahead, then the necessary thresholds might be reached for more secondary elements to appear. The Castlefield area has been placed in a wider tourism context in a strategic study (English Tourist Board/LDR, 1989). Geographically the area was linked to other areas along the River Irwell corridor, stretching from the cathedral area, where there are various proposals within the Northern Gateway Project, down to the old docks area, where

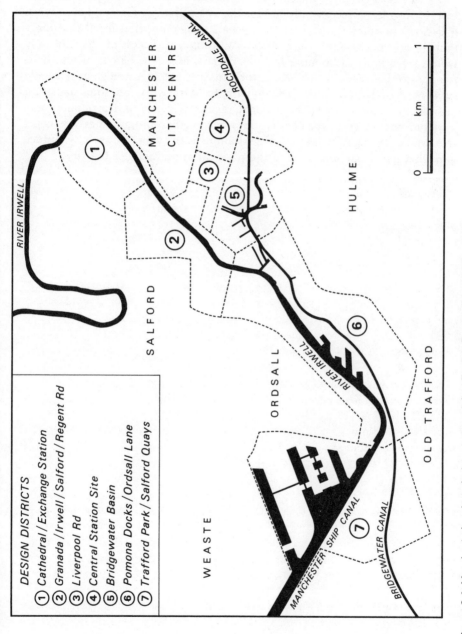

DESIGN DISTRICTS

1. Cathedral / Exchange Station
2. Granada / Irwell / Salford / Regent Rd
3. Liverpool Rd
4. Central Station Site
5. Bridgewater Basin
6. Pomona Docks / Ordsall Lane
7. Trafford Park / Salford Quays

Figure 8.4 Manchester's urban design strategy (after English Tourist Board/LDR, 1989).

tourism projects have been proposed (Figure 8.4). All of these proposals will require a great deal more public and private investment and sustained growth in the economy before they can be realized.

Manchester's Olympic ambitions have recently become a catalyst for action. In 1990 the city unsuccessfully bid for the 1996 Olympic Games. Later, when it decided to enter the race for the year 2000 games, it realized that more thought and preparation were necessary to make a successful bid. Not only would there have to be more facilities in advance, but the city would have to appear more ready to receive visitors. In early 1992 the British government gave Manchester an initial £55 million to start work on some facilities, including an indoor arena at the partly disused Victoria railway station, and a velodrome in east Manchester. However, other programmes are being reviewed in the light of the bid. One example is the way that the city council is paying particular attention to the physical appearance of the city.

9

Organization and funding

So far this book has been primarily concerned with the ideas behind urban tourism and the main branches of the industry. Little has been said about the means by which success in the industry is to be achieved or the appropriate forms of organization, a topic which will now be tackled. The organization of tourism in cities involves four main components (Pearce, 1992). First, there is planning, which includes the formulation of a strategy, the selection of activities such as attractions, culture and sport for expansion, and the improvement of the environment. Second, there is the development role, the implementation of the strategy and the obtaining of finance. It is relatively easy to come up with ideas, but often the main problem is finding the funding to implement them. Planning and development together should enable a city to have a product or products which it can offer to the rest of the world. Third, there is promotion and marketing, which includes the selling of the area to visitors through advertising, links with the trade and media and attracting conferences. Finally, there is the provision of visitor services such as tourist information centres and hotel booking services. Many of these activities will require the findings of research, either of a general industry-wide nature, or specific to the city. The latter could include market research, the monitoring of visitor flows, and assessments of the experience and satisfaction of visitors. Such research could be undertaken either by a promotional organization itself or by a specialized consultancy company.

The principal actors within the organization of tourism in cities may be drawn from either the public or private sectors. In addition to the local authority, the public sector may also include regional and national governments, development corporations, national and regional tourist boards, national museums and other semi-autonomous public organizations. The private sector includes the prime attractions, hotel and catering firms, retailers and travel organizations. These will now be considered in more detail.

The Public Sector

The local authority which is responsible for the city is the key actor in the local tourist industry. Its aim is to secure the benefits of tourism for the community, and it does this through its ability to control, coordinate and lead policy making. In a democracy its policies are determined by politicians and reflect both the ideology of the ruling political party and the views of the public. As has been mentioned earlier, some politicians have had negative views about tourism, perceiving the industry as being seasonal in character and providing low wages. According to this view the tourist industry is not a proper one to be developed and preference should be given to activities like manufacturing. In cities where this view has prevailed, such as Bristol and Liverpool, it has been difficult to bring a tourism organization into existence, whether inside or outside the local authority, and any failure has been used as an excuse for withdrawal of support (Bassett, 1986). The public may also have a negative view of tourism, thinking that it will result in congestion and higher taxes to pay for the needs and consequences of visitors. If either of these views prevails then the local authority is unlikely to promote tourism. However, as was discussed in Chapter 3, more and more local authorities are becoming persuaded of the desirability of tourism and are developing strategies. These strategies may be made explicit in published documents such as economic development strategies, or may be implicit and only observed through actions. The strength of commitment to tourism can be observed through the level of spending, which as always will be in competition with the other activities of local government and with the pressures to reduce public spending.

The activities of local government are undertaken by individual departments, and the exact departmental structure will vary from one authority to another. For tourism the boundaries of departments may be very important, since the activities which are significant for tourism are likely to be found within several sections. In theory, cross-departmental working should be easy, but in practice departments may be jealous of their independence and may have different policies and priorities. Successful tourism promotion will depend on the ability of departments to work together, which in turn may depend on the commonality of purpose which can be engendered across the local authority. In some cases it may be necessary to institute a coordinating committee, while in other cases the leadership role may be given to one department. Whether formalized or not, the ability of heads of department or sections to work together is very important, and may depend more on personalities than policies.

When tourism is considered widely it is obvious that a large number of departments could be involved. In the first place these might include museums, arts or culture (theatres), leisure (including sports facilities), parks (open spaces), halls (perhaps running a convention centre), planning, and economic development. All of these are responsible for activities which are particularly relevant to tourism and may include the organization of special events. Outside them are departments like engineering and cleansing, whose performance could make a great deal of difference to whether tourists enjoy their visit to the city. Other departments like education may have a role in the training of staff for the industry. In some local authorities, many, perhaps small, departments as indicated above have been grouped together to form super-departments. The nature of these groupings to form large departments could have important implications for tourism, giving rise to particular emphases.

So far no mention has been made of a tourism department itself. When a tourism section exists it is usually concerned with promotion and marketing as described above. Often it includes the general marketing and public relations of the city. It is rarely responsible for the activities which bring tourists to the city, such as museums or special events. While the promotion role is important, it is powerless to improve the tourist resources of the city in a way which will significantly help it to attract more visitors. It can advocate greater action and seek good relations with those departments where the decisions will be made. In this situation its ability to influence may be affected by where this small section is located within a bigger department, and whether there are formal structures for coordination.

It will be necessary for the local authority to work with other public sector bodies. In Britain urban development corporations have been set up in some cities with responsibility for key parts of the city centre. Their actions could have a significant impact on the development of tourism resources. Unfortunately, in some cities there is a conflict between the two bodies, which does not make for successful coordinated development of the industry. In the USA many cities have established redevelopment agencies, often with the role of managing the renewal of parts of the downtown area. Baltimore's Charles Center–Inner Harbor Management Inc. is an example of this type of organization.

In the USA and in Germany there is a higher intermediate tier of government, in the form of a state or Land, and these could complement the work and resources of the local authority. They will obviously be concerned to develop the tourist industry over a wider area, but may see the major cities as having a significant role to play, both as attractor and as a gateway to the region. Frequently these bodies have made resources available to major projects like museums, convention centres and stadiums. In Britain there is no regional tier of government as such, except in Scotland and Wales, but regional tourist boards have been established and these may also play a role in influencing tourist flows.

At the national level there are many branches of government which may influence tourism at the local level, including national tourist boards, various government departments, and national museums. In Britain responsibility for tourism has been moved several times in recent years, from the Department of Trade and Industry, to the Department of Employment and in April 1992 to a new Department of Heritage. For tourism development and promotion to be effective at the local level it is important that there is agreement about objectives and coordination of policies. Cities have frequently found there to be conflicts between themselves and regional and national tourist organizations (Pearce, 1992). The latter may promote the region or country with a theme which has very little connection with cities, such as the coast, the countryside, mountains or heritage, emphasizing villages, castles, country houses and churches. This is perhaps inevitable given the diversity of interests within a country or region, and the best that cities can hope for is that the themes are changed frequently so that they get their share of attention.

The Private Sector

There are a large number of operators in this sector, some small and some large. They are all autonomous, making decisions with respect to their own interests, and there is much competition between them, which might militate against cooperation. Some may have been influenced by local authority initiatives and the strategy of developing tourism. Sites may have been offered for particular uses, and grants made available. They all have the task of promoting themselves to the consumer, but success in this area may be affected by the general promotion of the area. It is this convergence of interest in the promotion of the area which may persuade rivals to join together in a common marketing organization.

Funding

As mentioned above, the attraction of finance is critical to the development of the tourist industry, both for capital development and running costs. It will be a test of the leadership and organization of the industry as to whether these funds are obtained. Some mention of finance has already been made in earlier chapters, but here the various elements are brought together.

Finance can be obtained from several sources. Many cities look to higher levels of government. In western Europe the European Community has provided grants to cities for tourist projects. Examples include Birmingham's International Convention Centre, Manchester's concert hall, and many types of infrastructure, such as airports, which could have an influence on the development of the industry. National governments are also important sources of finance. Grants may be available for urban regeneration, such as the former urban development action grants in the USA, and the current city grants in Britain. These governments also often make one-off grants for special projects which are of national importance. If a city is selected as the site for the Olympic Games or an international fair or expo then it could expect significant assistance. Help will also be given for national monuments or museums. In the USA the establishment of a national historic park in a city will bring capital and recurrent resources. St Louis benefited when its riverfront was designated as the Jefferson National Expansion Memorial Historic Park, and later when the Gateway Arch was built. Many British cities have benefited when national museums have either relocated or opened branches in their areas. Britain also has national tourist boards which are able to give grants to cities for new projects. In the USA, Germany and other countries there is a strong regional tier of government which can also make grants for tourist projects. Thus the museums of a city like Cologne have benefited from Land grants. In the USA many of the states have taken direct responsibility for the construction and running of tourist facilities. In Atlanta the State of Georgia established the Georgia World Congress Center Authority to build and operate the convention centre and later the Georgia Dome. In Baltimore the State of Maryland has built the new Oriole Park baseball stadium. In addition to grants, national and regional governments may help cities by granting tax exemptions, as in enterprise zones and with bond issues (see below).

With the decline of population and economic activity, central cities often find it difficult to fund tourist, cultural and leisure facilities. Most of these amenities are in fact used by the population of the entire metropolitan area, as well as tourists, and therefore one possible solution is to set up a voluntary organization to either run or contribute to the financing of these facilities. This does require the suburban municipalities to agree to some form of cross-financing, which is never easy. One example of this idea is the proposal in Pittsburgh for a regional fund for museums.

Cities themselves are usually the funders of both the capital and running costs of some of the main facilities used by tourists, as well as sometimes offering either grants or tax rebates to the private sector to encourage development. In the past, when the population and economic activity may have been larger, this was bearable, but with decline it may become more difficult to fund these amenities. National governments are cutting back on their subventions to local authorities so that the maintenance of basic welfare services has been put at risk. In this situation it may be difficult for city leaders to justify expenditure on facilities which are used greatly by non-residents, notwithstanding that they are bringing income into the area. In Britain, borrowing finance to pay for facilities is strictly controlled by the central government and has been restricted in recent years. In the USA a popular way of raising finance has been through tax-exempt bonds, with the national government forgoing income. Bond issues require voter approval, and in the case of some projects, such as convention centres, this has not always been given at the first time of asking (Sanders, 1992). Finding capital for new projects is critical for the success of a proactive local government seeking to expand its tourism industry.

One way used by American and some French cities to raise finance is through a tax on tourists. In the USA this is variously described as a hotel, lodging, bed or room tax, as it is charged only on those staying in hotels. Usually it is in the form of a percentage addition to the room bill. The money raised in this way can be used to fund both capital projects and the running costs of organizations like convention and visitors bureaus (see below). Power to raise finance in this way may reside with either the city or the state, depending on constitutional arrangements. In either case the government body concerned has the right to take a share of the proceeds, although often it is specified what percentage each organization will receive. Over the years, the rate of the tax has tended to be raised in order to pay for more facilities and more promotion. The amount of total tax raised varies from 8 per cent in Las Vegas to 21 per cent in New York (Figure 9.1). In recent years additional taxes have been levied which mainly fall on the tourist, such airport taxes, car rental taxes, sales taxes and restaurant taxes (Sanders, 1992). In the case of Atlanta, hotel and motel guests pay 13 per cent, broken down into a 6 per cent sales tax and a 7 per cent bed tax. This has increased from 8 per cent in 1986, to 12 per cent in April 1989, to 13 per cent in September 1989, and is one way that the city is financing its successful Olympic bid. The distribution of the tax is shown in Table 9.1, where it is seen that only the bed tax comes back directly into the tourism industry. The great advantage of this tax is that it is a user tax, paid by tourists and not residents. Politicians can be shielded from attack from residents claiming that they are paying for the facilities used by visitors. The major disadvantage of the tax is that it raises the cost of visiting a city, and could deter the tourists. For group visits and sometimes conventions, cost comparisons will be made between cities, and overall high costs could be a deterrent. It is likely, then, that strong tourist cities and those with low costs will be able to have relatively high tourist taxes, while cities with high costs and weak attractiveness will be able to

Table 9.1 The distribution of Atlanta's hotel/motel tax

Type	Destination	Share (%)
6% Sales tax	State	4
	Local option	1
	MARTA	1
7% Bed tax	ACVB	1.575
	City of Atlanta	2
	Georgia Dome	2.75
	GWCC	0.675

Notes: payable within the City of Atlanta and Fulton County.
ACVB, Atlanta Convention and Visitor Bureau; GWCC, Georgia World Congress Center; MARTA, Metropolitan Atlanta Rapid Transit Authority.

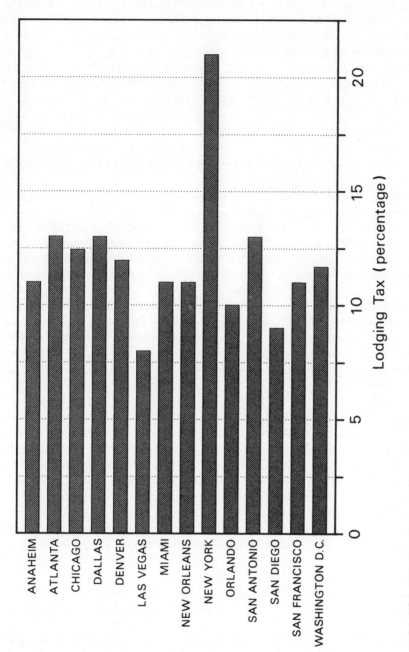

Figure 9.1 US hotel/lodging taxes 1991.
Source: Chicago Convention and Tourism Bureau.

charge only a low tax. Thus those cities which want to develop the industry but have only a weak base may find it difficult to raise funds from this source. In the UK there are no tourist taxes as such, but in 1992 hoteliers in Harrogate agreed to a levy on visitors to pay for necessary renovations on the town's conference and exhibition facilities.

The private profit-making sector is extremely important in the funding and organization of tourism facilities. It can be expected to finance hotels, shops, restaurants, clubs and sometimes major attractions. It will, of course, do so only if profits can be made. This will happen if tourists are coming in large numbers, which in turn puts the onus on the public sector to provide and maintain major attractions which are found within a good environment. In order to get private investment it will often be necessary to give either grants or tax exemptions for a limited period.

Finally, investment may come from philanthropic motivations, or from non-profit institutions. Large corporations may develop facilities in their home city, such as a company museum, or give grants for the development of public facilities such as an art gallery. Locally based, or perhaps non-locally based, charitable foundations may provide funds for a museum or other attraction. Many tourist attractions are the result of the work of voluntary organizations. Enthusiasts may gather artefacts to establish a museum and also raise money for its construction. In many cases these have later been taken over and run, wholly or partly, by the public sector. Finally, independent institutions like universities have often been responsible for the development of facilities such as museums, and, as at Cambridge and Oxford, may have buildings which are themselves part of the attraction of visiting a city.

Promotional Organizations

In the past the marketing and promotion of cities has often been left to the individual firm in the private sector and to whatever role the local authority has decided to play. In some cities, as mentioned above, the local authority has decided to play the lead role in developing and promoting the industry with or without the cooperation of the private sector. This is the case in many German cities, such as Cologne, and also in Britain (Queenan, 1992). However, in recent years an attempt has been made in many cities to develop a form of public–private partnership in which the two sectors are brought together. In the USA the widespread convention and visitors bureaus are an example. In Britain, examples include the Greater Glasgow Tourist Board and the recently formed Greater Manchester Visitor and Convention Bureau.

Most of these organizations cover the entire metropolitan area rather than just the central city. This makes sense, since boundaries are irrelevant to the tourist and it is often beneficial to market products jointly wherever they are found within the urban area. However, in a politically fragmented area where there is competition and conflict between local governments it can be a delicate task keeping all partners on board, since the outer areas may feel that the focus of marketing is on the downtown area. In all cases it is critical that these organizations have a good relationship with the local governments in their area.

These bodies are primarily marketing organizations and providers of visitor services, with little power to plan and develop. Their rationale is that by concentrating the marketing resources of the public and private sectors there will be a greater impact than would occur if each firm attempted its own advertising. They usually have independent legal status, such as not-for-profit corporations. The financing of these bodies is often a critical element in their success. In Britain and continental Europe, local authorities have made by far the largest contribution (Queenan, 1992; Touche Ross: Greene Belfield-Smith Division, 1991), while in the USA the hotel tax is the main source of income, although many cities pay a subvention to the bureau. The third source of finance is membership subscriptions. These are usually based on the type of organization and its size. Income can also be generated through sales.

In the USA the system of convention and visitor bureaus appears to work well. Convention and visitor bureaus have incomes which vary from about $5 million in Washington to $67 million in Las Vegas (Figure 9.2). Bureaus may have up to 1500 members whose contribution may equal up to 40 per cent of the budget. The work of these bureaus is shown by their departmental structure, which normally includes convention and tourism (leisure) sections as well as visitor services and administration. In contrast, in Britain this type of organization is relatively new and has not always had a good track record. It has been difficult to get private sector firms to contribute, although they have been willing to give support via advertising in brochures, or gifts in kind, as when hotels provide free accommodation for visiting travel writers. Consequently these organizations have relied very greatly on public sector finance. In a few cases these bodies have overspent, and when the local authority has not been willing to foot the bill they have been wound up. This has tended to confirm the local authority's fear that it is losing control over the use of funds. Even when the local authority makes by far the largest contribution, the membership of the ruling executive is usually divided equally between the two sectors. Budgets are much smaller than in the USA. Glasgow has one of the largest budgets at £2.2 million, followed by Birmingham with £1.4 million. The new Greater Manchester bureau has a budget of only £0.5 million, of which over half comes from local government. Obviously the size of the budget is important for these organizations, determining how much can be spent on advertising, staff and research (Touche Ross: Greene Belfield-Smith Division, 1991). Very little is spent by these organizations on development. In France the position is similar to that in Britain. The Office of Tourism in Lyon, established in 1976, receives 70 per cent of its funds from the public sector (Renucci, 1992).

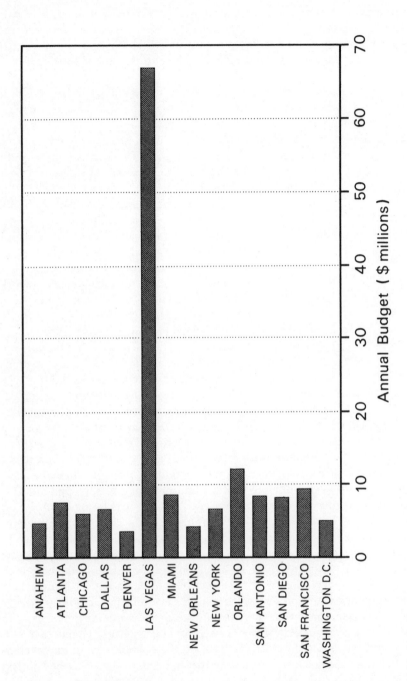

Figure 9.2 US convention bureau budgets 1991.
Source: Chicago Convention and Tourism Bureau.

Conclusion

It is interesting to compare the way that the tourist industry has developed in different cities and assess the role played by inherited resources, formal organization, leadership and the availability of finance. In a few cities the industry has appeared to develop almost spontaneously, without the need for formal organization, perhaps because of a good inheritance of resources. However, in many cities it has been necessary to be proactive to bring about the development of the industry. It has been seen that the public sector often has a very important role to play. It creates some of the main attractors and can place them in the right kind of environment. However, in comparing successful cities, there does not appear to be one particular model. In some cities the main thrust has come from a development agency which has assumed the leadership role for the whole city, as in Baltimore and Boston. In other cities one department has assumed a leadership role and carried the whole council along with it. In yet other cities there has been a strong corporate identity so that the different departments have wanted to work with others, with or without any formal structure. As in many other areas of life, progress may happen because two or three individuals have a vision of where they think the city should be going and work together to achieve particular ends. In some cities this leadership has come from outside the city council in the form of a private sector association or public–private partnership. This is the situation in many American cities, where a pre-dominantly private sector agenda has been imposed onto the public sector. However, from whatever source, a coherent vision and determination over many years can achieve significant results.

10

Assessing the impact of tourism in cities

The adoption of tourism as an economic development strategy by so many cities in the 1980s has not been without debate and questioning. Critics will need to be satisfied that the amount of public money being spent can be justified, and that the aims of an urban tourism strategy are being achieved. Such questions can be answered only through impact studies. Given the prominence of urban tourism in recent years it is surprising that so few have been undertaken, or at least so few that can be regarded as reliable. One reason for this situation may be that tourism is difficult to measure. When, say, a car factory or car factories are built in a city, it is relatively easy to see where the jobs have been created, although even here there is the problem of multiplier effects. However, the impact of tourism is spread across many sectors, from the attractions themselves, to hotels, restaurants, shops, transport and other activities, and so it is more difficult to calculate the impact. To be reliable, assessments of impact require many detailed surveys, which are both time-consuming and costly. There is thus a search for short cuts, the use of simple ratios, and the borrowing of results from other cities or wider surveys. In the USA in particular, many convention and visitor bureaus supply quantitative information about the state of the industry in their city, but in the absence of detailed impact studies it must be assumed that the consultants employed have used short-cut methods, and that these results are open to question (Hughes, 1982). Unfortunately, in many cases the results of these consultant studies are not available for detailed scrutiny.

The basic concerns of any impact study are: the number of visitors; how much income they inject into the economy; the number of jobs created; the kind of jobs created; the impact tourism has on the maintenance of amenities; the impact of tourism on physical regeneration; and the impact of tourism on the image of the city and its general attractiveness to economic investment. These concerns can be classified into what might be described as narrow economic impact and wider impact, the latter being more tenuous and therefore more difficult to measure, The questions to be asked can also be divided into those which can be answered by one survey and those which require more than one because they are examining the impact of the industry over time. This last aspect gets to the heart of the urban tourism strategy, which is to assist the economic and physical regeneration of the city. Only by reviewing the progress of tourism over a number of years can an assessment be made as to whether these objectives are being achieved. Asking whether the urban tourism strategy has been successful involves a series of related questions: is the number of visitors attracted increasing? what is the rate of growth of the different components? how does their rate of growth compare with national and international totals? is the income generated increasing? and have the policies been realized? Once these questions have been answered cities will be in a position to re-evaluate their policies.

So far it has been suggested that impact studies are concerned with the whole of the tourism industry, but, as has been seen in earlier chapters, they may be concerned with individual projects or with sectors of the industry. The viability of individual projects will almost certainly be studied by their sponsors before initiation, whether these be in the public or private sectors. After-studies may occur where there has been public funding, to ascertain that the investment made has been spent to good effect. Once again the project may be looked at in narrow economic terms or in terms of its wider impacts. In Britain the Department of the Environment commissioned a study of tourism to evaluate projects which had received some public assistance (Central London Polytechnic, Leisureworks and DRV Research, 1990). Sector studies may involve the convention industry, the arts or cultural industries, or sports, and these have been referred to in earlier chapters.

In essence the methodology of economic impact studies is relatively easy to understand, although its implementation is usually fraught with problems. First, these studies establish the number of visitors. Second these studies calculate the amount spent in the local economy by these visitors and its further impact thereafter through multiplier effects. The money spent in the local economy is used by firms to make purchases and to pay staff, with possible further impacts. Thus the monetary impact of tourists can be classified as direct, indirect and induced. Third, these studies attempt to calculate the number of jobs which have been created as a result of this spending, producing a figure which is likely to have the most significance for local politicians. In the rest of this chapter these topics will be examined in more detail, and will be illustrated with the results of impact studies. However, it will be apparent from what has already been said and what follows that because of different definitions and methods used, it is extremely difficult to compare the results of impact studies in different cities.

Visitors

The first task of any impact study is to decide who is to be counted as a visitor or a tourist, a definitional problem that has been discussed in earlier chapters. The official definition of a tourist is one who spends more than 24 hours away from home, but this excludes the day tripper, who is important for many cities. Since cities often draw in commuters from a wide area, it is necessary to be able to distinguish the regular commuter who may travel over 20 miles each day from the visitor who is coming to the city for a day out. Even in this latter category there can be the question as to whether the visitor whose sole purpose is shopping should be included. Many studies have excluded shoppers on the basis that shopping is a function for which the large city has always had a regional role. However, given that there are often several shopping centres in a metropolitan area and that shopping is increasingly perceived as a leisure activity, this distinction is not always easy to justify. In some studies the day tripper has been defined on the basis of an arbitrary distance, say 20 or 100 miles, beyond which it is assumed that anyone coming to the city is making a special trip. It is unlikely that there will ever be a universally agreed definition, but if the information about visitors can be classified in an agreed way then comparisons can be made.

Visitors staying overnight can be classified in various ways, the most obvious being between those who use serviced accommodation such as hotels and those who stay with friends and relatives. The great advantage of this division is that it can be related to expenditure patterns, there being a great difference between these categories. Visitors can also be classified by the purpose of their visit, primarily between the business traveller and the leisure tripper, but possibly with further divisions to include the conference and exhibition delegate. Another classification may be based on origin, and this may be important when there is a significant foreign element. Foreign visitors often spend more than people of the home country, but within the foreign component there could be differences. Within Britain, Americans are high spenders, but those from the continent of Europe are often low spenders, since there are many young people who have come to learn the language.

The calculation of visitor numbers is extremely difficult. There are no frontier posts around cities to record arrivals and departures. Visitors staying in hotels can be counted if cooperation can be obtained. In some European countries it is or has been in the past a legal requirement to register hotel guests, particularly foreigners, and this could be a reliable source for this type of visitor. Otherwise the cooperation of the hotel industry is required and this may not be given on the grounds of commercial confidentiality. In some areas sample surveys are done of hotel occupancy, and if the total stock of hotels is known, then through multiplication an estimate of the number of hotel room nights can be obtained. Further information from these surveys may provide details of the types of visitor and length of stay.

For the other types of visitor, those staying with friends and relatives and day trippers, there are no records, and some form of survey is required.

Most surveys of tourists take place at key visitor sites. The number of sites used will vary from city to city, depending on the nature of its attractions. Surveys could take place at locations where there is a popular vista or outside museums, theatres and sports events. The cost of these surveys means that they will be limited to a few days in the year, but every effort must be made to ensure that they are representative. Accordingly, they must be taken at different times of the year, different days of the week, and different hours of the day. The questionnaire will obtain information about the visitor, including age, sex, number in party, home area, purpose of visit, length of stay, places visited or to be visited, expenditure patterns, and impressions of city. The answers to these questions will need to be classified very carefully and may not be without problems. In particular there are often difficulties in categorizing the purpose of the visit. Indeed, there can be more than one reason for the visit. Should answers such as 'just for a change' be included with 'sightseeing'?

The reliability of these types of visitor survey is often questioned. Visitors interviewed in the middle of a visit cannot give a complete account of the whole trip. They may not be able to recall accurately the expenditures they have made. Indeed, in some cases they may not be aware of the details if payments have been made on their behalf by a tour operator. Alternative methods involve interviewing visitors only at the end of a visit, posting questionnaires to tourists after their visit, and giving visitors a diary to record the data required as they enter the city (Frechtling, 1987). However, all of these techniques suffer from similar problems and in addition it may be more difficult to obtain a representative sample.

This information can then be related to other statistical information to provide an estimate of the total number of visitors. Thus if 20 per cent of all tourists visit a particular museum or attraction and the total number of tourist, i.e. non-local, admissions is known from surveys, then a multiplier of five could be used to obtain the total number of visitors to the city. If one-sixth of the tourists are staying in hotels and the number of hotel stayers is known, then a multiplier could be used again (Merseyside Information Services, 1991). Once the total number of visitors has been calculated, the survey data can be used again to give estimates of the number of tourists by different categories. The reliability of this method will depend on the surveys picking up a representative sample. Street surveys might not pick up the business traveller or the convention delegate, or some other specialist type of visitor. Thus the technique when applied to an attraction may produce results only relevant to the pleasure tourist sector. To overcome this problem other surveys may be needed, either in hotels or at convention centres. There is clearly room for error in all these surveys from a failure to be representative. The flow of tourists may be uneven, perhaps because of special events or the weather, variations which cannot be picked up by the surveys. Outside researchers may not be aware of these variations and thus draw false conclusions about visitor flows.

In some countries national sample surveys of both domestic and foreign tourists can be disaggregated to provide information on the number of visitors to metropolitan areas. In the USA the US Travel Data Center developed a Travel Economic Impact Model (TEIM) in the early 1970s which estimates the economic benefits from travel to counties and cities (Frechtling, 1987). Given the size of the national sample, the data thus provided are subject to a degree of error.

Using the results of surveys from a number of cities, the number and nature of visitors to cities can be discussed. Merseyside, which includes the city of Liverpool, and Munich are among the few cities where there are statistics for all visitors (Table 10.1).

In terms of absolute numbers, day visitors are overwhelming in both cases, representing between 88 and 91 per cent of all visitors. The category of visitors to friends and relatives varied between 3 and 7 per cent, while those staying in hotels represented about 5 per cent. Further information shows that Munich had 2.2 million overnight business visitors and 16.1 million day business visitors, equal to one-third of all visitors. In contrast, Merseyside had only 137 000 overnight and 764 000 day business visitors, equalling just 3 per cent of all visitors. A strong economy like Munich's will thus attract many business visitors and be a good basis for the hotel trade. With a weak economy like Merseyside's there will be a poor basis for hotels. In the above examples the visitor numbers have simply been added up, but obviously hotel stayers have a greater impact as they stay longer and spend more. Further information about Munich non-business day visitors reveals that 73 per cent travelled from their homes, 20 per cent came from a holiday location, and the remaining 7 per cent were in transit, stopping *en route*. Munich attracted 11.3 million visitors for its festivals, including 6.7 million for its Oktoberfest.

As could be expected, many more cities have data about the number of visitors staying overnight in hotels. Figures for the late 1980s show that London received over 22 million visitors (as well as 40 million day visitors),

Table 10.1 Visitors to Merseyside and Munich

	Merseyside		Munich	
	No. (million)	%	No. (million)	%
Overnight hotel, etc.	1.4	4.7	3.1	5.7
VFR	2.1	7.1	1.6	2.9
Day	25.4	88.2	49.8	91.4
Total	28.9	100	54.5	100

Source: Merseyside Information Services (1991), and Munich City Tourist Office.

New York 16 million, Washington 6.5 million, Atlanta 4.9 million, Munich 3.1 million, Frankfurt 2 million, Glasgow also 2 million and Amsterdam 1.5 million. When only hotel-staying visitors are considered, then the significance of business travel and conventions greatly increases. In Munich (1988) 56 per cent of the hotel stayers were business travellers and 16 per cent were attending trade fairs and congresses. For Glasgow in 1985, 40 per cent of overnight stays were business people and conference delegates. Most overnight-staying visitors in cities are on a short visit only, the average length of stay being two nights.

In some cities research has been limited to a core tourist area and the results cannot be used for the entire city area. For Baltimore, annual surveys have been taken between 1980 and 1988 in and around the Inner Harbor (for the most recent, see Jeanne Beekhuis & Co., 1988). These suggest that after a rapid increase in the early 1980s, visitor numbers have stabilized at around 2.7 million a year from outside the metropolitan area, composed of 45 per cent day visitors and 55 per cent overnight stayers. About 25 per cent of the visitors come as individuals, 69 per cent in a party, average size 2.47, and only 6 per cent with group travel.

Income

Using the expenditure information obtained from the visitor surveys, an estimate of the income which tourists bring to the city can be made. This is usually done by classifying tourists into categories such as day visitors, those staying with friends and relatives, leisure tourists staying in hotels, business travellers and convention delegates. Each of these categories will have a different pattern of expenditure, as the figures for Hong Kong show (Table 10.2). The exact categories chosen will depend on the characteristics of tourism in the metropolitan area. If the numbers in each group have been estimated and their expenditure is known, then through multiplication an estimate of total tourist expenditure can be obtained. Using the details of expenditure, this can be broken down into figures for spend on hotels, restaurants, attractions, shops and local transport. This provides the data for direct expenditure. This, of course, is a misleading guide to economic impact, since much of the money will either be used to purchase goods from outside the area or be repatriated

Table 10.2 Average per capita expenditure per day by tourists in Hong Kong 1988

Type	Expenditure ($US)
Holiday makers	240
VFR	70
Convention delegates	470
Incentive travel	700

Source: HKTA Visitor Survey, quoted in Bull (1991, p. 13).

as profits to companies headquartered elsewhere (Frechtling, 1987). Once again, national models such as TEIM in the USA may be used to estimate expenditure in city areas. One problem for these models is to decide how to allocate transport expenditure, in either the home or destination area. Simpler simulation techniques may also be used if, say, the total income of hotels in an area is known and a ratio can be applied to estimate total expenditure.

The second stage is to make an estimate of indirect expenditure. This requires further survey work to ascertain how the income is used in the firms identified above as receiving the tourist expenditure. Some of this will be used to pay staff. Some will be used to make purchases, some of which will come from the local economy and some from outside. Those made from the local economy will create a further impact via employment and possible purchases from the local economy which could require survey work. Some of the income will be used to pay taxes, and again these will need to be divided between local and national ones. Using these results it is possible to obtain an estimate of the impact of second and subsequent rounds of expenditure in the local economy. As with the other surveys, there may be problems in obtaining cooperation and getting precise information, the absence of which could prejudice the results. If there are input–output tables for the metropolitan economy it may be possible to cut out some of the survey work.

The third stage of estimating the economic impact is to calculate the induced impact. This will come from the expenditure of those dependent on tourism for their income. The second round will have provided an estimate of this household income. Either through further survey work or through input–output tables the breakdown of this expenditure can be obtained, and the expenditure divided between local and non-local spend. This local spend will be the induced impact.

Adding the three effects together will provide the total impact, and if this is placed over the direct spend a simple ratio multiplier coefficient can be obtained. However, this would be very unreliable, since it ignores the income that has left the area. The normal or Keynesian multiplier takes only the income spent in the area and places it over direct expenditure to obtain a coefficient. For the general public these figures of total income for the tourist industry are usually fairly meaningless and if there are no comparable figures for the metropolitan economy their significance is difficult to evaluate.

In 1988 Munich's tourism generated DM 4.6 billion, of which nearly half was spent in retailing, one-third on hotels and catering, and the rest on entertainment, local transport and other items. About 10 per cent of this income is generated by congresses. For Amsterdam in 1987, tourism generated 1.5 billion guilders, of which 57 per cent was spent by international visitors (Pearce, 1992).

Ahmadi (1989) has classified visitors to Baltimore City in two ways, according to type of accommodation and purpose of activity (Table 10.3).

Table 10.3 Visitors to Baltimore City 1988

(a) By accommodation

Topic	Hotels	VFR	Day trippers
Numbers	654 000	165 000	3 143 000
Numbers (%)	16.5	4.2	79.3
Days	1 634 000	413 000	314 000
Days (%)	31.5	8.0	60.6
Daily spend ($)	143.61	58.87	49.43
Direct spend ($m)	234.71	23.99	155.32
Direct spend ($m)	56.7	5.8	37.5
Jobs	7 304	683	4 628

(b) By activity

	Conventions	Sightseeing	Shopping	Events
Days (%)	8.29	69.72	0.33	21.66
Direct spend ($m)	86.30	258.17	0.79	68.76
Direct spend (%)	20.8	62.4	0.19	16.6
Jobs	2 684	7 875	24	2 032
Jobs (%)	21.3	62.4	0.2	16.1

Source: Ahmadi (1989).

Hotel visitors formed 16.5 per cent of the total, but were responsible for 31.5 per cent of the tourist days, 56.7 per cent of the direct expenditure (and 57.9 per cent of the jobs). In contrast, 79.3 per cent of the visitors were day trippers, defined here as visitors travelling over 30 miles, but they accounted for only 37.5 per cent of the expenditure. In terms of the purpose of the trip, there were three main groups: conventioneers, sightseers and visitors to events. Conventioneers were relatively small in number but had a larger impact, while the greater number of events visitors had a smaller impact.

Jobs

The number and type of jobs that tourism generates are often the most important impact measure. They are also among the most difficult to calculate. As mentioned above, these jobs are scattered across many sectors and cannot easily be identified. The most relevant data for calculating the number of jobs come from the figure of the income which is devoted to employment, but this cannot always easily be translated into jobs. Usually some ratio drawn from national input–output tables is used to estimate the employment which a given amount of income will generate. More sophistication can be obtained if the components of income are used and the ratios applied. This still makes it difficult to identify the types of jobs, whether by sector, occupation or income, or whether they are full time, part time or seasonal. Some information on where tourist workers live would also be of interest, to see whether jobs are being created in the inner city. Once again, when figures are quoted for cities they are often not compatible because of different definitions.

The greatest number of tourism jobs are found in the major capital cities such as London and Paris. For 1985 it was estimated for London that there were between 210 000 and 230 000 jobs created directly by tourism and a further 150 000 indirectly, which equalled 10 per cent of all London's employment and about a quarter of all tourism jobs in Britain (London Tourist Board, 1987). Estimates of employment are available for most major US cities which use the US Travel Data Center's TEIM to calculate impact. In Atlanta in 1987 it was estimated that tourism created 65 000 jobs, of which 35 000 were generated by visitors staying in hotels, of whom 36 per cent were attending conventions. For Baltimore in 1988 about 20 000 jobs were created in the metropolitan area, and 16 400 in the city. Of the latter jobs, 62 per cent were created by sightseers, 21 per cent by conventioneers and 16 per cent by visitors to special events. In Britain there are estimates for only a few cities. Two studies of tourism in Merseyside suggested that the industry had created 13 500 jobs in 1985 and 14 000 in 1990 (DRV Research, 1986; Merseyside Information Services, 1991). For Bradford, where tourism became a key part of the economic development strategy in the early 1980s, Jeffrey (1990) suggests that the number of jobs increased only from 3772 in 1981 to 4133 in 1987. In Germany the 1988 study of Munich suggested that tourism created 57 000 full-time equivalent jobs or 7 per cent of all jobs. Unfortunately, there are few statistics which break down employment into full and part time, by industry type and by occupational level.

Other Methods

Owing to the cost of undertaking surveys, attempts have been made to develop simpler yet reliable methods of calculating impact. One such method is the use of the counterfactual. This was used by Barnett (1984) when calculating the employment impact of tourism in the city of York, England. The counterfactual method asks the basic question, what would be the situation if there were no tourism industry? To answer the question, a town of a similar size but without a tourist industry is taken and its employment structure is compared, highlighting those industries where tourism could be expected to have an impact. Thus the additional jobs in hotels could be presumed to arise from tourism. When these categories have been summed, an estimate of tourism impact is obtained. In the case of York, a small city, it was easy to compare it with, say, an industrial town, but the method would be more difficult to apply to larger cities, where it might be difficult to find a city for which tourism was of no importance at all.

Vaughan (1986) and Jeffrey (1989, 1990) have used two non-survey techniques to estimate employment in tourism. The first method relies on calculating the number of visitor nights. These may be obtained from sample surveys of hotel (and guest-house) occupancy, with the ratios then being applied to the

Table 10.4 Workforce per £100 000 of turnover in selected businesses in Merseyside

Business type	Direct workforce	Secondary workforce	Total
Hotel and guest houses	8.3	1.7	10.0
Rented self-catering	19.2	0.9	20.1
Restaurants and pubs	6.7	1.1	7.8
Shops	3.6	0.4	4.0
Attractions	8.7	1.6	10.3

Source: DRV Research (1986).

whole stock. Alternatively, national surveys of domestic and foreign tourists can be used to obtain visitor nights, although the disaggregated data to district levels may not be very reliable. Survey data, obtained from elsewhere, can then be used to estimate spend per 24 hours, and thus a figure of total expenditure broken down into the main categories can be obtained. Again using survey data from elsewhere, these totals can be converted into employment (Table 10.4). These figures cover only overnight tourists staying in serviced accommodation, and exclude visits to friends and relatives and day visitors.

The second technique applies ratios to relevant classes of employment figures. There is no class of employment which is solely tourist related, but national studies have attempted to estimate what proportion of each class could be so classified (Table 10.5). These ratios can then be applied to the statistics of employment for a particular urban area to estimate the total which is generated by tourism. Such a figure will cover all types of tourism, including day trips. However, since it is likely that the proportion of tourism-related employment in each class will vary from area to area, any estimate for a particular area must be subject to a degree of error. These figures also need to include estimates for the number of self-employed, seasonal employment and the induced effects on employment of workers' expenditure (Vaughan, 1986).

Table 10.5 The estimated proportion of total national employment which is directly related to tourism by employment class

Class	Proportion directly employed in tourism
Retail distribution 1	0.0803
Retail distribution 2	0.0803
Hotels and catering	0.4901
Railways	0.0627
Other inland trains	0.0254
Sea transport	0.1064
Air transport	0.8254
Transport supplementary services	0.1795
Miscellaneous transport	0.2200
Recreational services	0.2160
Personal services	0.0811

Source: Morrell (1985).

Wider Impacts

The wider impacts of tourism include the effects on the environment and the image of the locality (Central London Polytechnic, Leisureworks and DRV Research, 1990). As has been discussed earlier, cities are encouraging tourism as part of their efforts to regenerate the city centre and inner city. Very often, tourism projects are steered to the fringe of the city centre, where there are empty buildings and vacant land. Not surprisingly the new investment in these areas results in environmental improvement and often stimulates further investment, so that tourism development can be seen in many cities to have played a significant role in the physical and economic regeneration of run-down quarters. The second aspect of wider impact concerns the changing image and the effect this may have on inward investment. Again as discussed earlier, cities are seeking a higher profile in the outside world or greater visibility. There is no doubt that large projects with a tourism component, such as the Albert Dock in Liverpool or the Gateway Arch in St Louis, or large events do make an impact outside the city and help transform the image of a place. However, it will always be difficult to prove what effect this had on either retaining investment or attracting inward investment, although it is clearly positive.

So far the impact of tourism has been examined in terms of positive benefits, but there may be negative effects or costs (Frechtling, 1987). These spillover effects or externalities may take several forms. Direct effects may take the form of more rubbish on the streets, extra demand on public facilities where no charge is made to recoup the costs, and the costs of repair through wear and tear. Indirect costs which affect the quality of life of residents may include congestion on roads and in public spaces, and pollution. In some cities tourism has attracted criminal elements who threaten not only tourists but also residents. Finally, a successful and growing tourist industry could put pressure on the labour market and indirectly on the housing market, thereby raising prices and also creating demands for extra public facilities. However, given the poor state of many urban economies this appears unlikely.

Conclusion

In this chapter it has not been possible to provide very comprehensive information about the impact of tourism in cities, or about the progress of the industry in cities. Neither has it been possible to compare the state of the industry in different cities and evaluate the reasons for the different performances. This is because so few comprehensive and reliable surveys have been undertaken. Fragmentary evidence, such as the number of visitors to attractions, number of visitors to festivals, number of conference delegates and number of hotel rooms, leaves no doubt that tourism in large cities is growing, but in most cases it is impossible to quantify this growth precisely.

The methodology to undertake this research is available, as this chapter has shown, but few authorities have been willing to pay for the work to be done. Given the public funds which are being invested in tourism and related projects, this is unfortunate. Research could not only justify past expenditure but could be used to guide future policy.

11
Interpretation, problems and prospects

The previous chapters have chronicled the contemporary rise of tourism in large cities and discussed the main characteristics. Although generally unrecognized, tourism has become a significant activity in the economy of post-industrial cities and is likely to continue to grow in importance. In this chapter the various strands of urban tourism are drawn together, beginning with the interpretation of the growth in importance of the industry in cities.

The main emphasis in this book has been that of cities as competitors in the market-place and it is not necessary to repeat this perspective at length (see Chapter 2). The economy of cities has been undergoing significant changes in the past thirty years. The staple industries which often created the modern industrial city have gone into decline, at least as far as employment is concerned. Many of the newer and expanding activities are more footloose, and the old cities must compete not only with each other but with new emerging urban areas and many semi-urban areas. To obtain new employment and to reduce unemployment, cities must compete for the growing forms of economic activity. The need for economic regeneration is particularly acute in the core areas of cities, which are additionally competing against the suburbs. Tourism offers cities many advantages. It is perceived as a growth industry and one in which they already have some advantages. At a simple level, then, cities are developing the tourism industry in the same way as they might develop any other industry and in doing so are competing against other cities and other types of places. Because this strategy is relatively recent and because there have been few comprehensive studies at intervals of time, it is difficult to make any assessment of the success of this policy. However, the tourism industry is not like other industries. The elements of tourism include activities like museums, theatres and sports which can, of course, be considered as parts of other industries. When these elements are considered as parts of tourism, they have the ability to project an image of the city, thus assisting it to compete against others to attract new economic activities. Many of these elements enhance the lifestyle of residents and so may also help in persuading senior executives to come and live in the city and thus indirectly augment the arguments why firms should move to the area. From limited evidence it is possible to say that high-profile museums, theatres, sports and above all mega-events do help to transform the image of a city and thus help it in the market-place.

As important as these ideas are, many commentators would argue that they ignore another significant perspective, namely that of cities as places of consumption. As the standard of living rises for the individual, life becomes more than just meeting basic needs and buying essential goods. Non-essential consumption becomes more and more important and this can take many forms. For some, education in its broadest sense is important. This may take the form of learning about history, culture, the natural environment, hobbies and places. Another theme related to consumption is the idea of self-realization and the search for authentication. Individuals gain pleasure, confidence and self-esteem by knowing and feeling part of world events and history. A third aspect of consumption is the individual's desire for escapism, fun and entertainment.

The large city is well placed to meet these needs. It can meet the educational needs of the individual because it is the location for museums and art galleries, for universities and other establishments of learning, and it is often the venue for meetings and conferences. The city is also often the location for the events of history and the place where many famous buildings are found. The city has also always been well endowed with centres of legal and illegal forms of entertainment. It has theatres, clubs and sports, to name the more obvious.

The idea of the city as a place of entertainment has been incorporated in the concept of the city as a spectacle. Harvey (1989) and others see much that is happening in cities as an attempt to create spectacle. In contrast to television, cities can offer the excitement of live performances, in the theatre and, say, at pop concerts. There is often street theatre, and in the new living museums actors bring life to history. Sports events are another spectacle, and this is particularly so in the opening ceremonies of the mega-events like the Olympic Games. Cities also often have street parades and carnivals. Those cities that are fortunate enough to be on the coast or a large river can stage a pageant of ships, whether permanently as with a marina or in a special event as with the Tall Ships race. However, it is perhaps in architecture and urban design that the attempt to create a spectacle is most evident. Of course, many cities already have historic buildings, which are a form of spectacle. But architects are attempting to create the memorable through the construction of new landmark/signature/trophy buildings, which often take the form of towers. Older forms of the spectacular are reappearing, as with the Grand

Arch in Paris and the Gateway Arch in St Louis. The redevelopment of waterfront areas has enabled these spectacles of architecture to be set off. But it is not just the outsides of buildings which are important. Inside, the atrium and glass vaulted roof have been rediscovered, and the glass wall climbing lift added (sometimes on the outside of buildings as well). These features are present in those buildings which are emblematic of the modern city: the office block, the hotel, the shopping mall and the festival market-place. Some might argue that the city as a tourist attraction is attempting to copy one of its main rivals, namely the theme park. Through this urban design the scene for spectacles becomes a spectacle in itself.

The Characteristics of Urban Tourism

The varied characteristics of tourism in cities have been extensively described in earlier chapters, but it is useful at this point to summarize them succinctly. While urban tourism is primarily concerned with two motivations, broadly conceived, namely business and culture, it is in fact very diverse. People come to cities for a very large number of reasons: to see friends and relatives; to visit museums; to go to the theatre or attend a sports event; to see the sights; to find entertainment; to shop; to attend meetings and exhibitions; and so on. Any one of the reasons might explain only a small proportion of all visits, and obviously the exact shares would vary from city to city. However, given the fact that many trips are either multipurpose or have a strong secondary motivation, the sum is greater than the parts. When the city has a bundle of products, and when they are put together within a relatively small area, then perhaps it can be said that there is a city product, but again its exact composition would vary from one city to another. One of the many tasks for urban tourism research is to tease out the reasons why people visit cities, the links between the various motivations and the deeper reasons why people are attracted to cities.

The flow of visitors to cities is remarkably even throughout the year, in contrast to other types of tourism, and this, of course, is good news for those employed in the industry. Most visitors spend only a few days in the city, much less than the individual's one-or two-week main holiday. Cities attract people of all ages, although different activities have their own age and group profiles. Overall, visitors to cities tend to be more affluent and therefore higher spenders.

The Impact of Tourism in Cities

At a simple level and in an obvious way the impact of tourism in cities is easy to see, as cities build or enlarge conference and exhibition centres, museums and art galleries, festival market-places, theatres and concert halls, sports stadiums, hotels and tourist quarters. Clearly, some jobs are also being created. However, at a deeper level and in a more detailed way it is often very difficult to assess the impact of tourism on a city. There are several reasons for this. First, as discussed in Chapter 10, it is often very difficult to measure the flow of tourists, even when a definition has been agreed. Comprehensive surveys are expensive and short-cut methods are often unreliable and may, if repeated, come up with conflicting evidence. Secondly, the flow of income through the economy is difficult to trace, and it is difficult to calculate the number of jobs created. Tourism's impact is very diffuse and so not very visible, which is a problem for those campaigning for further support. Thirdly, the objectives of tourism development are also diffuse and often interlinked with other objectives, so that it is difficult to isolate its impact. A specific project may provide amenities for local people, attract tourists, raise the profile of the city, and be used to entice firms and their senior executives to the area. With multiple objectives it is difficult to isolate success in one area, and with the general objective of economic development it is difficult to determine what factor among many persuaded a company to move to the area. Notwithstanding these caveats, it is clear that in many cities more tourists are being attracted, more jobs are being created, physical regeneration is taking place, and the city is obtaining more attention in the outside world.

Success in Urban Tourism

This last statement ignores the fact that progress in cities is very variable. In the USA, cities such as Atlanta and Baltimore appear to be making considerable progress, while others, such as Detroit, are struggling to maintain what they have. Appearance and reality may, of course, be in conflict. In Britain, cities such as Birmingham and Glasgow have gained much publicity for what they have done, while until recently Manchester had obtained little, but in the absence of detailed impact studies it is difficult to be certain that there is a correlation with actual impact. In assessing success there is also the problem that a city may be successful in one area and not in another.

Several reasons can be postulated as to why some cities have been more successful than others. On the one hand, cities vary in their inheritance. Some have fine buildings, museums and urban landscapes. Others have discovered that they had potential, as when port areas became redundant, providing the opportunity for waterfront redevelopment. Negative factors include a poor urban landscape, few attractions, an industrial image, social disorder, administrative fragmentation, remoteness and downtown decay.

However, equally and perhaps more important has been the degree of drive, determination and vision to develop a tourism industry using all the resources available. An early start, imagination, sustained drive over many years, the cooperation of the public and private sectors and the ability to extract public funds from higher levels of government have all been important. No two cities are exactly alike and therefore no precise formula can be put forward to explain why some cities have been successful and others not, or how cities should proceed in the future.

Problems

Even with the right approach the task of developing tourism in cities is not easy. There are a number of problems along the way, which can be listed:

1 The problem if all cities become alike, or as Harvey (1989) has termed it, the problem of 'serial reproduction'. Once an idea for city economic development is seen to work, it is likely to diffuse very quickly to other cities. This is certainly the case for tourism in general and also for the component parts. A development policy almost always results in buildings; hence the proliferation across American cities of convention centres, stadiums and festival market-places. The trouble with this is that all too easily all cities could become alike, just as high streets have with the same multiple stores. It is very unlikely that visitors will want to travel to clone cities; hence the need for cities to develop something either distinctive or specialized. This can be based on something inherent in the place and its history, or on a theme which has been identified. The example of Indianapolis illustrated how this could be done.

2 The problem of visibility and attractiveness to visitors. In the competition for visitors the winners are likely to be those which have a relatively high degree of visibility and high standards in their attractions. A few cities like London and Paris already tower over other cities. As centres of the media and government they are frequently being shown on the television and in the press. Most second-tier cities have a battle to obtain attention; hence the desire to stage mega-events. It is these high-profile cities that tourists will want to visit in order to authenticate their lives. The public will hold information about only a relatively few cities and in the competition that exists between cities those with less visibility and those with less newsworthy attractions are likely to lose out.

3 The problem of keeping moving forward. The public will not necessarily remain loyal to cities. Standards are rising all the time and there is a need to invest to renovate and keep up to date. The public are looking for something new and different and this again means that cities must continually invest in their product or see their visitor numbers fall. This raises the question of where cities will find the necessary resources. The example of Atlanta suggests that those cities that developed tourism early have been able to make profits that can then be reinvested to keep their facilities up to date and consequently maintain their position in the industry. The problem for those who entered the industry late may be that they may never become profitable enough to have the funds to keep up their investment in the product.

4 The problem of competition from other types of places. At the beginning of the book it was indicated that the tourism resources of large cities were by no means unique to them. Resorts and small historic cities have convention centres, museums and entertainments. Orlando in the USA, built around a

theme park, has in the space of twenty years become one of the leading convention centres. Resorts can offer the seaside and often better weather as well. Major cities cannot afford, therefore, to ignore this competition.

5 The problem of the link with property development and economic cycles. Many urban tourism projects are parts of mixed-use building schemes. Frequently in cities, a concert hall, hotel or a specialty shopping centre is part of a mega-structure which also includes a large component of office space. Sometimes in practice the tourism project is being cross-subsidized by the office component. The demand for office space is very much related to the economic cycle, and supply as shown by the office development cycle fluctuates even more greatly because of the pipeline effect. Thus at present, at the end of a recession, there is considerable oversupply and consequently investment is greatly reduced. The knock-on effect is that investment in tourism projects may also be stopped. Through this cross-subsidization large cities may obtain projects they otherwise would not have, but equally they may face frustration at certain points in the economic cycle.

6 The problem of the conflict between growth and welfare objectives in city politics. In many British cities there has been perceived to be a conflict between the idea of pushing for growth and that of using resources for welfare. In the USA this conflict appears as one of investing in either the downtown area or inner city neighbourhoods. Politicians who must win votes somehow have to square the circle. There is a problem that the greater the scale of poverty, the greater the claims for welfare measures, and thus the greater the likelihood that a policy for urban tourism will be either weakened or abandoned. Here, as in so many areas, the prospects of the urban economy lie outside the control of local people and are dependent on the state of the national and world economy.

7 The problem of sustainable or green tourism. Many of the comments that have been made in recent years about sustainable or green tourism relate to non-urban areas, i.e. the destruction of soils in the countryside. In cities the problems are usually different. They are more likely to concern wear and tear on the urban fabric, the problem of parking, traffic congestion, air pollution, rubbish, and sometimes the land use conflicts between housing, hotels and other tourist uses. As concern with the environment rises, these are issues that will have to be faced by those planning tourism in cities.

And Finally

An implicit premise underlying this book is that tourism in cities is a growth industry; it is growing and is likely to keep on growing. However, the comments above suggest that possibly a more cautious approach should be adopted. Cities will generally want tourism to develop and they have some good resources. But growth is by no means assured either in all cities or even in aggregate. They will have to work hard at it if they are to beat the various competitors they face.

All cities will want to assess their strengths and weaknesses and the progress they are making. In this situation a firm statistical base would be useful, but it is so often lacking. As mentioned above, there are severe methodological and practical problems in making an assessment of the impact of tourism, but frequently the greatest problem is the unwillingness of people in the industry to supply data, usually on the grounds of commercial confidentiality. This contrasts with firms in many other industries, where statistics are collected with confidentiality guaranteed. Until this problem can be overcome, any assessment of tourism in cities will either be elementary or subject to error because of the short cuts used.

REFERENCES

Abbey, J.R. (1987) The convention and meetings sector: its operation and research needs. In J.R.B. Ritchie and C.R. Goeldner (eds) *Travel, Tourism and Hospitability Research*. New York: John Wiley.

Ahmadi, M. (1989) *The 1988 Economic Impact of Tourism in Maryland: A Multiregional Analysis*. Baltimore: Maryland Department of Economics and Employment Development.

American Association of Museums (1992) *Data Report from the 1989 National Museums Survey*. Washington, DC: American Association of Museums.

Arbel, A. and Pizam, A. (1977) Some determinants of hotel location: the tourist's inclinations. *Journal of Travel Research*, 15, 18–22.

Ashworth, G.J. (1989) Urban tourism: an imbalance in attention. In C.P. Cooper (ed.) *Progress in Tourism, Recreation and Hospitality Management*. London: Bellhaven.

Ashworth, G.J. and Goodall, B. (eds) (1990) *Marketing Tourism Places*. London: Routledge.

Ashworth, G.J. and Voogd, H. (1990) *Selling the City: Marketing Approaches in Public Sector Urban Planning*. London: Belhaven.

Astroff, M.T. and Abbey, J.R. (1991) *Convention Sales and Services*. 2nd edn. New Jersey: Waterbury Press.

AUMA (1991) *Handbuch Messeplatz Deutschland*. Cologne: AUMA.

Baade, R.A. and Dye, R.E. (1988a) An analysis of the economic rationale for public subsidization of sports stadiums. *Annals of Regional Science*, 23, 37–42.

Baade, R.A. and Dye, R.E. (1988b) Sports stadiums and area development: a critical review. *Economic Development Quarterly*, 2, 265–275.

Baade, R.A. and Dye, R.E. (1990) The impact of stadiums and professional sport on metropolitan area development. *Growth and Change*, 21(2), 1–14.

Bagguley, P. (1990) Gender and labour flexibility in hotel and catering. *Service Industries Journal*, 10, 737–747.

Bale, J. (1991) Sport and local economic development: a review of the literature. Paper presented at the IBG Annual Conference, Sheffield, January 1991.

Ball, R.M. and Metcalfe, M. (1992) Tourism development at the margins: pits, pots and potential in the Potteries locality. Paper presented at the Tourism in Europe conference, Durham, July 1992.

Bamberger, R.J. and Parham, D.W. (1984) Leveraging amenity infrastructure: Indianapolis' economic development strategy. *Urban Land*, 43(11), 12–18.

Barnett, R.R. (1984) Tourism's contribution to employment in York. Unpublished report to York City Council.

Bassett, K. (1986) Economic restructuring, spatial ambition and local economic development strategy, a case study of Bristol. *Political Geography Quarterly*, 5 (Supplement), 163–178.

Bennett, B. (1991) The shape of things to come: Expo 88. *Cultural Studies*, 5(1), 30–51.

Berkowitz, B.L. (1987) Rejoinder to downtown redevelopment. *Journal of Urban Affairs*, 9(2), 133–138.

Berry, B.J.L. (ed.) (1976) *Urbanization and Counterurbanization*. Beverly Hills: Sage.

Bianchini, F. (1991) Urban renaissance? The arts and the urban regeneration process. In S. MacGregor and B. Pimlott (eds) *Tackling the Inner Cities: The 1980s Reviewed, Prospects for the 1990s*. Oxford: Clarendon Press.

Bianchini, F., Fisher, M., Montgomery, J. and Walpole, K. (1988) *City Centre Culture: The Role of the Arts in the Revitalization of Towns and Cities*. Manchester: Centre for Local Economic Strategies.

Birmingham City Council (1987) *Action Programme for Tourism in Birmingham*. Birmingham: Birmingham City Council.

Birmingham City Council (1991) *International Convention Centre: Commemorative Book*. Birmingham: Birmingham City Council.

Blank, U. and Petkovich, M.D. (1987) Research on urban tourism destinations. In J.R.B. Ritchie and C. Goeldner (eds) *Travel, Tourism and Hospitality Research*, Chapter 14. New York: John Wiley.

Blau, J.R. and Hall, R.H. (1986) The supply of performing arts in metropolitan places. *Urban Affairs Quarterly*, **22**, 42–65.

Boggs, B. and Wall, G. (1984) Economic impact of a recreational facility: perspectives from Canada's Wonderland (Toronto). *Operational Geographer*, **5**, 42–46.

Boorstein, D. (1964) *The Image: A Guide to Pseudo-events in America*. New York: Harper.

Bradford Metropolitan District Council (1991) *Economic Development Strategy*. Bradford: Bradford Metropolitan District Council.

Brawn, B.M. (1992) The economic contribution of conventions: the case of Orlando. *Journal of Travel Research*, **30**(3), 32–37.

Bristol City Council Planning Department (1990) *Proposed Tourism Strategy for Bristol (Draft)*. Bristol: Bristol City Planning Department.

British American Arts Association (1989) *Arts and the Changing City: An Agenda for Urban Regeneration*. London: British American Arts Association.

British Tourist Authority (1988) *The Short Break Market*. London: British Tourist Authority.

British Tourist Authority (1991) *Digest of Tourist Statistics* No. 15. London: British Tourist Authority.

British Tourist Authority (1992) *The British on Holiday*. London: British Tourist Authority.

British Tourist Authority and English Tourist Board (annual) *Visits to Tourist Attractions*. London: British Tourist Authority and English Tourist Board.

British Tourist Authority and English Tourist Board (1988) *The Visiting Friends and Relatives Market*. London: British Tourist Authority and English Tourist Board.

Brown, J. (1992) Oceanapolis. *Leisure Management*, **12**(7), 26–29.

Buckley, P.J. and Witt, S.F. (1985) Tourism in difficult areas: case studies of Bradford, Bristol, Glasgow and Hamm. *Tourism Management*, **10**, 138–152.

Buckley, P.J. and Witt, S.F. (1989) Tourism in difficult areas II: case studies of Calderdale, Leeds, Manchester and Scunthorpe. *Tourism Management*, **10**, 138–152.

Bull, A. (1991) *The Economics of Travel and Tourism*. Melbourne: Pitman.

Business Ratios (1989) *The Hotel Industry*. Hampton, Middlesex: Business Ratios.

Butler, R.W. (1991) West Edmonton Mall as a tourist attraction. *Canadian Geographer*, **35**, 287–295.

Capstick, B. (1985) Museums and tourism. *International Journal of Museum Management and Curatorship*, **4**, 365–372.

Central London Polytechnic, Leisureworks and DRV Research (1990) *Tourism and the Inner City: An Evaluation of the Impact of Grant Assisted Tourism Projects*. London: HMSO.

Chadwick, P. A. (1987) Concepts, definitions and measures used in travel research. In J. R. B. Ritchie and C. R. Goeldner (eds) *Travel, Tourism and Hospitality Research*. New York: John Wiley.

Champion, A. G. (ed.) (1989) *Counterurbanisation*. London: Edward Arnold.

Champion, A. G. and Townsend, A. R. (1990) *Contemporary Britain*. London: Edward Arnold.

Chetwynd, K. (1984) Garden festivals: planning potential. *The Planner*, **70**(7), 23–25.

Clevedon, R. and O'Brien, K. (1988) *International Business Travel 1988*, Economist Intelligence Unit Special Report 1140, London.

Collinge, M. (1989) Tourism and urban regeneration. Vision for Cities conference paper. London: English Tourist Board.

Collins, M. F. (1991) The economics of sport and sport in the economy: some international comparisons. In C. P. Cooper (ed.) *Progress in Tourism, Recreation and Hospitality Management*, Vol. 3. London: Belhaven.

Comedia (1991) *Out of Hours: A Study of the Economic and Cultural Life in Twelve Town Centres in the UK*. London: Comedia.

Comedia Consultants (1989) *Developing a Cultural Industries Strategy for Coventry*. Coventry: Coventry City Council.

Cooper, C. P. (ed.) (1990) *Progress in Tourism, Recreation and Hospitality Management*, Vol. 2. London: Belhaven.

Coopers & Lybrand Deloitte Tourism Leisure Consultancy Services (1990) *UK Conference Market Survey 1990*, London: Coopers & Lybrand Deloitte.

Cossens, N. (1991) Innovation of new types of European museums as tourist attractions. In *Seminar on New Forms of Demand and New Products*, World Tourist Organization, Nicosia, Cyprus.

Cwi, D. (1980) Models of the role of arts in economic development. In W. Hendon, J. Shanahan and A. McDonald (eds) *Economic Policy for the Arts*, pp. 308–316. Cambridge, MA: Abt Books.

Davies, L. (1987) If you've got it, flaunt it: making the most of city tourism. *Employment Gazette*, April, 167–171.

Denman, R. (1988) *A Response to the Visits to Friends and Relatives Market*. London: English Tourist Board.

Donnison, D. and Middleton, A. (eds) (1987) *Regenerating the Inner City: Glasgow's Experience*. London: Routledge & Kegan Paul.

Drabble, M. (1991) A vision of the real city. In M. Fisher and U. Owen (eds) *Whose Cities?* London: Penguin.

DRV Research (1986) *An Economic Impact Study of the Tourist and Associated Arts Developments in Merseyside*. Bournemouth: DRV Research.

Economic Research Associates (1984) *Community Economic Impact of the Olympic Games in Los Angeles*. Los Angeles: Economic Research Associates.

English Tourist Board (1980) *Tourism and the Inner City*. London: English Tourist Board.

English Tourist Board (1984) *The UK Conference Market: Providing for the Future*. London: English Tourist Board.

English Tourist Board/LDR (1989) *Manchester, Salford, Trafford Strategic Development Initiative: A Framework for Tourism Development*. London: English Tourist Board.

Exhibition Industries Federation (1989) *The UK Exhibition Industry: The Facts.* London: Polytechnic of North London.

Exhibition Industries Federation (1990) *The UK Exhibition Industry: The Facts.* London: Polytechnic of North London.

Exhibition Industries Federation (1991) *The UK Exhibition Industry: The Facts,* Vol. 3. London: Polytechnic of North London.

Fainstein, S.S., Gordon, I. and Harloe, M. (1992) *Divided Cities: New York and London in the Contemporary World.* Oxford: Blackwell.

Falk, N. (1986) Baltimore and Lowell: two American approaches. *Built Environment,* 12, 145–152.

Farrell, K. (1980) Insights into site selection. *Restaurant Business,* 1 July, 115–120.

Federation of British Industries (1959) *Exhibition Facilities in the UK.* London: FBI.

Foley, P. (1991) The impact of the World Student Games on Sheffield. *Environment and Planning, C,* 9, 65–78.

Ford, L.R. (1979) Urban preservation and the geography of the city in the USA. *Progress in Human Geography,* 3, 211–238.

Ford, L.R. (1992) Reading the skyline of American cities. *Geographical Review,* 82, 180–200.

Frechtling, D.C. (1987) Assessing the impacts of travel and tourism – introduction to travel impact estimation. In J.R.B. Ritchie and C.R. Goeldner (eds) *Travel, Tourism and Hospitality Research.* New York: John Wiley.

Frey, B.S. and Pommenehne, W.W. (1989) *Muses and Markets: Explorations in the Economics of the Arts.* Oxford: Blackwell.

Frieden, B. and Sagalyn, L.B. (1989) *Downtown Inc.: How America Rebuilds Its Cities.* Cambridge, MA: MIT Press.

Getz, D. (1989) Special events. *Tourism Management,* 10, 125–137.

Getz, D. (1991a) *Festivals, Special Events and Tourism.* New York: Van Nostrand.

Getz, D. (1991b) Festivals, special events and tourism. In D.E. Hawkins and J.R.B. Ritchie (eds) *World Travel and Tourism Review,* Vol. 1, pp. 183–184. Wallingford: CAB International.

Getz, D. (1992) Trends in event tourism. In J.R.B. Ritchie and D.E. Hawkins (eds) *World Travel and Tourism Review,* Vol. 2, pp. 183–186. Wallingford: CAB International.

Gilbert, D.C. (1990) Conceptual issues in the meaning of tourism. In C.P. Cooper (ed.) *Progress in Tourism, Recreation and Hospitality Management,* Vol. 2. London: Belhaven.

Glaser, J.R. (1986) USA museums in context. In Scottish Museums Council (ed.) *The American Museum Experience: In Search of Excellence.* London: HMSO.

Go, F. (1991) The international conventions and meetings market. In D.E. Hawkins and J.R.B. Ritchie (eds) *World Travel and Tourism Review,* Vol. 1, pp. 127–128. Wallingford: CAB International.

Goodall, B. (1989) Tourist accommodation: a destination area perspective. *Built Environment,* 15, 78–81.

Gratton, C. and Taylor, P. (1988a) The Olympic Games: an economic analysis. *Leisure Management,* 8(3), 32–34.

Gratton, C. and Taylor, P. (1988b) The Seoul Olympics. *Leisure Management,* 8(12), 54–59.

Graveline, D. (1984) Convention centers. *Urban Land,* 43(7), 2–5.

Gray, H.P. (1970) *International Travel–International Trade.* Lexington: Heath Lexington.

Greater Manchester Visitor and Convention Bureau (1992) *Marketing Audit 1992.* Manchester: GMVACB.

Greenhill, E.H. (1988) Counting visitors or visitors who count? In R. Lumley (ed.) *The Museum Time Machine*. London: Routledge.

Gunn, C. (1988) *Tourism Planning*. New York: Taylor & Francis.

Gupta, S. (1984) Types of tourists. In R.W. McIntosh and C.R. Goeldner (eds) *Tourism: Principles, Practices and Philosophies*. New York: John Wiley.

Guskind, R. (1988) The biggest photo opportunity of them all. *Planning (APA)*, 54(7), 4–11.

Guskind, R. (1990) Fish or foul: just how many aquariums does the world really need? *Planning (APA)*, 56(5), 10–14.

Guskind, R. and Pierce, N.R. (1988) Faltering festivals. *National Journal*, 20(38), 2307–2311.

Hague, D., Jones, T., Pandit, N.R. and Richardson, P.K. (1990) The economic impact of the Manchester Olympics. Unpublished report to the Manchester Bid Committee.

Hall, P. (1987) Urban development and the future of tourism. *Tourism Management*, 8, 129–130.

Harvey, B. (1987) *Visiting the National Portrait Gallery*. London: HMSO.

Harvey, D. (1989) *The Urban Experience*. Oxford: Basil Blackwell.

Heady, P. (1984) *Visiting Museums*. London: HMSO.

Healey & Baker (1990, 1991, 1992) *Europe's Top Cities: European Real Estate Monitor*. London: Healey & Baker.

Heeley, J. (1990) *Sheffield Tourism Initiative*. Sheffield: Sheffield Partnerships Ltd.

Henderson, D.M. (1975) *The Economic Impact of Tourism: A Case Study of Greater Tayside*. Edinburgh: Tourism and Recreation Research Unit, University of Edinburgh.

Hendon, W. and Shaw, D. (1987) The arts and urban development. In G. Gappert (ed.) *The Future of Winter Cities*. Beverly Hills: Sage.

Herron Associations Inc. (1991) *1991 World Gymnastics Championships Impact Report*. Indianapolis: Herron Associates Inc.

Hewison, R. (1989) Heritage: an interpretation. In D.L. Uzzel (ed.) *Heritage Interpretation*, Vol. 1, pp. 15–23. London: Belhaven.

Horwath International (1990) *Worldwide Lodging Industry*. New York: Horwath International.

Hoyle, B.S., Pinder, D.A. and Hussain, M.S. (1988) *Revitalising the Waterfront: International Dimensions of Dockland Development*. London: Bellhaven.

Hudson, K. (1975) *A Social History of Museums*. London: Macmillan.

Hughes, C.G. (1982) The employment and economic benefits of tourism reappraised. *Tourism Management*, 3, 167–176.

Hughes, C.G. (1988) Conference tourism: a salesman's dream. *Tourism Management*, 9, 235–238.

Hughes, G. (1991) Conceiving of tourism. *Area*, 23, 203–207.

Hughes, H.L. (1986) Tourism and the live performance of opera and classical music. *Journal of Arts Policy and Management*, 2(3), 12–16.

Hughes, H.L. (1989a) Tourism and the arts. *Tourism Management*, 10, 97–99.

Hughes, H.L. (1989b) Entertainment. In S.F. Witt and L. Moutinho (eds) *Tourism, Marketing and Management Handbook*, pp. 127–130. Englewood Cliffs NJ: Prentice-Hall.

Jansen-Verbeke, M. (1986) Inner city tourism, resources, tourists, and promoters. *Annals of Tourism Research*, 13, 79–100.

Jansen-Verbeke, M. (1988) *Leisure, Recreation and Tourism in Inner Cities*. Amsterdam: Netherlands Geographical Studies.

Jansen-Verbeke, M. (1989) Inner cities and urban tourism in the Netherlands: new challenges for local authorities. In P. Bramham *et al.* (eds) *Leisure and Urban Processes*. London: Routledge.

Jansen-Verbeke, M. (1990) Leisure + Shopping = Tourism product mix. In G. Ashworth and B. Goodall (eds) *Marketing Tourism Places*. London: Routledge.

Jeanne Beekhuis & Co. (1988) *Expenditures and Characteristics of Visitors to the Inner Harbor and Related Downtown Sites in Baltimore, Maryland.* Washington, DC: Jeanne Beekhuis and Co.

Jeffrey, D. (1989) *The Impact of Tourism in Yorkshire and Humberside.* Bradford: Department of Environmental Science, University of Bradford.

Jeffrey, D. (1990) Monitoring the growth of tourism-related employment at the local level: the application of a census based non-survey method in Yorkshire and Humberside, 1981–1987. *Planning Outlook*, 33, 108–117.

Johnson, A.T. (1986) Economic policy implications of hosting sport franchises. *Urban Affairs Quaterly*, 22, 411–433.

Johnson, P. and Thomas, B. (1990) Measuring the local employment impact of a tourist attraction: an empirical example. *Regional Studies*, 24, 395–403.

Jones Lang Wootton (1989) *Retail, Leisure and Tourism.* London: English Tourist Board.

Judd, D.R. (1979) *The Politics of American Cities: Private Power and Public Policy.* Boston: Little, Brown.

Judd, D.R. and Collins, M. (1979) The case of tourism: political coalitions and redevelopment in central cities. In G. Tobin (ed.) *The Changing Structure of Cities: What Happened to the Urban Crisis?* Beverly Hills: Sage.

JURUE (1977) *The Impact of the National Exhibition Centre.* Birmingham: JURUE.

JURUE (1981) *The Economic Impact of an Exhibition Centre at Manchester Central Station.* Birmingham: JURUE.

JURUE (1983) *The Economic Impact of the International Convention Centre.* Birmingham: JURUE.

JURUE (1984). *The Economic Impact of the National Exhibition Centre in 1984.* Birmingham: JURUE.

Karski, A. (1990) Urban tourism: a key to urban regeneration? *The Planner*, 6, 15–17.

Karver, J.R. (1982) There's more to lodging than location. *Urban Land*, 41(10), 14–17.

Kent, W.E. (1984) Underground Atlanta: the untimely passing of a major tourist attraction. *Journal of Travel Research*, 22, 2–7.

Kent, W.E. and Chestnutt, J.E. (1991) Underground Atlanta: resurrected and revisited. *Journal of Travel Research*, 29(4), 36–39.

Kent, W.E., Shock, J. and Snow, R.E. (1983) Shopping: tourism's unsung hero(ine). *Journal of Travel Research*, 21(4), 2–4.

Kerslake, B. (1988) Garden festivals: good for tourism? In H. Cameron (ed.) *The Tourism Industry 1988/9.* London: The Tourism Society.

Kim, J-G. *et al.* (1989) *The Impact of the Seoul Olympic Games on National Development.* Seoul: Korean Development Institute.

Knack, R.E. (1986) Stadiums: the right game plan? *Planning (APA)*, 52(9), 6–11.

Kotas, R. (ed.) (1975) *Market Orientation in the Hotel and Catering Industry.* Guildford: University of Surrey Press.

Labasse, J. (1984) Les congrès; activité tertiaire de villes privilégiées. *Annales de Géographie*, 88, 688–703.

Laventhol & Horwath (1984) Checking into hotel development. *Urban Land*, 43(2), 12–14.

Law, C.M. (1985a) Urban tourism: selected case studies. *Urban Tourism Project Working Paper* No. 1. Department of Geography, University of Salford.

Law, C.M. (1985b) Urban tourism in the United States. *Urban Tourism Project Working Paper* No. 4. Department of Geography, University of Salford.

Law, C.M. (ed.) (1988a) *The Uncertain Future of the Urban Core.* London: Routledge.

Law, C.M. (1988b) From Manchester Docks to Salford Quays: a progress report on a redevelopment project. *Manchester Geographer, N.S., 9,* 2–15.

Law, C.M. (1991a) Tourism as a focus for urban regeneration. In S. Hardy, T. Hart and T. Shaw (eds) *The Role of Tourism in the Urban and Regional Economy.* London: Regional Studies Association.

Law, C.M. (1991b) Tourism and urban revitalisation. *East Midland Geographer,* 14, 49–60.

Law, C.M. (1992) Urban tourism and its contribution to urban regeneration. *Urban Studies,* 29, 599–618.

Law, C.M. and Grime, E.K. (1993) Salford Quays in context. In K.N. White *et al.* (eds) *Urban Waterside Regeneration: Problems and Prospects.* Chichester: Ellis Horwood.

Law, C.M. and Tuppen, J.N. (1986) *Tourism and Greater Manchester: The Final Report of the Urban Tourism Research Project.* Department of Geography, University of Salford.

Lawrence, P. and Rosenthal, L. (1990) Employment experiences following the Stoke-on-Trent Garden Festival. *Local Economy,* 5(2), 154–158.

Lawson, F.R. (1982) Trends in business tourism. *Tourism Management,* 3, 298–302.

Lawson, F.R. (1985a) *Exhibition Trends 1984.* Guildford: University of Surrey.

Lawson, F.R. (1985b) *Major UK Exhibitions 1983 and 1985.* Guildford: University of Surrey.

Lawson, F.R. and Wilkie, B. (1985) *Major UK Exhibitions 1983 and 1984.* Guildford: University of Surrey.

Levine, M.V. (1987) Downtown redevelopment as an urban growth strategy: a critical appraisal of the Baltimore renaissance. *Journal of Urban Affairs,* 9(2), 103–123.

Ley, D. and Olds, K. (1988) Landscape as spectacle: world fairs and the culture of heroic consumption. *Environment and Planning D. Society and Space,* 6, 191–212.

Listokin, D. (1985) The convention trade: a competitive economic prize. *Real Estate Issues,* 10, 43–46.

Loftman, P. and Nevin, B. (1992) *Urban Regeneration and Social Equity: A Case Study of Birmingham 1986–92.* Birmingham: University of Central England in Birmingham.

Lohmann, M. (1991) Evolution of short break holidays. *Tourist Review,* 46, 14–22.

Lundberg, D.E. (1984) *The Hotel and Restaurant Business,* 4th edn. New York: Van Nostrand.

Lyall, K. (1982) A bicycle built for two: public/private partnerships in Baltimore's renaissance. In R.S. Fosler and R.A. Berger (eds) *Public–Private Partnerships in American Cities.* Lexington: Lexington Books.

MacCannell, D. (1976) *The Tourist: A New Theory of the Leisure Class.* New York: Schocken Books.

McNulty, R. (1985) Revitalizing industrial cities through cultural tourism. *International Journal of Environmental Studies,* 25, 225–228.

Manchester City Council (1991) *Manchester: City of Drama: Bid for the Arts 2000 Initiative*. Manchester: Manchester City Council.

Manchester Polytechnic (1985) *Manchester City Centre Theatre Survey*. Manchester: Manchester Polytechnic.

Martin, B. and Mason, S. (1988) The role of tourism in urban regeneration. *Leisure Studies*, 7, 75–80.

MAS Research Marketing and Consulting (1989) *North West Area Short Break Holidays*. London: MAS Research Marketing and Consulting.

MAS Research Marketing and Consulting (1991) *A Report on the Short Break Market in England's North West*. London: MAS Research Marketing and Consulting.

Massey, D. (1984) *Spatial Divisions of Labour*. London: Macmillan.

Medlik, S. (1980) *The Business of Hotels*. London: Heinemann.

Merriman, N. (1991) *Beyond the Glass Case: The Past, the Heritage and the Public in Britain*. Leicester: Leicester University Press.

Merseyside Information Services (1991) *Visitors to Merseyside 1990*. Liverpool: Merseyside Information Services.

Merseyside Tourist Board (1987) *Tourism: A Flagship for Merseyside: Consultation Draft Strategy*. Liverpool: Merseyside Tourist Board.

Middleton, V. (1990a) Irresistible demand forces. *Museums Journal*, 90, 31–34.

Middleton, V. (1990b) *New Visions for Independent Museums*. Chichester: Association of Independent Museums.

Miestchovich, I.J. and Ragas, W.R. (1986) Stadium parking attracts office developers in New Orleans. *Urban Land*, 45(6), 14–17.

Morrell, B. (1985) *Employment in Tourism*. London: British Tourist Authority.

Morton, R. (1985) A city pulled up by its bootstraps. *Town and Country Planning*, February, 60–62.

Myerscough, J. (1988a) *The Economic Importance of the Arts in Britain*. London: Policy Studies Institute.

Myerscough, J. (1988b) *The Economic Importance of the Arts in Glasgow*. London: Policy Studies Institute.

Myerscough, J. (1991) *Monitoring Glasgow 1990*. Glasgow: Glasgow City Council.

NOP Market Research Ltd (1985) *Survey of Visitors to the Liverpool Garden Festival 1984: Final Report*. London: NOP Market Research Ltd.

NOP Market Research (1987) *Stoke National Garden Festival Visitor Survey: Final Report*. London: NOP Market Research.

O'Connell, C. (1986) The Stoke National Garden Festival. *The Planner*, 72(1), 11–13.

Office of Population Censuses and Surveys (1991) *Leisure Day Visits in Great Britain 1988/9*. London: HMSO.

O'Toole, M. and Robinson, F. (1990) *Garden Festivals and Urban Regeneration*. Newcastle: University of Newcastle upon Tyne.

Owen, C. (1990) Tourism and urban regeneration. *Cities*, 194–201.

PA Cambridge Economic Consultants (1990) *An Evaluation of Garden Festivals*. London: HMSO.

Pannell Kerr Forster (1984) *Glasgow Tourism Development Study*. Glasgow: Scottish Development Agency.

Pannell Kerr Forster (1987) *Trends in the Hotel Industry*, US edn. Houston. London: Pannell Kerr Forster.

Parkinson, M. and Bianchini, F. (1990) Cultural policy and urban regeneration in Liverpool: a tale of missed opportunities. *Liverpool Urban Studies Working Paper* No. 19. Liverpool University.

Pearce, D. (1987) *Tourism Today: A Geographical Analysis*. London: Longman.
Pearce, D. (1989) *Tourist Development*, 2nd edn. Harlow: Longman.
Pearce, D. (1992) *Tourist Organisation*. Harlow: Longman.
Peat Marwick McLintock (1989) *The Impact of Visitors and Exhibitors at the National Exhibition Centre*. London: Peat Marwick McLintock.
Perloff, H. (1979) *The Arts in the Economic Life of the City*. New York: American Council for the Arts.
Petersen, D.C. (1988) Thinking about a downtown stadium for Baltimore. *Urban Land*, 47(9), 21–23.
Petersen, D.C. (1989) *Convention Centers, Stadiums and Arenas*. Washington, DC: Urban Land Institute.
Petersen, D.C. (1992) Convention center performance. *Urban Land*, 51(1), 42–45.
PIEDA (1987) *The Greater Belfast Tourism Development Study*. Belfast: Northern Ireland Tourist Board.
Pillsbury, R. (1987) From Hamburger Alley to Hedgerose Heights: towards a model of restaurant location dynamics. *Professional Geographer*, 39(3), 326–344.
Pillsbury, R. (1990) *From Boarding House to Bistro: The American Restaurant Then and Now*. Boston: Unwin Hyman.
Plog, S.C. (1987) Understanding psychographics in tourism research. In J.R.B. Ritchie and C.R. Goeldner (eds) *Travel Tourism and Hospitality Research*. New York: John Wiley.
Polytechnic of Central London, Leisureworks, and DRV Research (1990) *Tourism and the Inner City: An Evaluation of the Impact of Grant Assisted Tourism Projects*. London: HMSO.
Pred, A.R. (1966) *The Spatial Dynamics of US Urban-Industrial Growth, 1800–1914*. Cambridge, MA: MIT Press.
Price Waterhouse (1991) *Annual Convention Report*, Tampa, FL.
Pyo, S., Cook, R. and Howell, R. (1988) Summer Olympic tourist market: learning from the past. *Tourism Management*, 9(2), 137–144.
Pysarchik, D.T. (1989) Tourism retailing. In S.F. Witt and L. Moutinho (eds) *Tourism Marketing and Management Handbook*. Englewood Cliffs, NJ: Prentice-Hall.
Queenan, L. (1992) *Conference Bureaux: An Investigation into their Structure, Marketing Strategies and Business*. Birmingham: British Association of Conference Towns.
Ragas, W.R., Miestchovich, I.J., Nebel, E.G., Ryan, T.P. and Lacho, K.J. (1987) Louisiana Superdome public costs and benefits, 1975–1984. *Economic Development Quarterly*, 1, 226–239.
Redmond, G. (1991) Changing styles of sports tourism: industry/consumer interactions in Canada, the USA and Europe. In M.T.S. Sinclair and M.J. Stabler (eds) *The Tourism Industry: An International Analysis*, pp. 107–112. Wallingford: CAB International.
Renucci, J. (1992) Aperçus sur le tourisme culturel urbain en région Rhône-Alpes: l'exemple de Lyon et de Vienne. *Revue de Géographie de Lyon*, 67(1), 5–18.
Rice, B.R. (1983) Atlanta: if Dixie were Atlanta. In R.M. Bernard and B.R. Rice (eds) *Sunbelt Cities: Politics and Growth since World War II*, Chapter 2. Austin: University of Texas Press.
Richards, G. (1991) English conference venues: market trends and prospects. *Investment in Tourism (ETB)*, Jan.–June, 29–34.

Rines, M. (1979) The business of conferences. *Management Today*, February, 99–108.

Ritchie, J.R.B. and Coeldner, C.R. (eds) (1987) *Travel Tourism and Hospitality Research*. New York: John Wiley.

Ritchie, J.R.B. and Smith, B.H. (1991) The impact of a mega event on host region awareness: a longitudinal study. *Journal of Travel Research*, 30, 3–10.

Ritter, W. (1985) Hotel location in big cities. In F. Vetter, (ed.) *Big City Tourism*. Berlin: Reiner Verlag.

Rolfe, H. (1992) *Arts Festivals in the UK*. London: Policy Studies Institute.

Rosentraub, M.S. (1988) Public investment in private business: the professional sports mania. In S. Cummings (ed.) *Business Elites and Urban Development: Case studies and Critical Perspectives*. New York: State University of New York Press.

Rosentraub, M.S. and Nunn, S.R. (1978) Suburban city investment in professional sports. *American Behavioral Scientist*, 21, 393–414.

Rouse, J. (1984) Festival market places: bringing new life to the center city. *Economic Development Commentary*, 8, 3–8.

RPA Management (1985) *The Conference and Exhibition Market Survey*. London: RPA Management.

Safavi, F. (1971) A cost benefit model for convention centers. *Annals of Regional Science*, 2, 221–237.

Sanders, H.T. (1992) Building the convention city: politics, finance and public investment in urban America. *Journal of Urban Affairs*, 14, 135–159.

Sawicki, D.S. (1989) The festival marketplace as public policy: guidelines for future policy decisions. *APA Journal*, 55, 347–361.

Scotinform Ltd and Leisure Research Services (1991) *Edinburgh Festivals Study, 1990–1*. Edinburgh: Scottish Tourist Board.

Scottish Tourist Board (1992) *Edinburgh Festivals Study 1990–1991: Summary*. Edinburgh: Scottish Tourist Board.

Shanahan, J.L. (1980) The arts and urban development. In W. Hendon, J. Shanahan and A. McDonald (eds) *Economic Policy for the Arts*, pp. 295–305. Cambridge, MA: Abt Books.

Sheffield Joint Tourism Initiative (1990) *A Programme for Action*. Sheffield: Sheffield Partnerships Ltd.

Smith, G.V. (1989) The European conference market. *Travel and Tourism Analyst*, 4, 60–76.

Smith, S.L.J. (1983) Restaurants and dining out: geography of a tourism business. *Annals of Tourism Research*, 10, 515–549.

Smith, S.L.J. (1985) Location patterns of urban restaurants. *Annals of Tourism Research*, 12, 581–602.

Smyth, B. and Ayton, B. (1985) *Visiting the National Maritime Museum*. London: HMSO.

Speakman, L. and Bramwell, B. (1992) *Sheffield Works: An Evaluation of a Factory Tourism Scheme*. Sheffield: Centre for Tourism Research, Sheffield City Polytechnic.

Stevens, T. (1988) The Baltimore Story: the rebirth and emergence of a maritime city. *Leisure Management*, 8(11), 54–61.

Stevens, T. (1992) Barcelona: the Olympic city. *Leisure Management*, 12(6), 26–30.

Syme, G.J., Shaw, B.J., Fenton, D.M. and Mueller, W.S. (1989) *The Planning and Evaluation of Hallmark Events*. Aldershot: Avebury.

Tibbalds, Colbourne, Karski (1988) *Cardiff Tourism Study: Final Report*. London: Tibbalds, Colbourne, Karski.

Tighe, A.J. (1985) Cultural tourism in the USA. *Tourism Management*, **6**, 234–251.

Touche Ross: Greene Belfield-Smith Division (1991) *Survey of Tourist Offices in European Cities*. London: Touche Ross.

Tourism Canada (1986) *The US Travel Market Study*. Ottawa: Tourism Canada.

Travis, A.S. (1989) Tourism destination area development. In S.F. Witt and L. Moutinho (eds) *Tourism Marketing and Management Handbook*. Englewood Cliffs, NJ: Prentice-Hall.

Trinity Research (1989) *The UK Short Break Holiday Market*. Trinity Research.

Urry, J. (1990) *The Tourist Gaze: Leisure and Travel in Contemporary Society*. London: Sage.

Var, T., Cessario, F. and Mauser, G. (1985) Convention tourism modelling. *Tourism Management*, **6**, 194–200.

Vaughan, R. (1977) *The Economic Impact of the Edinburgh Festival*. Edinburgh: Scottish Tourist Board.

Vaughan, R. (1979) Does a festival pay? A case study of the Edinburgh Festival in 1976. Tourism Recreation Research Unit, Working Paper No. 5, University of Edinburgh, Edinburgh.

Vaughan, D.R. (1980) Does a festival pay? In W. Hendon, J. Shanahan and A. McDonald (eds) *Economic Policy for the Arts*. Cambridge, MA: Abt Books.

Vaughan, R. (1986) *Estimating the Level of Tourism Related Employment: An Assessment of Two Non-Survey Techniques*. Bournemouth: DRV Research.

Vaughan, R. (1991) Assessing the economic impact of tourism. In S. Hardy, T. Hart and T. Shaw (eds) *The Role of Tourism in the Urban and Regional Economy*. London: Regional Studies Association.

Vetter, F. (1985) *Big City Tourism*. Berlin: Reimer Verlag.

Wall, G. and Sinnott, J. (1980) Urban recreational and cultural facilities as tourist attractions. *Canadian Geographer*, **24**, 50–59.

Wall, G., Dudycha, D. and Hutchinson, J. (1985) Point patterns analysis of accommodation in Toronto. *Annals of Tourism Research*, **12**, 603–618.

Waters, S.R. (Annual) *Travel Industry World Yearbook: The Big Picture*. New York: Child & Waters.

Whitehall, W.M. (1977) Recycling Quincy Market. *Ekistics*, **256**, 155–177.

Whitt, J.A. (1987) Mozart in the metropolis: the arts coalition and the urban growth machine. *Urban Affairs Quarterly*, **23**, 15–36.

Whitt, J.A. (1988) The role of the arts in urban competition and growth. In S. Cummings (ed.) *Business Elites and Urban Development: Case Studies and Critical Perspectives*. Albany: State University of New York Press.

Wilkie, E. (1988) *UK Exhibitions and Their Evaluation*. Privately published, Midhurst, Sussex.

Wilkie, E. and Lawson, F.R. (1983) *Major UK Exhibitions 1982*. London: British Exhibition Promotion Council.

Wilkinson, J. (1990) Sport and regenerating cities. In Sports Council (ed.) *Sport: An Economic Force in Europe*. London: Sports Council.

Williams, A.M. and Shaw, G. (1988) Tourism: candyfloss industry or job creator? *Town Planning Review*, **59**, 81–103.

Wishart, R. (1991) Fashioning the future: Glasgow. In M. Fisher and V. Owen (eds) *Whose Cities?* London: Penguin.

Witt, S.F. (1988) Mega events and mega attractions. *Tourism Management*, **9**(1), 76–77.

Wood, R.C. (1992) Hospitality industry labour trends: British and international experience. *Tourism Management*, 13, 297–304.

Wynne, D. (ed.) (1992) *The Culture Industry: The Arts in Urban Regeneration.* Aldershot: Avebury.

Index